# SINGING BAPTISTS
## STUDIES IN BAPTIST HYMNODY IN AMERICA

Harry Eskew
David W. Music
Paul A. Richardson

## CHURCH STREET PRESS
NASHVILLE, TENNESSEE

ISBN 0-8054-9824-9
Dewey Decimal Classification: 782.27
Subject Headings: HYMNS–HISTORY AND CRITICISM

*Printed in the United States of America*

Church Leadership Services Division
The Sunday School Board of the Southern Baptist Convention
127 Ninth Avenue, North
Nashville, Tennessee 37234

Production Staff
Jere V. Adams, *editor*
Deborah Hickerson, Connie Powell, *textual editing*
O. Dixon Waters, *artist designer*
M. Lester McCullough, *manager*
Mark Blankenship, *director*
Music Department of the Church Leadership Services Division

*In honor of*
Hugh T. McElrath *and*
William J. Reynolds
*and in memory of*
Edmond D. Keith, 1903-1992
Exemplary Baptist Hymnologists

# Contents

*Acknowledgments* ..............................................................................*vii*
*List of Illustrations* ............................................................................*viii*
*Preface*
   *Paul A. Richardson* ........................................................................*xi*

## PART I:
### EARLY NEW ENGLAND DEVELOPMENTS

Introduction
   *David W. Music* ..............................................................................15
OLIVER HOLDEN (1765-1844): An Early Baptist Composer in America
   *David W. Music* ..............................................................................17
The First American Baptist Tunebook
   *David W. Music* ..............................................................................26
Music in the First Baptist Church of Boston, Massachusetts, 1665-1820
   *David W. Music* ..............................................................................34

## PART II:
### PASTOR-HYMNISTS OF THE 19TH-CENTURY SOUTH

Introduction
   *Paul A. Richardson* ........................................................................49
ANDREW BROADDUS and Hymnody
   *Paul A. Richardson* ........................................................................51
ELEAZAR CLAY'S *Hymns and Spiritual Songs* (1793)
   *Paul A. Richardson* ........................................................................66

STARKE DUPUY: Early Baptist Hymnal Compiler
  *David W. Music* ................................................................78
The Hymns of RICHARD FURMAN
  *David W. Music*.................................................................86
BASIL MANLY, JR.: Southern Baptist Pioneer in Hymnody
  *Paul A. Richardson* ...........................................................94

## PART III:
## SINGING-SCHOOL TUNEBOOKS OF THE
## 19TH-CENTURY SOUTH

Introduction
  *Harry Eskew* ...................................................................115
WILLIAM WALKER and His *Southern Harmony*
  *Harry Eskew* ...................................................................117
WILLIAM WALKER'S *Southern Harmony:* Its Basic Editions
  *Harry Eskew*....................................................................129
ELI BALL, of Virginia
  *Paul A. Richardson* ...........................................................139
J. R. GRAVES' *The Little Seraph* (1874): A Memphis Tunebook
  *David W. Music* ................................................................155
*Christian Harmony* Singing in Alabama: Its Adaptation and Survival
  *Harry Eskew*....................................................................165

## Part IV:
## Southern Baptist Hymnody

Introduction
  *Harry Eskew* ...................................................................179
Use and Influence of Hymnals in Southern Baptist Churches up to 1915
  *Harry Eskew* ...................................................................181
Southern Baptist Contributions to Hymnody
  *Harry Eskew* ...................................................................194


*Southern Baptist Contributors to (The) Baptist Hymnal* ........................*205*
*Suggested Additional Readings in Baptist Hymnody* ...........................*209*
*Index* ..............................................................................*215*

# Acknowledgments

The authors wish to express their thanks to the following journals for permission to reprint these articles:

*Baptist History and Heritage*
- "William Walker and His *Southern Harmony*," 21, 4 (October 1986), 19-26.
- "Use and Influence of Hymnals in Southern Baptist Churches up to 1915," 21, 3 (July 1986), 21-30.
- "Southern Baptist Contributions to Hymnody," 19, 1 (January 1984), 27-35.
- "Basil Manly, Jr.: Southern Baptist Pioneer in Hymnody," 27, 2 (April 1992), 19-30.

*Foundations*
- "The First American Baptist Tunebook," 23, 3 (July 1980), 267-273.

*Inter-American Music Review*
- "*Christian Harmony* Singing in Alabama: Its Adaptation and Survival," X, 2 (Spring-Summer 1989), 169-175.

*Journal of the South Carolina Baptist Historical Society*
- "The Hymns of Richard Furman," 16 (November 1990), 31-38.

*Latin American Music Review*
- "William Walker's *Southern Harmony:* Its Basic Editions," 7, 2 (Fall/Winter 1986), 137-148.

*The Quarterly Review*
- "Oliver Holden (1765-1844): The First Baptist Composer in America," 41, 1 (October 1980), 46-52.
- "Music in the First Baptist Church of Boston, Massachusetts, 1665-1820," 42, 3 (April 1982), 37-44.
- "Starke Dupuy: Early Baptist Hymnal Compiler," 45, 1 (October 1984), 43-47.

*The Virginia Baptist Register*
- "Andrew Broaddus and Hymnody," 24 (1985), 1198-1211.
- "Eleazar Clay's *Hymns and Spiritual Songs* (1793)," 29 (1990), 1457-1468.
- "Eli Ball, of Virginia," 25 (1986), 1240-1256.

*The West Tennessee Historical Society Papers*
- "J. R. Graves' *The Little Seraph:* A Memphis Tunebook," 35 (October 1981), 40-50.

# List of Illustrations

1. Portrait of Oliver Holden, 1765-1844. Bostonian Society, Old State House, Boston, Massachusetts, 18.

2. The tune CORONATION as it appeared in Oliver Holden's *Union Harmony* (Boston, 1793). Photo courtesy of the American Antiquarian Society, Worcester, Massachusetts, 21.

3. Title page from Samuel Holyoke's *The Christian Harmonist* (Salem, Massachusetts, 1804). The Music Division, The New York Public Library for the Performing Arts. Astor, Lenox, and Tilden Foundations, New York, New York, 30.

4. Portrait of James Winchell [original source unknown]. From Nathan E. Wood, *The History of the First Baptist Church of Boston* (Philadelphia, 1899), 37.

5. William Billings' tune STILLMAN from John Rippon's *Selection of Psalm and Hymn Tunes,* 6th ed., (London, n. d.). Bowld Music Library, Southwestern Baptist Theological Seminary, Fort Worth, Texas, 41.

6. Self-portrait of Andrew Broaddus, 1770-1848. Virginia Baptist Historical Society, Richmond, Virginia, 52.

7. Title page from Andrew Broaddus' *The Dover Selection* (Richmond, 1828). James P. Boyce Centennial Library, Southern Baptist Theological Seminary, Louisville, Kentucky, 53.

8. "Amazing Grace" from Andrew Broaddus' *The Dover Selection* (Richmond, 1828). James P. Boyce Centennial Library, Southern Baptist Theological Seminary, 56.

9. Title page from Andrew Broaddus' *The Virginia Selection,* Second edition (Richmond, 1840). James P. Boyce Centennial Library, Southern Baptist Theological Seminary, 59.

10. Title page from Eleazar Clay's *Hymns and Spiritual Songs* (Richmond, 1793). Photo courtesy of the Virginia Baptist Historical Society, 66.

11. Title page from Starke Dupuy's *Hymns and Spiritual Songs* (Nashville, Tennessee, 1825). James P. Boyce Centennial Library, Southern Baptist Theological Seminary, 81.

12. "Wondrous Love" from Starke Dupuy's *Hymns and Spiritual Songs* (Nashville, Tennessee, 1825). James P. Boyce Centennial Library, Southern Baptist Theological Seminary, 82-83.

13. Portrait of Richard Furman, 1755-1825. South Carolina Baptist Historical Collection, Furman University, Greenville, South Carolina, 86.

14. Portrait of Basil Manly, Jr., 1825-1892. Henry S. Burrage, *Baptist Hymn Writers and Their Hymns* (Portland, Maine, 1888), facing page 425. Provided by Andrew Rawls, Media Services, Southern Baptist Theological Seminary, 94.

15. Title page from Basil Manly and Basil Manly, Jr.'s, *The Baptist Psalmody* (Charleston, 1850). James P. Boyce Centennial Library, Southern Baptist Theological Seminary, 97.

16. Pages from *The Baptist Psalmody* (Charleston, 1850), including "Holy, holy, holy Lord," by Basil Manly, Jr., and "Eternal God! Almighty Power," by Abram M. Poindexter. James P. Boyce Centennial Library, Southern Baptist Theological Seminary, 99.

17. Title page from Basil Manly, Jr., and A. Brooks Everett's *Baptist Chorals* (Philadelphia, 1860). James P. Boyce Centennial Library, Southern Baptist Theological Seminary, 101.

18. Pages from *Baptist Chorals* (Philadelphia, 1860) showing the format, with a traditional tune on the left and a new tune (in this case by by Basil Manly, Jr.) on the right. James P. Boyce Centennial Library, Southern Baptist Theological Seminary, 102.

19. Title page from *Manly's Choice: A New Selection of Approved Hymns for Baptist Churches with Music* (Louisville, 1892). James P. Boyce Centennial Library, Southern Baptist Theological Seminary, 107.

20. Portrait of William Walker, 1809-1875. Walker family records now in the Spartanburg County Regional Museum, 118.

21. Title page from *Southern Harmony* (New Haven, Connecticut, and Spartanburg, South Carolina, 1835). Personal library of Harry Eskew, New Orleans, Louisiana, 121.

22. NEW BRITAIN ("Amazing Grace") from *Southern Harmony* (New Haven, Connecticut, and Spartanburg, South Carolina, 1835). Personal library of Harry Eskew, 122.

23. THE PROMISED LAND ("On Jordan's stormy banks I stand") from *Southern Harmony* (New Haven, Connecticut, and Spartanburg, South Carolina, 1835). Personal library of Harry Eskew, 123.

24. WONDROUS LOVE from *Southern Harmony* (Philadelphia, 1840) [2nd edition]. Personal library of Carl Shull on loan to the Eastern Mennonite College Library, Harrisonburg, Virginia, 125. Photo courtesy of the Eastern Mennonite College Library.

25. Title page from Eli Ball's *The Manual of the Sacred Choir* (Richmond and Philadelphia, 1849). James P. Boyce Centennial Library, Southern Baptist Theological Seminary, 146.

26. GOOD SHEPHERD ("Let thy kingdom, blessed Saviour") from Eli Ball's *The Manual of the Sacred Choir* (Richmond and Philadelphia, 1849). James P. Boyce Centennial Library, Southern Baptist Theological Seminary, 150.

27. Portrait of J. R. Graves, 1820-1893. *The Baptist Encyclopedia,* ed. William Cathcart (Philadelphia, 1881), provided by Andrew Rawls, Media Services, Southern Baptist Theological Seminary, 155.

28. Title page from J. R. Graves' *The Little Seraph* (Memphis, 1874). Bowld Music Library, Southwestern Baptist Theological Seminary, 157.

29. Title page from William Walker's *The Christian Harmony* (Philadelphia, 1867). Personal library of Harry Eskew, 166.

30. Title page from the Deason-Parris revision of Walker's *The Christian Har-*

*mony* (Birmingham, 1958). Personal library of Harry Eskew, 168.

31. THE HEAVENLY THRONG from the Deason-Parris revision of Walker's *The Christian Harmony* (Birmingham, 1958). Personal library of Harry Eskew, 169.

32. NOT MADE WITH HANDS from the Deason-Parris revision of *The Christian Harmony* (Birmingham, 1958). Personal library of Harry Eskew, 173.

33. Title page from William C. Buck's *Baptist Hymn Book* (Louisville, 1842). James P. Boyce Centennial Library, Southern Baptist Theological Seminary, 183.

34. Title page from Robert Lowry and William H. Doane's *Pure Gold* (New York and Chicago, 1871). Personal library of Harry Eskew, 188.

35. Title page from W. E. Penn's *Harvest Bells Nos. 1, 2, and 3 Combined* (Cincinnati, 1892). Martin Music Library, New Orleans Baptist Theological Seminary, 189.

36. Title page from Lansing Burrows' *Baptist Hymn and Praise Book* (Nashville, 1904). Martin Music Library, New Orleans Baptist Theological Seminary, 190.

37. Title page of Robert H. Coleman and W. W. Hamilton's *The Evangel* (Philadelphia, 1909). Personal library of Harry Eskew, 191.

38. "Bringing in the Sheaves" with George A. Minor's tune from his *Golden Light No. 1, for Sunday Schools* (Richmond, 1879). Photo courtesy of the Virginia Baptist Historical Society, 196.

39. W. E. Penn's "The Sheltering Rock" from *Harvest Bells Nos. 1, 2, and 3 Combined* (Cincinnati, 1892). Martin Music Library, New Orleans Baptist Theological Seminary, 197.

40. Title page from B. B. McKinney's *The Broadman Hymnal* (Nashville, 1940). Martin Music Library, New Orleans Baptist Theological Seminary, 199.

# SINGING BAPTISTS:
## STUDIES IN BAPTIST HYMNODY IN AMERICA

# Preface

## Paul A. Richardson

EVEN THE MOST CASUAL observer of worship in Baptist churches today will notice the rich variety of congregational song. There are hymns from the present and those with origins that extend over centuries. These hymns come from a multitude of authors, known and unknown, whose beliefs and worship patterns range far beyond Baptist contexts. There are psalms that connect today's singers with the worship of Jesus and His forebears; there are gospel songs; there are contemporary pieces in a wide range of idioms. Out of the broad range of Christian hymnody, each congregation has developed its own particular mix of hymnic expressions.

This variety reflects differing ways of speaking to and about God, differing preferences for musical styles, and differing patterns of worship. More broadly, it reveals differing cultural contexts, differing theological perspectives, and differing historical legacies—all of them parts of Baptist heritage and embodiments of Baptist piety and polity.

Such diversity is not a new development. The tapestry of Baptist hymnody is woven of many different strands, each lending its own color, texture, and character to the weave. While present discussions about hymnody among Baptists often address what is "best" in a general sense or focus on what is "right" for a particular congregation, the presence of singing by Baptists in worship is assumed. It was not always so! At the time that Baptists emerged in England in the early 17th century, many congregations permitted no singing; others tolerated only spontaneous solos. Those that allowed participation by the assembly sang only psalm paraphrases and warned against the "promiscuous" singing together of men and women or of believers and unbelievers.

How have we moved from this situation to the point where Baptists are widely known as "a singing people"? That story has many chapters.

This book does not purport to trace the development of hymn singing among Baptists. It is a collection of studies of certain aspects of the hymnic practices of some Baptists in America. These "snapshots" do not tell the whole story of the Baptist family at worship. Instead, they offer greater insight into some of the ways in which certain Baptists have written texts and tunes, compiled hymnals and tunebooks, and used hymns in their common life. This hymnological evidence reflects the diversity of Baptist worship, devotion, belief, witness, and culture.

The studies that make up this book take a variety of approaches. Some focus on the content of a particular collection; others discuss the life and work of an individual. Some tell the story of hymn singing in a particular place; others provide a glimpse of the bigger picture.

The chapters are clustered under broad headings that indicate some common trait of time, place, or purpose. Three articles explore different facets of Baptist hymn singing in "Early New England Developments." Five essays examine the work of representative "Pastor-Hymnists of the 19th-Century South." The significant contributions of Baptist compilers are seen in five studies of "Singing-School Tunebooks of the 19th-Century South." Two chapters look more broadly at "Southern Baptist Hymnody." Each section of the book has a brief introduction to offer some context for its content.

All of these essays have appeared previously in a variety of journals. The first publication is acknowledged in each case. Each of the articles has been updated for inclusion in this book. The authors are grateful to the original publishers both for the opportunity to share their work with particular audiences and for permission to revise and reprint the material here for a larger readership.

To help make the greater story of Baptist hymnody in America more accessible, a selected and annotated bibliography of supplemental readings follows the articles. There is much yet to be explored. The authors of *Singing Baptists* hope to entice their readers to become students, scholars, and singers of this heritage.

*Soli Deo gloria!*

# PART I:

# EARLY
# NEW ENGLAND
# DEVELOPMENTS

# Introduction

## David W. Music

THE FIRST BAPTIST CHURCH in America was founded at Providence, Rhode Island, in 1639. From this point to the end of the 17th century, nine other churches were formed in the northern colonies, though one of these, the congregation at Kittery, Maine, moved to Charleston, South Carolina, in 1696.

The early churches were mostly small in membership, poor in resources, and often under persecution from secular or religious authorities. These and other factors militated against the development of elaborate church music programs and, in some instances, even against the practice of congregational singing.

During the course of the 18th century, however, Baptists in the northern colonies began to rise in both numbers and economic prosperity. Their religious views became more widely tolerated and ultimately were protected by law. By the early decades of the 19th century, Baptists had become a "respectable" denomination.

These developments were naturally reflected in their church music. Toward the end of the 18th century, several northern churches had formed choirs; in the early 19th century, instruments were introduced into some congregations.

The materials and practices of congregational song were also affected by the rising status of Baptists in the North. Baptists abandoned psalmody and the practice of lining-out during the late 18th and early 19th centuries. They began to compose and publish music for their own congregations and choirs; furthermore, composers of other denominations also sought to fill the demand created by the new conditions.

The tunes sung by Baptists during this period included a number of European tunes which are still found in American hymnals, such as OLD 100TH and ST. THOMAS. Two tunes found in recent Southern Baptist hymnals were written by American composers of the late 18th century: LENOX, a fuging tune by Lewis Edson, appeared in *Baptist Hymnal* 1956; the tune CORONA-TION by Oliver Holden, a Baptist composer, was printed in *Baptist Hymnal,* 1956, *Baptist Hymnal,* 1975, and *The Baptist Hymnal,* 1991.

Certain aspects of these developments are discussed in the following group of essays. Chronologically, the essays cover the period from the founding of the First Baptist Church of Boston in 1665 through the early decades of the 19th century, with particular attention given to the years ca. 1790–ca. 1810. Geographically, the articles are restricted to New England, specifically the colony and state of Massachusetts. The general practices of Baptists in this time and place are reflected in these discussions, as are a number of innovative features which eventually became standard for Baptist churches in other eras and areas of the country.

# OLIVER HOLDEN (1765-1844): An Early Baptist Composer in America

## David W. Music

Reprinted, with revisions, from *The Quarterly Review,* October-December 1980. © Copyright The Sunday School Board of the Southern Baptist Convention. All rights reserved. Used by permission.

CONTEMPORARY BAPTISTS ARE FORTUNATE to have in their ranks a number of composers who are widely recognized as leaders in the church music field. The compositions of these men and women are found in the catalogs of most major church music publishers in the United States. Hardly a year passes in an evangelical church without the performance of at least one piece written or arranged by a Baptist. Baptist composers write in almost every conceivable style and form. Their recognition is interdenominational, and they are frequently requested to compose music for use in churches of denominations other than Baptist.

This is quite a contrast to conditions among Baptists during the 18th century when there were few Baptist composers. The reasons for the lack of interest in writing music are not difficult to discover: Baptists were frequently rather poor and had neither the time nor money to become proficient in music. In addition, they generally regarded organs and choirs as "popish innovations" in the worship of a New Testament church. They also frowned upon secular music, particularly that associated with dancing and the theater. Thus, for economic, social, and theological reasons, 18th-century Baptists were not called upon to supply new music for their services.

Most Baptists at least accepted and participated in the congregational singing of metrical psalms and hymns. Though restricted to metrical psalmody in the earlier part of the 18th century, Baptists began introducing the hymns of Isaac Watts and other English writers as the century progressed. They also wrote new hymns which mainly dealt with the distinctive

Baptist doctrines of baptism and the Lord's Supper. By the end of the century, Baptists had published a number of hymnals, some of which were reprints of earlier English Baptist books.[1]

This interest in providing new hymns did not extend to the tunes. Baptists generally took the music for their hymns from a fairly standard body of tunes which were widely used by all denominations in America. This is evident from a list of tunes approved for use in the First Baptist Church of Philadelphia, Pennsylvania, in 1789, which included 31 more or less traditional psalm and hymn tunes.[2]

The influence of the singing schools that became popular as the century progressed, together with the resultant rise of a group of American composers, could not be ignored by the Baptists. Some of these early composers, sensing the presence of a largely untapped market in American Baptist churches, began to write music specifically for Baptists. For example, *The Cashaway Psalmody,* a tunebook by Durham Hitts known only in a 1770 manuscript copy by Evan Pugh, contained a tune named CASHAWAY written expressly for the Baptist Church at Cashaway, South Carolina.[3] No evidence suggests that Hitts himself was a Baptist.

The first music collection published especially for Baptists appears to have been Samuel Holyoke's *The Christian Harmonist* (1804). This collection contained a large number of new tunes, most of which were probably by Holyoke himself. While *The Christian Harmonist* revealed the growing interest in new music on the part of Baptists, Holyoke was not a Baptist. His book was strictly a commercial venture and, as such, was apparently a failure.[4] Thus, neither Hitts nor Holyoke could lay claim to being the first Baptist composer in America.

That distinction apparently belonged to Holyoke's friend, and sometime associate, Oliver Holden. Holden was both a prolific composer and an active Baptist. Very little of his music was written specifically for Baptists, but this is not surprising in view of the rather limited music market in Baptist churches of that time. In fact, his music was like that of most early American composers in that it could be performed in churches of almost any denomination. Many of Holden's compositions were likely used in Baptist churches, particularly those with which he was closely associated.

**Portrait of Oliver Holden**
**1765–1844**

Holden was born on September 18, 1765, in Shirley, Massachusetts. At the age of 21 he moved to Charlestown, Massachusetts, a community located across the Charles River from Boston. The battle of Bunker Hill was fought near Charlestown and the town was burned by the British. Holden was trained as a carpenter and assisted in the rebuilding of the town. He later opened a general store and after that began dealing in real estate. Through his many business pursuits he became well-to-do. Holden was inclined toward politics, serving several terms in the Massachusetts House of Representatives.[5]

Despite Holden's prominent place in business and governmental affairs, it was as a musician that he achieved his fame. By his own admission his musical training was slight, consisting of only "2 month's instruction in a Singing School in 1783."[6] Soon thereafter he began teaching singing schools himself. His lack of formal musical education seems to have been at least partly offset by a natural talent for composing and performing music. Holden has often been ranked alongside his contemporary, the musician-tanner William Billings,[7] as one of the best New England composers of the 18th century.[8] Holden's compositions included psalm and hymn tunes, "odes," anthems, and instrumental music. He also wrote hymn texts.[9]

### Membership in the First Baptist Church of Boston

Almost nothing is known about Oliver Holden's conversion and baptismal experiences. According to Nathan Wood, Holden was baptized in the First Baptist Church of Boston in 1791.[10] However, the church minutes note only that Holden was "recd." into the church, without defining the manner: "After ye afternoon service, before the communion was administered, the following persons were recd. into ye chh, viz., *Jacob Foster, Oliver Holdon,* [*sic*, etc.]."[11]

Holden seems to have had some previous connection with the Baptists, for in 1790 he had an important part in the calling of Thomas Baldwin to the pastorate of Boston's Second Baptist Church.[12] However, his name did not appear in the alphabetical list of church members, leaving his exact relationship to the Second Baptist Church unclear.[13]

At any rate, Holden evidently took an active part in the First Baptist Church of Boston following his acceptance into its membership. On November 5, 1792, he and another member, John Waite, were appointed to look into the "unhappy affair" of Sarah Cheever, who was "evidently insane at times."[14] The same two men were appointed on April 6, 1795, to check on a church member who had reportedly embraced the doctrine of universal salvation.

They reported back to the church on May 5 of that year that the brother had, indeed, become a universalist; he was excluded from the church.[15] Holden, Waite, and David Goodwin were elected a committee on July 31, 1797, to make provisions for the horses of messengers to the annual associational meeting which was being hosted by the First Baptist Church.[16]

**Musical Activities.** Holden took an active part in the musical life of his church. Though records of musical activity in the First Baptist Church of Boston are scarce for this period, the extant sources indicate that this church had a music program far in advance of that in other Baptist churches of the time. In fact, the church's music program seems to have been one of the best of any late 18th-century church in New England.

The reason for such excellence is not difficult to discover: Oliver Holden was the leader of the choir.[17] The choir of the First Baptist Church of Boston had been in existence at least since 1771 when three anthems were sung at the rededication of the renovated meetinghouse.[18] Since few Baptist churches had a choir at this early date (the music being mainly congregational), the First Baptist Church of Boston was a pioneer in sponsoring choral music among Baptists in America.

Exactly when Holden took over the choir is not known, but it was probably soon after he joined the church. That Holden did an excellent job with the music is indicated by the diary of William Bentley, pastor of the East Congregational Church in Salem, Massachusetts. The entry dated June 1, 1797, said, "On the last evening, I was at the first Baptist church, & the vocal music was excellent. Dr. Stillman preached with his usual animation."[19] Bentley certainly had no reason to paint a brighter picture than was called for by the facts, so his analysis can probably be accepted at face value.

**Holden's Early Music Collections.** Unfortunately, the details of the music program at the First Baptist Church are not known. Most of the music sung by the choir was probably written by Holden himself. During his membership at the church, he published a number of sacred music collections: *American Harmony* (1792), *The Union Harmony* (1793), *The Massachusetts Compiler* (1795, with Holyoke and Hans Gram), *The Worcester Collection* (6th ed., 1797; 7th ed. 1800), *Sacred Dirges, Hymns, and Anthems* (1800), *The Modern Collection of Sacred Music* (1800), and *Plain Psalmody* (1800). Holden may have introduced many pieces from these collections to his choir in manuscript form prior to their publication. More than likely, some or all of these collections formed the bulk of the music at the church.

Holden's famous hymn tune, CORONATION, written for and still sung to

The tune CORONATION as it appeared in Oliver Holden's *Union Harmony* (1793). Note the incorrect attribution of the text to "the Rev. Mr. Medley."

Edward Perronet's hymn, "All hail the power of Jesus' name," was composed about one year after Holden joined the First Baptist Church, and was first published in his *Union Harmony* of 1793.[20] Holden derived the name of the tune from the last line of each stanza: "And crown Him Lord of all." The tune has been continually popular since its first printing and has appeared in almost every major American hymnal to the present time. Though the harmonization has been modernized in most hymnals, the tune has lost none of its characteristic vigor and sturdiness. The choir at the First Baptist Church of Boston may have particularly enjoyed singing this fine tune.

### Membership in First and Second Baptist Churches of Charlestown

**First Baptist Church, Charlestown.** Oliver Holden's official connection with the First Baptist Church of Boston ended in April, 1801, when he and 13 other members of the church who lived in Charlestown asked for their letters in order to form the First Baptist Church of Charlestown.[21] On May 12 a meetinghouse for the new congregation was dedicated with the blessings of the Baptist church in Boston. According to Benedict, Holden "gave the lot, was treasurer to the association, by whom it was built, and had made large advances towards its erection."[22] The dedication service for the new building included the singing of a "DEDICATORY POEM," a "DEDICATORY HYMN," and "an ANTHEM from 48th Psalm."[23] All these pieces were probably by Holden. The "Dedicatory Poem" was first printed in 1794 and appeared in several of Holden's later collections.[24] An anthem on Psalm 48, "Great is the Lord," by Holden, appeared in his *Plain Psalmody* (1800) with a note that it was "Composed for the Dedication of the New Meeting-House in Charlestown." The "Dedicatory Hymn" also appeared in *Plain Psalmody*. Since the new church had only 20 members,[25] the choir of Boston's First Baptist Church undoubtedly furnished the music under Holden's direction. This was probably his "swan song" with the famous Baptist choir.

At first glance it seems strange that such an active composer and musician would leave a large, well-established, and musically inclined church to help found a church of 20 members whose musical resources and opportunities would be few. However, Holden seems to have been endowed with a missionary spirit that was at least as strong as his love for music. His interest in missions led him the next year to become one of the original 12 trustees of the Massachusetts Baptist Missionary Society, the forerunner of the Massachusetts Baptist Convention.[26]

The First Baptist Church of Charlestown called Thomas Waterman as its pastor in late 1802, but he ministered there only eight months before resigning. In 1804 the church called William Collier as pastor. Benedict noted that the church "moved on in harmony from the commencement of Mr. Collier's ministry until 1809, when a series of difficulties began respecting church order, &c."[27]

**Second Baptist Church, Charlestown.** These "difficulties" soon resulted in a split, with Oliver Holden being among those who left the church. The main issue seems to have been a claim by the dissidents that the First Baptist Church was too lax in disciplining its members.[28] The splinter group formed the Second Baptist Church of Charlestown which, for obvious reasons, soon was nicknamed "the Puritan Society." Oliver Holden, who appears to have been one of the guiding spirits in the separation, became pastor of the new church, which was constituted with nine members.

Unfortunately, the friction between the two Charlestown groups did not end with this separation. Holden, who had been largely responsible for building the meetinghouse of the First Baptist Church, had never transferred ownership of the land to the church; thus, when he and the other dissident members left the church, a question arose concerning the use of the property. The First Baptist Church offered to buy the title from Holden but apparently thought his terms were too high. The church then offered to give up all claim to the land if Holden would relieve them of any debts on the building, which he accepted. To Holden's credit, he allowed the First Baptist Church to continue meeting in "his" building until they had erected one of their own. The Second Baptist Church was too small in numbers to need such a large building, so it met in a schoolhouse. Thus, the building erected by Holden soon stood empty.[29]

By 1813 Holden's "Puritan Society" numbered 25 members, most of whom had joined from other churches.[30] Besides maintaining strict discipline, the church practiced weekly communion. Holden served as minister to the church until its demise in 1836, only eight years before his death on September 4, 1844. At the time of his death, Holden was listed as a pewholder at the Baldwin Place (Second) Baptist Church in Boston, perhaps indicating membership in that congregation.[31]

**Holden's Later Music Collections.** Holden's interest in sacred music seems to have declined after he left the First Baptist Church of Boston, because the number of sacred music collections he published dropped off sharply after 1801. Perhaps other concerns engaged his time. The lack of a trained choir in his two Charlestown churches certainly prevented him from being able to try out new pieces in a worship setting. In addition, the style of church music was changing. European upheavals brought large numbers of refugees to America. Many of these refugees were musicians who, quite naturally, brought with them European ideals of church music. Compared to Handel, Haydn, and Mozart, the music of largely self-taught men like Oliver Holden sounded rough and uncouth.

Holden's only major collections of sacred music published after 1801 were *The Charlestown Collection of Sacred Songs* (1803) and *The Worcester Collection* (8th ed., 1803). During this period he also published *Occasional Pieces, Adapted to the Opening of a Place of Worship, the Constituting of a Church, and the Ordination of a Minister. Respectfully Inscribed to the Third Baptist Society, Boston.* Though the publication was undated, it probably was from the year 1807 when the Third Baptist Church opened its meetinghouse and ordained its pastor.[32] These pieces, together with the anthem on Psalm 48, mentioned previously, were among the few pieces Holden seems to have written especially for use by Baptists.

## Conclusion

Despite Holden's obvious shortcomings, Baptists have reason to be proud of him and the role he played in the religious and musical life of early America. He showed a genuine interest in the welfare and program of his churches and was committed to the cause of missions. Holden has been regarded as one of the best of the "Yankee tunesmiths" in the late 18th and early 19th centuries. More importantly, he made a direct contribution to contemporary worship through his hymn tune CORONATION. Though enjoyed today by Christians of all denominations, the tune has remained a particular favorite of Baptists.

Hamilton C. MacDougall has succinctly observed that:
> Out of the hundreds of tunes written in New England from 1770 to 1823 (the latter being the year Lowell Mason wrote his tune MISSIONARY HYMN), CORONATION is the only one now in general and approved use in the United States.[33]

As Baptists across America rise to sing the sturdy rhythm and soaring melody of CORONATION, it is hoped they will remember to be grateful for one of their own whose music helps them crown Jesus "Lord of all."

[1]See the bibliography of "Baptist Collections of Hymns Published in America" in *Handbook to The Baptist Hymnal*, Jere V. Adams (ed.) (Nashville: Convention Press, 1992), 48-49.
[2]William Williams Keen (ed.), *The Bicentennial Celebration of the Founding of the First Baptist Church of Philadelphia* (Philadelphia: American Baptist Publication Society, 1899), 180-81.
[3]Leah Townsend, *South Carolina Baptists, 1670-1805* (Florence, SC: Florence Printing Co., 1935), 89.
[4]See "The First American Baptist Tunebook" in Part I of this volume.
[5]Frank J. Metcalf, *American Writers and Compilers of Sacred Music* (New York: Russell & Russell, 1967), 125; David W. McCormick, "Oliver Holden, 1765-1844," *The Hymn,* 14:69-73, July 1963.
[6]David P. McKay and Richard Crawford, *William Billings of Boston* (Princeton: Princeton University Press, 1975), 25.
[7]William Billings (1746-1800) was a colorful Bostonian who published several collections of music for use in singing schools and churches. He was best known as the composer of CHESTER, a tune which he set to a Revolutionary text of his own authorship.
[8]Ralph T. Daniel, *The Anthem in New England before 1800* (Evanston: Northwestern University Press, 1966), 129.
[9]Henry S. Burrage, *Baptist Hymn Writers and Their Hymns* (Portland, ME: Brown Thurston & Co., 1888), 235-37.
[10]Nathan E. Wood, *The History of the First Baptist Church of Boston (1665-1899)* (Philadelphia: American Baptist Publication Society, 1899), 278-79.
[11]*Minutes,* First Baptist Church of Boston, August 7, 1791.
[12]*A Concise History of the Baldwin Place Baptist Church* (Boston: Wm. H. Hutchinson, 1854), 27.
[13]Ebenezer T. Andrews, a copartner in the firm of Thomas and Andrews which published most of Holden's music, became a member of this church. However, he did not join the church until 1816. See Ibid., 80.
[14]*Minutes,* First Baptist Church of Boston.
[15]Ibid.
[16]Ibid.
[17]Henry Wilder Foote, *Three Centuries of American Hymnody* (Cambridge: Harvard University Press, 1940; reprint ed., Archon Books, 1968), 121-22.
[18]Wood, 265-66.
[19]William Bentley, *The Diary of William Bentley, D.D.,* II (Salem: The Essex Press, 1907; reprint

ed., Gloucester, MA: Peter Smith, 1962), 224.

[20]P[aul] R[ichardson], "All hail the power of Jesus' name," in *Handbook to The Baptist Hymnal* (Nashville: Convention Press, 1992), 87.

[21]Wood, 286.

[22]David Benedict, *A General History of the Baptist Denomination in America,* I (Boston: Lincoln & Edmands, 1813), 414.

[23]*Sacred Performances at the Dedication of the Baptist Meeting-House in Charlestown, May 12, 1801* (Boston: Manning & Loring, n.d.), n.p.

[24]David W. McCormick, "Oliver Holden, 1765-1844," 77.

[25]A few charter members were from churches other than the First Baptist Church of Boston.

[26]W. H. Eaton, *Historical Sketch of the Massachusetts Baptist Missionary Society and Convention, 1802-1902* (Boston: Massachuetts Baptist Convention, 1903), 12.

[27]Benedict, *A General History,* I, 414.

[28]Ibid., II, 408-09. Benedict observed (p. 409) that "the real cause of the separation has probably not been disclosed."

[29]Ibid., I, 414-15.

[30]Ibid., II, 408.

[31]David W. McCormick, "Oliver Holden, Composer and Anthologist" (D.S.M. dissertation, Union Theological Seminary, New York City, 1963), 52.

[32]McCormick, "Oliver Holden, 1765-1844," 76.

[33]Hamilton C. MacDougall, *Early New England Psalmody* (Brattleboro, VT: Stephen Daye Press, 1940; reprint ed., New York: Da Capo Press, 1969), 74.

PART I:
EARLY NEW ENGLAND DEVELOPMENTS

# The First
# American Baptist Tunebook
## David W. Music

Reprinted, with revisions, from *Foundations*, July 1980, with permission of The American Baptist Historical Society, Valley Forge, PA 19482-0851.

IT IS GENERALLY THOUGHT that Baptists in America during the 18th and early 19th centuries were a poor, uneducated, and musically backward people. Such, indeed, was probably the case for the majority of early Baptists, particularly those in rural areas. As the end of the 18th century neared, however, Baptists began to rise in their economic, social, and educational levels, not to mention their phenomenal numerical growth.

The rising fortunes of the Baptists were reflected in the music of their churches. Baptists began to compile hymnals, form choirs, purchase musical instruments, and hire leaders to provide music that was suitable for their worship. Much research remains to be done on the music of the early American Baptists, but it is evident that if they were not in the forefront of musical progress in America, at least they were not in the rear guard. This chapter singles out one aspect of early church music among American Baptists—the publication in 1804 of the first tunebook designed specifically for Baptist churches in the New World.

### Tunes Used by Baptists Before 1804

Unfortunately there are few indications as to which tunes were sung by American Baptists during the 18th century. When early Baptist writers mentioned music at all, they generally described or quoted the texts to which the music was set. Another hindrance to our knowledge of Baptist music is the lack of Baptist composers and tunebook compilers during the 18th and early 19th centuries;[1] nevertheless, a few references to the music used by early Baptists in America may be noted here.

The fact that the name of "James Maning, *Student of N. H.*" appears in the list of subscribers to James Lyon's *Urania, or a Choice Collection of Psalm-tunes, Anthems, and Hymns* (Philadelphia, 1761)[2] implies that the tunes in Lyon's book were acceptable to Baptists. Manning was, of course, a future graduate of Princeton (N. H. stands for Nassau Hall), pastor of the First Baptist Church of Providence, Rhode Island, and first president of Rhode Island College (Brown University). Manning was chiefly responsible for reintroducing singing into Providence's First Baptist Church;[3] whether or not he did so by using *Urania* is unknown.

Three anthems sung at the First Baptist Church of Boston on December 22, 1771, seem to have been taken from Josiah Flagg's *Sixteen Anthems* (Boston, 1766); Flagg's was the only book published in America before 1772 which contained anthems on all three texts mentioned in the account of the performance.[4] Flagg's book also contained a few psalm and hymn tunes. Some 20 years later the composer Oliver Holden joined this church. Holden published most of his collections of sacred music while he was a member of the First Baptist Church of Boston, and some of his music books were undoubtedly used by that church.[5]

Perhaps the most significant indication of musical materials used by 18th-century American Baptists is found in the records of the First Baptist Church of Philadelphia. Two years after the publication of *Urania* in that city, a dispute arose in the church concerning the use of two tunes which were not acceptable to some of the members. A committee was appointed to look into the matter; strangely enough, the committee did not report until 26 years had elapsed. On March 2, 1789, the committee recommended the use of the following 31 psalm and hymn tunes:

**Common Meter:** ISLE WHITE, BRUNSWICK, COLESHILL, MUR [MEAR], BANGOR, ROCHESTER or ST. MICHAL, ST. HUMPHRY, ST. MARTIN'S, 98TH, 5TH, 34TH, SUFFIELD, VIRGINIA.
**Particular Meter:** LENOX, AMHURST.
**Long Meter:** 136TH, OLD 100, NEW 100, GREENS 100, WELLS, BROOKFIELD, WELLINGTON, MORNING HYMN, ANGLE HYMN, BATH, SAVANAH.
**Short Meter:** LITTLE MARLBOROW, NEW EAGLE STREET, WORKSWORTH or AILSBOROW, ST. THOMASES, ORANGE.[6]

Most of these were popular English tunes, but several were written by American composers: SUFFIELD (King); VIRGINIA (Oliver Brownson); 136TH

(Deaolph); NEW 100 (John Tufts?); BROOKFIELD, SAVANNAH, and AMHERST (William Billings); and LENOX (Lewis Edson). All these tunes, whether English or American, were popular in the New World during the 18th century; most of them can be found in several early American collections of sacred music.[7] Two of them, OLD 100 and ST. THOMAS, are still found in most hymnals.

In addition to these concrete references to the music used by Baptists, we may infer that they drew from the stock of melodies common to most English-speaking congregations in early America. There is little reason to suppose that Baptist congregations used a tune repertoire that was radically different from that of their fellow denominations. Since these tunes were so familiar, there was little need to mention them—though few tunebooks could afford to omit them. Thus, such common tunes as AMSTERDAM, ST. ANNE, and SOUTHWELL probably also entered the 18th-century Baptist tune repertoire.

The first tunebook published specifically for American Baptists was Samuel Holyoke's *The Christian Harmonist* (Salem: Joshua Cushing, 1804). While Holyoke's was neither the best nor the most influential tunebook compiled for Baptist use, its position as the first of its kind deserves more attention from Baptists than it has previously received.

## Samuel Holyoke

Samuel Holyoke was born on October 15, 1762, in Boxford, Massachusetts. His father, Elizur Holyoke, was pastor of the Boxford Congregational Church for almost a half-century. From 1783 to 1785, Samuel attended Phillips Andover Academy in Massachusetts. He entered Harvard in 1785, graduating with an A. B. in 1789. Two years later he received an honorary A. M. from Dartmouth College, New Hampshire. Holyoke was justly proud of his college education—a distinction achieved by few musicians in early America—and included the initials of his degrees on each of his musical publications.

Upon his graduation from Harvard, Holyoke began teaching in singing schools, primarily in Massachusetts and New Hampshire. According to Frank J. Metcalf, Holyoke had a fine voice, but in later years "it became so harsh that in the teaching of his vocal classes he was obliged to use a clari-onet."[8] Holyoke was a member of the Essex Musical Association and a teacher at Phillips Andover Academy.

In addition to his teaching activities, Holyoke was known as a performer and composer of music. One of his first tunes, ARNHEIM, was far and away his most popular composition, becoming part of the standard American tune repertoire in the last decade of the 18th century. He compiled a number of tunebooks and other musical publications, the most significant of which were:

*Harmonia Americana* (Boston, 1791)

*The Massachusetts Compiler* (Boston, 1795),

    with Hans Gram and Oliver Holden

*The Instrumental Assistant, Vol. I* (Exeter, 1800)

*The Columbian Repository* (Exeter, 1802)

*The Christian Harmonist* (Salem, 1804)

*The Instrumental Assistant, Vol. II* (Exeter, 1807)

*The Vocal Companion* (Exeter, 1809).

Holyoke is perhaps most famous for his criticism of the "fuging tune," an English musical form that was widely adopted by American composers and singers. The fuging tune usually consisted of four musical phrases. In phrases one, two, and four, the voices often sang homophonically.[9] The third phrase was generally the "fuging" section, in which the voices entered successively in an imitative fashion.[10] Despite the popularity of this form, Holyoke claimed that such pieces produce a "trifling effect," "confuse the sense, and render the performance a mere jargon of words."[11] This did not, however, prevent him from including fuging tunes in some of his later books.

According to Louis C. Elson, Holyoke "was a more versatile musician than most of his contemporaries, but he scarcely possessed as much natural talent as Billings, Law, or Kimball."[12] His tunes have been called "almost unremittingly bland;"[13] none have survived into modern use. Samuel Holyoke died, unmarried, on February 7, 1820, at Concord, New Hampshire.[14]

### The First American Baptist Tunebook

*The Christian Harmonist* was entered for copyright in the District Court of Boston, Massachusetts, on December 24, 1803.[15] Some nine months later, on September 21, 1804, the Salem *Gazette* carried the following advertisement:

*Baptist Music.*

Just Published, by SAMUEL HOLYOKE, and for Sale by Cushing & Appleton, a Collection of Tunes adapted to Rippon's[,] Smith and Sleeper's, and other Hymns made use of in Baptist Societies.[16]

The complete title of the book reads as follows:

The Christian Harmonist: Containing a Set of Tunes Adapted to all the Metres in Mr. Rippon's Selection of Hymns, in the Collection of Hymns by Mr. Joshua Smith, and in Dr. Watts's Psalms and Hymns. To which are added, Hymns on Particular Subjects, Set Throughout; Two anthems, and a Funeral Dirge; with a Concise Introduction of Practical Principles. The Whole in a Familiar Style, Designed for the Use of the Baptist Churches in the United States.

Holyoke's choice of texts from the collections of Rippon, Smith, and Watts was a felicitous one, for these books were among those most widely used by American Baptists. Watts' *Psalms and Hymns* had gone through numerous American printings, while Rippon's *Selection of Hymns* (1787) had been reprinted in New York and New Jersey in 1792. Joshua Smith was a Baptist lay preacher from Brentwood, New Hampshire, whose *Divine Hymns, or Spiritual Songs* was first published in Norwich, Connecticut, in 1784. *Divine Hymns* reached its 11th edition in the year *The Christian Harmonist* was entered for copyright.[17] All three of the hymnals used by Holyoke served as text sources for later compilers of American folk-hymn tunes.

It is not known what prompted Holyoke to prepare a tunebook for the Baptists, since he seems to have remained a Congregationalist throughout his

Title page from Samuel Holyoke's *The Christian Harmonist* (Salem, Massachusetts, 1804).

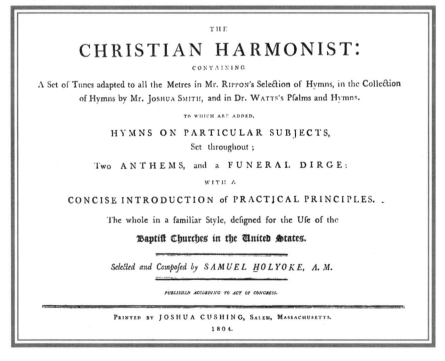

THE

# CHRISTIAN HARMONIST:

CONTAINING

A Set of Tunes adapted to all the Metres in Mr. RIPPON's Selection of Hymns, in the Collection of Hymns by Mr. JOSHUA SMITH, and in Dr. WATTS's Pſalms and Hymns.

TO WHICH ARE ADDED,

HYMNS ON PARTICULAR SUBJECTS,

Set throughout ;

Two ANTHEMS, and a FUNERAL DIRGE:

WITH A

CONCISE INTRODUCTION of PRACTICAL PRINCIPLES.

The whole in a familiar Style, deſigned for the Uſe of the

Baptiſt Churches in the United States.

Selected and Compoſed by SAMUEL HOLYOKE, A. M.

PUBLISHED ACCORDING TO ACT OF CONGRESS.

PRINTED BY JOSHUA CUSHING, SALEM, MASSACHUSETTS.
1804.

life. Oliver Holden, with whom Holyoke collaborated in the publication of *The Massachusetts Compiler,* was a Baptist. Holyoke is known to have given at least one concert in a Baptist meetinghouse.[18] In view of Holyoke's activities in New Hampshire, it is not impossible that his compilation was prompted by some association with Joshua Smith. At any rate, it is likely that he sensed the presence of a largely untapped market for music among the Baptist churches and that his publication of *The Christian Harmonist* was mainly a commercial venture.

The index of *The Christian Harmonist* lists 257 tunes,[19] 168 of them being marked "not before published." A wide variety of composers are represented, including Billings, Holden, Kimball, and other American writers, as well as the usual English composers. Five tunes are credited to Holyoke's earlier *Harmonia Americana,* two are from his *The Columbian Repository,* and one is marked simply "S. H." All except three of the new tunes carry no composer attribution.[20] It can be assumed that most or all of the unattributed new tunes were written by Holyoke himself.[21]

In view of Holyoke's stated opposition to the fuging tune, it is surprising to find that a large portion of *The Christian Harmonist* is devoted to this type of music. Forty-one tunes have more or less extensive fuging sections, including 28 that are probably of Holyoke's composition. The reason for this inclusion of a large number of fuging tunes is not difficult to determine: Holyoke was simply bowing to popular demand. Baptists, like their evangelical brothers and sisters of other denominations in America, were apparently fond of fuging tunes; this is evidenced not only by Holyoke's book, but by later tunebooks compiled by and for Baptists, particularly in the South.[22] On the title page of *The Christian Harmonist,* Holyoke indicated that "the whole [is] in a familiar style." It is apparent that Holyoke's primary purpose in this book was to provide music for Baptist worship.[23] This implies that Baptists frequently sang fuging tunes in their services, though it is not clear whether these were sung congregationally or by choirs.

The increasing number of choirs found in Baptist churches is reflected in the presence of two pieces designated "anthem" in *The Christian Harmonist.* Both anthems were probably written by Holyoke. The first, "Hear our prayer," opens with a lengthy section in three voice parts; a fourth part joins midway through the piece.[24] The other anthem is "O be joyful in the Lord," written "For Thanksgiving," which is in three parts throughout. Two other pieces in *The Christian Harmonist* were obviously designed for choir; they are "The Christian Warrior" (probably by Holyoke) and "Hymn for the New Year" (attributed to "S. H."). Both pieces are anthem-like in their structure and are much longer and more complex than the hymn and fuging tunes in the book.

Irving Lowens has theorized that some of the newly printed tunes in *The Christian Harmonist* might have been "notated directly from the oral tradition," thus making this book one of the first to include American folk hymn tunes. It is more likely that Holyoke simply "attempted to compose in the folk idiom."[25] None of the original tunes in *The Christian Harmonist* appear to have been reprinted by later compilers of folk hymnody, implying that these melodies were not a part of that body of oral song.

In fact, Holyoke's book seems to have been almost ignored following its publication. Lowens states that "it does not seem to have been known outside of northeastern Massachusetts and southeastern Vermont and New Hampshire."[26] The absence of reprintings of new tunes from *The Christian Harmonist* certainly bespeaks a lack of popularity for the book. This unpopularity is probably due to several factors, including the presence of too many new tunes (nearly two-thirds of the book), the popularity of other books among Baptists, and the denominational restriction implied in the title and contents of the book.

Nevertheless, Holyoke's book was probably not wholly without influence. In 1805, Jeremiah Ingalls published *The Christian Harmony* (Exeter: Henry Ranlet), which is generally thought to have been the first major publication of American folk-hymn tunes. Lowens noted several similarities between the books by Holyoke and Ingalls, including their choice of texts, use of the same tune names, and likeness of titles.[27] It should also be noted that Henry Ranlet, the publisher of Ingalls' book, published a large number of Holyoke's music books, and that the list of subscribers to Holyoke's *The Columbian Repository* included Ingalls' name. Unfortunately, *The Christian Harmonist* did not include a subscriber's list, but it is not unreasonable to assume that Ingalls knew of Holyoke's book and perhaps modeled his after it.

Holyoke's book was not popular in its own day, nor does it seem to have stimulated other compilers to publish books for the use of Baptists; thus, its influence on the development of Baptist church music appears to have been negligible. Despite these shortcomings, however, *The Christian Harmonist* deserves to be remembered as the first Baptist tunebook in America.

---

[1]In 1791 the English Baptist preacher John Rippon had published a selection of tunes, but "apparently this did not find favor in America." See William J. Reynolds, *Companion to Baptist Hymnal* (Nashville: Broadman Press, 1976), 13.
[2]Facsimile edition issued in 1974 by Da Capo Press, New York.

[3]David Benedict, *A General History of the Baptist Denomination in America,* I (Boston: Lincoln & Edmands, 1813), 480.

[4]See "Music in the First Baptist Church of Boston, Massachusetts, 1665-1820" in Part I of this volume.

[5]See "Oliver Holden (1765-1844): The First Baptist Composer in America" in Part I of this volume.

[6]William Williams Keen, ed., *The Bi-centennial Celebration of the Founding of the First Baptist Church of Philadelphia* (Philadelphia: American Baptist Publication Society, 1899), 180-81.

[7]For example, 23 of the above tunes appeared in Andrew Adgate's *Rudiments of Music* (Philadelphia: John M'Culloch, 1789).

[8]Frank J. Metcalf, *American Writers and Compilers of Sacred Music* (New York: Abingdon Press, 1925; reprinted, New York: Russell & Russell, 1967), 119.

[9]That is, they sang the same text at the same time.

[10]For examples of the fuging tune form, see Irving Lowens, *Music and Musicians in Early America* (New York: W. W. Norton, 1964), 240. For a detailed listing of early English and American fuging tunes, see Nicholas Temperley and Charles G. Mann's *Fuging Tunes in the Eighteenth Century,* No. 49 of Detroit Studies in Music Bibliography (Detroit: Information Coordinators, Inc., 1983).

[11]Samuel Holyoke, *Harmonia Americana* (Boston: Isaiah Thomas and Ebenezer T. Andrews, 1791), Preface.

[12]Louis C. Elson, *The History of American Music* (New York: Macmillan Co., 1925; reprinted, New York: Burt Franklin, 1971), 22.

[13]David P. McKay and Richard Crawford, *William Billings of Boston* (Princeton: Princeton University Press, 1975), 61.

[14]For more extensive biographical data on Holyoke see Metcalf, *American Writers and Compilers,* 114-120; Louis Pichierri, *Music in New Hampshire, 1623-1800* (New York: Columbia University Press, 1960), 183-90; and J. Laurence Willhide, "Samuel Holyoke, American Music Educator," Ph.D. dissertation, University of Southern California, 1954.

[15]H. Earle Johnson, *Musical Interludes in Boston, 1795-1830* (New York: Columbia University Press, 1943; reprinted, New York: AMS Press, Inc., 1967), 345.

[16]Henry M. Brooks, *Olden-Time Music* (Boston: Ticknor and Company, 1888; reprinted, New York: AMS Press Inc., 1973), 254.

[17]Reynolds, *Companion to Baptist Hymnal,* 13.

[18]This occurred in 1809. See Brooks, *Olden-Time Music,* 227-28, and William Bentley, *The Diary of William Bentley D.D.* (Salem: The Essex Press, 1905-1914; reprinted, Gloucester, MA: Peter Smith, 1962), III, 414.

[19]One tune was omitted from the index, making a total of 258 tunes in the book.

[20]The three tunes are FREEPORT and RESURRECTION by Jacob Kimball, and ROCK by Oliver Holden.

[21]McKay and Crawford, *William Billings,* 61.

[22]Several of the tunes mentioned in the 1789 list from the First Baptist Church of Philadelphia were fuging tunes, (e.g. Joseph Stephenson's 34TH and Lewis Edson's LENOX).

[23]Neither the advertisement for the book nor its title page implies its use as a singing-school manual. On the contrary, it was "designed for the use of the Baptist churches." However, the presence of a short (3 pages) introduction to music indicates that use of the book in a singing school was not completely ruled out.

[24]In Elwyn A. Wienandt and Robert H. Young's *The Anthem in England and America* (New York: The Free Press, 1970), 224, the impression is left that the anthem is in three parts throughout.

[25]Lowens, *Music and Musicians,* 142.

[26]Ibid., 142.

[27]Ibid., 142.

PART I:
EARLY NEW ENGLAND DEVELOPMENTS

# Music in the First Baptist Church of Boston, Massachusetts, 1665–1820

## David W. Music

THE STORY OF MUSIC in the Baptist churches of early America is, in many respects, the same as that found in many other denominations of the same time and place. Most early American churches were composed of psalm singers who gradually began to admit the use of hymns. A singing school, formed to encourage the better performance of psalms and hymns, would soon lead to the organization of a choir and the performance of anthems, an innovation that was not always pleasing to the congregation. Eventually the choir leader would have the temerity to introduce musical instruments into the choir loft, generally setting off a hue and cry of "popery" from the pews. Such, in fact, is the story in most Baptist churches of early America.

Nevertheless, the history of Baptist church music in America is not without its interesting and instructive aspects. In general, Baptists were much slower than other denominations to pick up musical innovations for use in their worship. To an outside observer, the music of most early Baptist churches must have sounded distressingly out of date. In a few places, however, the musical side of Baptist worship was equal to or better than that in other churches possessing a much longer heritage of church music. One of the Baptist churches of the latter type was the First Baptist Church of Boston, Massachusetts.

The First Baptist Church of Boston was founded in June 1665, the fourth Baptist church organized in the American colonies. The church came under immediate and prolonged persecution, but a succession of able ministers and the numerical growth of the congregation soon made this one of the leading Baptist churches in America.

The period of the church's greatest prosperity coincided with the calling of Samuel Stillman as pastor in 1764. Stillman was one of the most popular Baptist preachers of his day and attracted large crowds to the church until his death in 1807. During his long pastorate, the church was characterized by a missionary spirit which resulted in many conversions and additions to the membership. Later pastors of the church who also achieved a measure of prominence included James M. Winchell, Francis Wayland, William Hague, and Rollin H. Neale.

A study of music in this church is of interest for several reasons. Besides being the only Baptist church founded in America before 1700 whose records are preserved in reasonably complete form, the church's activities frequently revealed the general musical trend among other Baptist churches, thereby illuminating the history of early Baptist church music. During some periods, however, the First Baptist Church of Boston became a leader in establishing certain musical precedents which were adopted by other Baptist churches in America.

Another point of interest is that at least one important early American composer was an active member of the church. Also, one of the church's pastors was the compiler of a popular hymnal. Finally, it should not be overlooked that the church's history was the subject of a valuable book which, though containing some errors and omissions, sought to do justice to the musical side of the church's life.[1]

### Congregational Singing

No records of musical activity have been discovered for the first 63 years of the First Baptist Church's existence. According to Nathan Wood, the church "had no singing" in its earliest years, "perhaps lest it should attract too much attention" in those times of persecution.[2] Singing was by no means unanimously approved by the English and American Baptists of the 17th century. Probably no music was used during the years immediately following the founding of the church.

**Hymnals Used by the Church.** At any rate, the church had adopted the practice of singing by 1728, for on September 8 of that year it was "voted that our Brother Skinner Russell be desired from that time forward to Set the Psalm in Publick."[3] Metrical psalmody—the Book of Psalms translated, set into meter, and rhymed—was the backbone of English and American congregational singing from the 16th through the early 18th century. The most popular books of psalmody were *The Whole Book of Psalms* by Thomas Sternhold and John Hopkins (1562), *A New Version of the Psalms of David* by Nahum Tate and Nicholas Brady (1696), and the so-called *Bay Psalm Book* (1640), compiled by a group of New England Puritan divines.

Identification of the psalter used by the Boston Baptists at this date is somewhat uncertain. Wood implied that the church was using the *Bay Psalm Book*.[4] However, William J. Reynolds pointed out that the ministers who compiled the *Bay Psalm Book* were the very ones responsible for much of the persecution suffered by the early New England Baptists.[5] For this reason, it is doubtful that the church would have used this book. More likely, they used the Sternhold and Hopkins psalter, commonly referred to as the "Old Version." The Old Version was far and away the most popular psalter ever published and was quite commonly found in Baptist churches of the 18th century.

On July 7, 1740, the church voted to "Sing that Version of the Psalms done by Dr. Brady & Mr. Tate so long as no objections should be offered against it, & Wn. any should, then this vote to be reconsidered."

The poetic quality of the Old Version was not very high and, with time, the almost fanatical attachment to it on the part of churchgoers lessened. When a church finally gave up its beloved Sternhold and Hopkins, it usually chose Tate and Brady as the replacement. The so-called "New Version" was more poetic in quality (Nahum Tate was one of England's poet laureates) and gradually surpassed the Old Version in popularity during the later 18th century. The people of Boston's First Baptist Church apparently liked the New Version, for despite the loophole left for objectors, the matter does not seem to have been "reconsidered" until a new book was adopted 31 years later.

This new book was chosen on December 10, 1771, when it was "Voted. That for the Future Dr. *Watts's* Psalms together with his three Books of Hymns, which are commonly bound up in one Volume, be sung in Public, instead of the Version of Tate & Brady."

Isaac Watts has almost universally been accorded the title "Father of English Hymnody," for through his writing of hymns and paraphrased psalms, he almost single-handedly broke down the monopoly of metrical psalm singing in congregational worship. His influence was so far-reaching that his own psalms and hymns nearly created a monopoly of their own.

The adoption of Watts' "three books of Hymns" by the First Baptist Church signaled the church's acceptance of hymn singing. A few hymns had been appended to the Old and New Version psalters, but the hymns were never more than a small fraction of the whole. Watts' *Psalms and Hymns,* on the other hand, relegated the metrical psalms to a secondary position. In reference to the adoption of Watts by the congregation, Wood noted that "It is easy to believe that the smooth metres of Dr. Watts' Hymns made singing in public worship a more delightful exercise."[6]

A further step in the development of hymn singing at the church occurred on September 26, 1791, when it was "Voted. That ye Selection of Hymns by the Revd. Mr. *Rippon* of *London,* be used at baptisms and communion seasons, as a supplement to Dr. Watts's Hymns." That there was as yet no dissatisfaction with "Dr. Watts," who had been in use at the church for 20 years, is shown by the fact that Rippon's book was to be used merely as an adjunct to the *Psalms and Hymns.* In fact, as the title of Rippon's collection shows, the English Baptist minister did not intend for his book to replace Watts, but to supplement his: *A Selection of Hymns from the Best Authors, Intended to be an Appendix to Dr. Watts's Psalms and Hymns.* Rippon's *Selection* was the most modern hymnal the church had ever used, for it had been published only four years before its adoption by the congregation. By way of contrast, Tate and Brady's New Version was 46 years old and Watts' *Psalms and Hymns* some 52 years old when adopted by the church.

Portrait of James Winchell
1791–1820

A major milestone in the hymnody of the First Baptist Church was reached with the publication of James M. Winchell's *An Arrangement of the Psalms, Hymns, and Spiritual Songs of...Watts* in 1818. Winchell was pastor of the First Baptist Church when this collection was published. It found immediate acceptance among the Baptists of New England and quickly became the standard hymnal for Baptists in that area, a position it retained until the 1843 printing of Baron Stow and Samuel F. Smith's *The Psalmist.* "Winchell's Watts," as the book came to be called, contained 687 psalms and hymns by Watts, together with 327 hymns by other authors.[7] In 1819, Winchell published his *Sacred Harmony*, which provided tunes for use with his hymnal.

**Setting the Psalm and Lining-out.** One of the unusual practices connected with psalm singing during the 17th and 18th centuries was that of "lining-out." Psalm books were not provided by the church and many people were too poor to own one; thus, the leader, usually called the "deacon" or "precentor," would read two lines of the psalm text, then lead the people in singing them. This process would be repeated until the entire psalm had been sung. Quite frequently the leader was no more musically inclined than the rest of the congregation and was chosen for his position by such qualities as faithfulness and willingness to serve.

In congregations where the leader was more skilled, the practice of "setting the psalm" held sway. This was similar to lining-out, except that instead of simply reading the lines the leader *sang* the two lines of the psalm.

The action taken by the First Baptist Church of Boston on September 8, 1728, authorizing Skinner Russell to "Set the Psalm in Publick" implies that Russell must have been more skilled in psalm singing than the average deacon or precentor. In fact, an advertisement in the *Boston Gazette* of January 29, 1751, showed that Skinner Russell was skilled enough in music to be a teacher of singing schools:

> TO BE TAUGHT By Messirs Skin[n]er Russell and Moses Deshon, at the House of the said Deshon's in Dock Square. Psalmody in the best Manner, where any young Gentlemen and Ladies may apply for Information on what Condition they are to be Taught, or at Mr. Russel[l]'s Shop a little below the Draw-Bridge, Boston.[8]

Skinner Russell's tenure as leader of the singing at the Boston church is not known, but he remained a faithful member of the church until his death in 1753.

Apparently, however, the church adopted the lining-out procedure sometime before 1759, for on March 11 of that year the following note appeared in the church minutes: "This Day the Congregation began to Sing, without the Psalms being read, Line by Line; it being found most agreeable, tho the Church did not pass any Vote respecting it." This attempt to eliminate lining-out seems to have been unsuccessful, for the congregation had to deal with the issue again on February 8, 1767, when it was "Concluded without a Vote of the Church to sing in the Congregation without Reading out the Line." However, lining-out continued to be a source of annoyance to the church. On June 2, 1789, "The affair of singing on lecture evenings without reading ye lines was considered, & referred to ye next chh-meeting; as was ye choice of another deacon."

At the meeting of June 29, 1789, the matters of lining-out and deacon selection were again "deferred for future consideration," but no further mention of lining-out appears in the church records. Lining-out was probably finally abandoned shortly after this, for the choir seems to have taken a major role in leading the singing at the church during the last decade of the century. Choirs were notoriously adverse to the practice of lining-out. In their view, the increasing availability of hymnals, tunebooks, and musical education had eliminated the need for lining-out.[9]

## The Choir

The music used in the Baptist churches of 18th-century America was almost exclusively restricted to congregational singing of psalms and hymns, with choirs being virtually nonexistent. This stemmed in part from a lack of trained singers. Early Baptists in America were frequently poor and could ill-afford music lessons. Baptist churches were small and had neither the personnel nor financial resources to sustain a choral program.

Also, some early Baptists had serious doubts about the propriety of using choirs in worship. In 1699, Philadelphia Baptists went on record as being opposed to choirs of *"singing men and boys."*[10] As late as 1868, some Baptist churches were still struggling with the problem of admitting choirs into the worship service.[11] The theological and cultural objections to choirs, coupled with a lack of trained personnel, tended to stifle any movement toward the use of special groups of singers in Baptist worship before 1800.

Nevertheless, a few 18th-century Baptist churches did accept choirs into their services. A choir was in existence at the First Baptist Church of Haverhill, Massachusetts, as early as 1786,[12] and one was formed in the First Baptist Church of Providence, Rhode Island, by 1791.[13] One of the earliest Baptist church choirs in America was that of the First Baptist Church of Boston.

The choir at the Boston church was evidently formed in 1771 to assist in the rededication of the church's enlarged meetinghouse. The *Boston Evening Post* for December 23, 1771, reported that

> The new Baptist Meeting House in this Town being finish'd was opened Yesterday. We hear that the Exercises of the Day were introduced by Singing an Anthem taken out of the 122d Psalm... The Solemnity was then concluded with a second Anthem well adapted to the Occasion. The Singing was performed incomparably well by a select Company which gave great Satisfaction to a crowded Audience.

According to the church's "Pew Proprietor's Book," the second anthem was "taken out of 29 Psalm." The Pew Proprietor's Book also mentioned that "an Anthem taken out of the 104 Psalm" was sung during the afternoon service.[14] These three anthems were probably sung from Josiah Flagg's *Sixteen Anthems* (Boston, 1766), for this was the only New England book published before 1772 which contained anthems on all the psalm texts mentioned in the accounts of the service.[15] Flagg's book also included a few psalm and hymn tunes which might have been used in the worship services of the First Baptist Church.

The "select Company" of singers possibly disbanded after this performance, for the choir was not mentioned again until near the end of the 18th century. More likely, the choir continued to play a part in the worship of the church. The compliments paid the choir in both the *Boston Evening Post* and the Pew Proprietor's Book following the 1771 performance indicate the congregation was pleased with the choir and its music. Some 20 years later, the famous composer and singing-school teacher Oliver Holden joined the church—a natural leader for the choir. Finally, the late 18th- and early 19th-century references to the choir mentioned its excellence, probably indicating a tradition of good choral singing. The 1771 performance likely represented only the beginning of the choir, which continued to fill a leadership role in worship at the First Baptist Church for the remainder of the century.

**The Oliver Holden Years.** A number of native American composers were active during the last quarter of the 18th century, but only two of these men achieved any lasting fame. The first was William Billings, a musician-tanner who was one of the most remarkable characters ever to appear on the American musical scene. With typically American independence, he declared himself to be free of all "rules" of composition, though he still leaned heavily on traditional methods. The result was a music of rugged, individualistic character which seemed to typify the early American spirit.

It is interesting to speculate on the possibility of a direct relationship between Billings and the First Baptist Church of Boston. The composer was not a Baptist, and there is no record of him teaching a singing school at a Baptist church, though the possibility cannot be ruled out. On the other hand, Billings was an active participant in Boston's musical life and would almost certainly have been known to many members of the First Baptist Church, some of whom might even have attended one of his singing schools at another institution.

One piece of circumstantial evidence perhaps points to an association

William Billings' tune STILLMAN from John Rippon's *Selection of Psalm and Hymn Tunes,* 6th ed. (London, n.d.).

between the composer and the church. In 1778, Billings published his *Singing Master's Assistant,* which included a tune of his composition named CONSOLATION. When John Rippon published *A Selection of Psalm and Hymn Tunes* in London in 1791, he included a variant of this tune, attributing it to "W. Billings." However, instead of using Billings's original title for the tune, Rippon called it STILLMAN, most likely after the pastor of Boston's First Baptist Church, Samuel Stillman. Indeed, Stillman himself might have sent the tune—perhaps without including its title—to Rippon as a specimen of American composition, with the London minister then naming it after his correspondent. The implication is that this tune could well have been known and used in the First Baptist Church of Boston during Billings's lifetime. However, until more precise information is available, this must remain conjectural.

The other famous composer was Oliver Holden. Holden, like Billings, was essentially self-educated in music and concerned himself primarily with sacred music. However, he was more inclined to the imitation of current European styles and techniques of music composition. His music, while retaining certain of the rugged characteristics of Billings's works, was somewhat smoother and more "professional" than that of his older contemporary. Holden is still remembered today as the composer of CORONATION, a tune which is usually sung to Edward Perronet's hymn "All hail the power of Jesus' name."

Oliver Holden became a member of the First Baptist Church of Boston on August 7, 1791. He was a faithful and active member and was sometimes called upon to investigate cases involving church discipline.[16]

Holden had not yet published any music when he joined the First Baptist Church, but the very next year (1792) he issued his *American Harmony*. This book contained seven psalm and hymn tunes, two odes, and four anthems, all of them apparently by the compiler. This was followed by his two-volume *Union Harmony* (1793), which included CORONATION. Holden may have acquired the "All hail the power" text from Rippon's *Selection,* which the church had adopted just one month after Holden's admission to membership. While still a member at the First Baptist Church, Holden issued six additional music collections.

Holden, the choir director at the church, must certainly have used his own music with the choir. Indeed, he is known to have used three pieces of his own composition when the choir sang at the 1801 dedication of the new Baptist meetinghouse in Charlestown, Massachusetts, where Holden became a charter member.[17] Holden was evidently a good choir director, for William Bentley noted in his diary for June 1, 1797, that the First Baptist Church of Boston's "vocal music was excellent."[18]

**The Early 19th Century.** The quality of the choir at the First Baptist Church does not seem to have diminished after Holden's transfer of membership in 1801. On May 25, 1803, William Bentley again visited the church and noted in his diary that "The vocal music of this Congregation far exceeds any thing which I ever heard in any other. The closing anthem was well performed."[19]

The choir continued to be a "vigorous organization" during the first two decades of the 19th century. According to Wood, the choir

> usually met one evening in the week, and also before the services, to practice the tunes. They carefully rehearsed Mear, China, Wyndham, Wantage, Jourdan, Silver Street, Oporto, Windsor, Plympton, St. Asaphs, etc., but seldom ventured upon an anthem, except on special occasions.[20]

As was customary at that time, the choir was located in the gallery or balcony facing the pulpit.[21] The choir was given a prominent place at the funeral of Samuel Stillman on March 16, 1807, and at the ordination of Francis Wayland on August 21, 1821.[22] Daniel Badger, the choir director during the early years of the 19th century, was paid "a very small salary" in the second decade of the century.[23]

Another person who might have been of some importance in the choral program of the First Baptist Church was James Loring, who was "recd. into ye church" on July 1, 1792, became a deacon, and was elected church clerk on June 16, 1809.[24] There is no evidence that Loring himself was particularly inclined to music; however, he was a partner in the firm of Manning and Loring, one of the important publishing companies of early 19th-century Boston. This firm issued a number of music books, some of which might have been used by the First Baptist Church choir through the courtesy of Loring.

### Instrumental Music

Instrumental music does not seem to have been used at the First Baptist Church of Boston until the second decade of the 19th century. Opposition to musical instruments was characteristic of many Baptist churches until well into the 19th century. Organs and orchestral instruments were often derogatorily referred to as "mechanical music" or "wooden music." Only through a long and sometimes painful process did musical instruments come to be accepted in Baptist churches in America.[25]

If some members of the First Baptist Church were opposed to musical instruments, Oliver Holden did not share that feeling. Holden owned an organ which can still be seen at the Bostonian Society in the Old State House, Boston.[26] However, there is no evidence that Holden ever played this organ in the church.

The first instrument used in the church seems to have been a bass viol, introduced in 1818. Wood remarked that "the introduction of the bass viol was not without some opposition, but it soon became a regular accompaniment of the choir."[27] The bass viol was later supplemented by a violin, a flute, and a clarinet; this "gallery orchestra" was succeeded several years later by an organ. The function of the bass viol and gallery orchestra was to accompany the choral and congregational singing. Independent instrumental music (such as preludes and offertories) was probably not used until the installation of the organ.

### Conclusion

The First Baptist Church of Boston was typical of most early American Baptist churches in its early rejection of instrumental music and in its successive use of the Sternhold and Hopkins psalter, the *New Version,* Watts' *Psalms and Hymns,* Rippon's *Selection,* and "Winchell's Watts." The church was one of the first to introduce several of these books into Baptist worship in America, thereby assuming a position of musical leadership in the denomination. The early establishment of a choir at the First Baptist Church was somewhat unusual for that time and place and represented an innovative step that was not quickly imitated by other Baptist churches, except in a few places.

Credit for the leadership role played by the First Baptist Church of Boston in early Baptist church music belongs to a succession of able ministers and music leaders. Samuel Stillman, James Winchell, and other pastors of the church encouraged and supported the use of hymnody and choral music in the church. With their backing, capable music leaders such as Skinner Russell and Oliver Holden were able to build music programs which foreshadowed the future of the art in the entire denomination. These twin pillars of pastoral support and competent leadership are still the foundation for the establishment and maintenance of an effective church music program.

[1]Nathan E. Wood, *The History of the First Baptist Church of Boston (1665-1899)* (Philadelphia: American Baptist Publication Society, 1899).

[2]Ibid., 9.

[3]*Minutes,* First Baptist Church, Boston, Massachusetts. Succeeding references to the original minutes will not be footnoted, but will be identified by date.

[4]Wood, *The History,* 218-19. See also Louis F. Benson, *The English Hymn* (New York: George H. Doran Co., 1915; reprinted, Richmond, VA: John Knox Press, 1962), 196.

[5]William J. Reynolds, "Baptist Hymnody in America," in *Handbook to The Baptist Hymnal* (Nashville: Convention Press, 1992), 32.

[6]Wood, *The History,* 266.

[7]Ibid., 309.

[8]Quoted in Robert Francis Seybolt, The *Private Schools of Colonial Boston* (New York: Arno Press & The New York Times, 1969; reprint of 1935 edition), 33-34.

[9]George Hood, *A History of Music in New England* (Boston: Wilkins, Carter & Co., 1846; reprinted, New York: Johnson Reprint Corporation, 1970), 188-90.

[10]Morgan Edwards, *Materials Towards a History of the Baptists in Pennsylvania* (Philadelphia: Joseph Crukshank, and Isaac Collins, 1770), 101.

[11]W. C. James, *Leigh Street Baptist Church, 1854-1954* (Richmond, VA: Whittet and Shepperson, 1954), 82.

[12]John Woolman Brush, *Heritage of Faith and Freedom: A Short History of the First Baptist Church, Haverhill, Massachusetts* (Groveland, MA: Boyd-James Press, Inc., 1964), 64.

[13]Norman M. Isham, *The Meeting House of the First Baptist Church in Providence* (Providence: Akerman-Standard Co., 1925), 19-20.

[14]Wood, *The History,* 265-66.

[15]Ralph T. Daniel, *The Anthem in New England before 1800* (Evanston: Northwestern University Press, 1966), 54, 58, 63.

[16]See "Oliver Holden (1765-1844): The First Baptist Composer in America," in Part I of this volume.

[17]Ibid.

[18]William Bentley, *The Diary of William Bentley, D.D.* (Salem, MA: The Essex Press, 1905-1914; reprinted, Gloucester, MA: Peter Smith, 1962), II, 224.

[19]Ibid., III, 25.

[20]Wood, *The History,* 307.

[21]Ibid., 307-08.

[22]Ibid., 299, 314. James Winchell's support for the choir may be assumed from the publication of his *An Address on Music, Delivered before the Singing Society of the Second Baptist Church in Boston, on the Evening of the 7th April, 1814* (Boston: Manning and Loring, [1814]). This sermon reveals a considerable knowlege of music on the part of Winchell.

[23]Ibid., 374.

[24]Ibid., 304.

[25]See David Music, "The Introduction of Musical Instruments into Baptist Churches in America," *The Quarterly Review,* 40: 55-62, October 1979.

[26]William J. Reynolds, *Companion to Baptist Hymnal* (Nashville: Broadman Press, 1976), 339.

[27]Wood, *The History,* 307.

# PART II:

# PASTOR–HYMNISTS OF THE 19TH-CENTURY SOUTH

# PART II:
## PASTOR–HYMNISTS OF THE 19TH-CENTURY SOUTH

# Introduction
## Paul A. Richardson

I N THE LATE 18TH AND 19TH centuries, Baptists in the South produced many collections of hymn texts. Most of these were local to some degree, each serving a congregation, an association, or whatever churches in a region could be persuaded to purchase it. This pattern reflected Baptist congregational polity, regional preferences for certain types of materials, limited means for distribution and sales, provincial attitudes, and the limited connections that were being developed for association and cooperation. Among the leading collections, in addition to those discussed in the following studies, were books by Jesse Mercer (Georgia), Silas Noel (Kentucky), William Dossey (South Carolina), John Purify (North Carolina), Staunton Burdett (South Carolina), and William Buck (Kentucky).

The persons, hymns, and compilations discussed in the following five articles illustrate the range of content and circulation. Eleazar Clay's *Hymns and Spiritual Songs* was compiled in a rural congregation in Virginia. Richard Furman's three hymns were written for a specific religious commemoration of a civic celebration in South Carolina. Starke Dupuy's collection, which went through numerous editions published in at least three cities, served the western frontier. Andrew Broaddus' three extant books, ranging over nearly a half century, show progressive enlargement in scope and repertory, from a small volume of informal "sacred ballads" to larger collections for wide distribution that integrated standard hymns for corporate worship with folk materials for social singing and revivals. The high point in size and intended circulation was reached in *The Baptist Psalmody,* an anthology for more-formal worship that was compiled by Basil Manly and Basil Manly, Jr., as the first hymnbook issued by the publication society of the young Southern Baptist Convention.

Emerging from these differing sources and practices was an identifiable body of diverse hymnody that still, to some degree (coupled with the gospel song, a later borrowing from the North), forms a common core of hymnic repertory among Southern Baptists. This includes the psalms and hymns of Isaac Watts ("Am I a soldier of the cross"); the contributions of the British Baptist writers of the "Golden Age" ("Come, thou fount of every blessing"); the hymns of Charles Wesley ("Love divine, all loves excelling"), John Newton ("Amazing grace! How sweet the sound"), and others who energized the religious awakenings; and the anonymous folk hymns of rural America ("What wondrous love is this").

# ANDREW BROADDUS
## and Hymnody
### Paul A. Richardson

Reprinted, with revisions, from *The Virginia Baptist Register*, 1985. Used by permission.

ANDREW BROADDUS (1770-1848) was, by all accounts, a multifaceted, many-gifted individual. Garnett Ryland succinctly identifies him as "scholar, writer, poet, painter, preacher."[1] Woodford B. Hackley broadens this, characterizing him as "pre-eminently a preacher" but also "a skilled draughtsman, a painter of portraits and landscapes, a hymnologist, somewhat of a poet, a school teacher, and a clean and forceful writer of prose."[2]

Most historical studies of Broaddus have focused on his preaching and writing. It is the purpose of this article to examine his work in the area of hymnody. He will be seen to be a writer of hymns, a compiler of hymnals, and an advocate of hymn singing in a formative period in the use of hymns in the worship and fellowship of Virginia Baptists.

### Hymns and Broaddus' Conversion

Hymn singing was important in Andrew Broaddus' life from the time of his conversion. His father, John, was a staunch Episcopalian who had intended that his eldest son, William, enter the priesthood. When William died as a young man, Andrew, the fifth and youngest son, became the object of this desire.[3]

The third son in the Broaddus family, Reuben, had already disappointed his father by becoming a Baptist. Andrew, apparently attracted to this brother's faith, was forbidden by his father even to attend Baptist meetings. Compromising the spirit, if not the letter, of this law, Andrew would listen to the hymn singing coming from meetings at Reuben's house. The impressions of this singing were significant in his spiritual decision.[4]

According to Jeter, Broaddus said later that "he had never listened to anything which sounded more like the music of heaven."[5] Considering the enthusiasm and the tonal quality that must have characterized these performances, Jeter observes (perhaps tongue in cheek) that the music must have been "softened by distance, and rendered more impressive by the stillness and solemnity of the night."[6]

Broaddus' conversion came during the Great Revival of the late 1780s, which was particularly strong in the areas of King and Queen and Caroline counties under the ministry of Theodoric

Self-portrait of
Andrew Broaddus,
1770–1848

Noel.[7] It was during this awakening that hymn singing became an enthusiasm among Virginia Baptists.[8] The record of the singing at Reuben Broaddus' home suggests that this was a method of Noel's evangelism. Certainly this was true later in the career of this illustrious pastor, who in a meeting at Piscataway about 1812 eschewed preaching in favor of the singing and testimony of young converts brought from Upper King and Queen.[9]

Noel baptized Broaddus on May 28, 1789. The young Christian was soon exhorting at meetings and preached his first sermon on December 29 of that same year.[10] He was ordained on October 16, 1791, in a service led by his mentor, Noel, and his long-time colleague, Robert Semple.[11]

### Collection of Sacred Ballads

Even at this early point in his life and ministry, Broaddus was active in shaping the hymnic practices of Virginia Baptists. Together with his half cousin, Richard, he published a *Collection of Sacred Ballads* in 1790.[12] Richard Broaddus, the son of John's eldest half brother, was a school teacher and farmer identified in the family history as "a Baptist preacher of some local note."[13]

This *Collection* was a fairly small volume, containing 107 texts. In its preface, the compilers "lament the labor and inconveniency which it hath hitherto cost to retain the many excellent songs of praise, lately composed, and now extant among us."[14] The intent, evidently, was to prepare a convenient book of songs for the use of Christians in social settings, such as the one at the house of Reuben Broaddus. Lumpkin tells us that in this era of revival, "Family and community groups went singing to meetings, sang in the meetings, especially after preaching, and sang on the way home."[15] This application of the literature is made clearer by the citation later in the preface of "a few select hymns… suitable for any occasion whatever," that is, useful for worship as well as for exhortation and fellowship.

No authors are identified in the *Collection.* The leading contributors are Isaac Watts, with 18 texts, and Charles Wesley, with 13. There is little historic Baptist hymnody, though there are three texts by the American Baptist preacher, John Leland. *The Baptist Hymnal,* 1991,[16] includes seven hymns that appeared in the *Collection;* its predecessor, *Baptist Hymnal,* 1975,[17] had eight. Among the enduring hymns are "Am I a soldier of the cross" (Isaac Watts); "Come, thou fount of every blessing" (Robert Robinson); and "Love divine, all loves excelling" (Charles Wesley).

The Virginia Baptist Historical Society holds what appears to be a manuscript of the *Collection.* Though it bears no identification or title page, its contents are largely the same, with only minor differences, as those of the published book.[18] Further, the elegant script in which the manuscript is written matches that of letters known to be from Broaddus' pen.

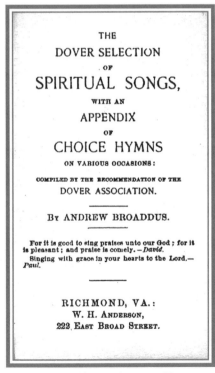

Title page from Andrew Broaddus'
*The Dover Selection* (Richmond, 1828).

### A Selection of Hymns and Spiritual Songs

There is no surviving evidence of Broaddus' hymnic activity over the next 37 years. However, *A Selection of Hymns and Spiritual Songs from the Best Authors* by Andrew Broaddus was advertised by Richmond printer Samuel Pleasants in several issues of *The Virginia Argus* in late 1798. Based on this advertisement, Charles Evans listed the book in *American Bibliography.* Edward Starr repeated Evans' citation in *A Baptist Bibliography.* Unfortunately, the hymnbook is not extant, and the bibliographers give no clue as to its contents.

### The Dover Selection

During the nearly four decades between the *Collection of Sacred Bal-*

*lads* and *The Dover Selection,* Broaddus served churches in King and Queen and Caroline counties (with a brief stint as assistant to John Courtney at First Church, Richmond), while declining invitations to several prominent pastorates along the east coast. He became a prominent and influential figure in the Dover Association.

The changes in the repertory of his collections after this interval suggest that Broaddus continued to explore and to experience a wide range of hymnic literature. The introduction to *The Dover Selection* shows his acquaintance with both Rippon's and Winchell's editions of Watts.[19] He is known to have corresponded both with John Leland, who wrote hymns, and with Jesse Mercer, who edited an important hymnal, and may well have exchanged information about hymnody with them.[20] Three of his colleagues in Virginia— Eleazar Clay, John Courtney, and Eli Ball—also compiled hymnals. It seems likely that his contacts with them would have included discussions about hymns.

At the 1827 annual session of the Dover Association, the 20th item in the minutes reads:

> *Resolved.* That A. Broaddus, Wm. Todd, and John Spencer be appointed a committee to select and publish such Hymn Books as they may think useful, (if to them it should be thought expedient) and report to the next Association.[21]

Broaddus' status in the association may be gauged from his mention six times in the minutes for this year. Hackley notes that he preached at the association meeting every year that he was in attendance from 1797 to 1843.[22]

It is not clear what role the other committee members played in the design of the book. Only Broaddus' name appears on the title page of *The Dover Selection of Spiritual Songs.* In the preface, he refers to himself as "the Compiler of this Work," while acknowledging parenthetically that he was "associated with two others, as a Committee of Inspection."[23] Neither Todd nor Spencer is identified by name or position.[24]

The 1828 minutes record that:

> The Committee appointed concerning the publication of a Hymn Book made report, which is received as satisfactory. And this Association hereby recommends to the Christian public the said Hymn Book.[25]

Thus *The Dover Selection of Spiritual Songs* was authorized. The recommendation by the largest association in Virginia,[26] soon to become the largest in the world,[27] lent the work prominence.

The public must have registered suggestions for improvement, however, for a second edition was soon prepared. It carries an "advertisement" from the compiler, dated May 2, 1829, which notes that the songs are newly distributed under their topics, that some corrections have been made, and that "a few songs (favourite compositions with many persons)" have been added.[28] This is the more widely circulated and, in some sense, definitive edition of this collection.

*The Dover Selection,* second edition, contains 291 texts. These are arranged in two sections: "The Spiritual Songs,"[29] comprising 204 entries related to 19 topics; and the "Appendix containing a Choice Collection of Hymns,"[30] including 87 items under 15 heads.

This anthology is "principally intended for popular use and not as a standard book for the desk, or the leader of the hymn in public worship."[31] Thus the term "spiritual songs" is to be related to the social singing discussed earlier. Broaddus, citing the Rippon and Winchell hymnals, says that "we have good standard Hymn Books in general use in the Baptist Churches."[32]

Later in the preface, Broaddus admits that though some of these spiritual songs "may well commend themselves to the critic's taste, and may challenge the critic's eye, this, it is acknowledged, is not always, nay, not *generally* the case."[33] He argues for a limited place for such and asserts that he has chosen only the best. His objective is set forth this way: "The Compiler, for his own part, wishes to see cultivated a devotion, *lively* without *levity,* and *solemn* without *dulness.*"[34] The appendix of hymns has been included "so that the book might be used, if required, in any of the common exercises of public or social worship."[35]

The range of textual sources is broader than in the 1790 *Collection.* Of special interest are hymnists of the British Baptist heritage, such as John Fawcett, Samuel Stennett, and Joseph Swain; American Baptist contemporaries of Broaddus, such as Joseph Cook, Robert Daniel, and Thomas Baldwin are also of special interest.

*The Baptist Hymnal,* 1991, contains 22 hymns that were in *The Dover Selection; Baptist Hymnal,* 1975, had 24. Among these are such favorites as: "Amazing grace! How sweet the sound," "Blest be the tie," and "On Jordan's stormy banks."

"Amazing Grace" from Andrew Broaddus' *The Dover Selection*, (Richmond, 1828).

Three of Andrew Broaddus' own hymns are found in *The Dover Selection*. Marked "original" is "Help thy servant, gracious Lord" (192):

Help thy servant, gracious Lord
    Who comes in Jesu's [*sic*] name;
Only thou canst strength afford,
    Thy gospel to proclaim:
Grant his soul a heavenly ray,
    Fill his heart with holy fire;
Help thy servant, Lord, we pray—
    Regard our souls' desire.


CHORUS.
O, for sanctifying grace!
    O, for love's inspiring power!
Lord, we beg, for Jesus' sake,
    A sweet refreshing shower.

Give us to receive the word,
    With love, and joy, and fear;
Grant thy quickening grace, O Lord,
    On all assembled here:
Seal the truth on all to-day;
    All our hearts with heaven inspire.
Help thy servant, Lord, we pray—
    Regard our souls' desire,

O, for sanctifying grace, &c.[36]

Labeled "chiefly original" is "How solemn the signal I hear" (183):

How solemn the signal I hear!
    The summons that calls me away,
In regions unknown to appear:—
    How shall I the summons obey!
What scenes in that world shall arise,
    When life's latest sigh shall be fled
And darkness has seal'd up my eyes,
    And deep in the dust I am laid?

No longer the world I can view,
    The scenes which so long I have known:
My friends, I must bid you adieu,
    For here I must travel alone:—
Yet here my Redeemer has trod.
    His hallowed footsteps I know;
I'll trust for defence to his rod,
    And lean on his staff as I go.

Dear Shepherd of Israel, lead on;
    My soul follows hard after thee;
The phantoms of death are all flown.
    When Jesus my shepherd I see.
Dear brethren and sisters, I go
    To wait your arrival above:
Be faithful, and soon you shall know
    The triumphs and joys of his love.[37]

"Soldiers of the cross, arise" (152) is also "original."

> Soldiers of the cross, arise!
> Lo! your Captain from the skies
> Holding forth the glittering prize,
>     Calls to victory:
> Fear not, though the battle lower;
> Firmly stand the trying hour;
> Stand the tempter's utmost power,
>     Spurn his slavery.
>
> Who the cause of Christ would yield?
> Who would leave the battle-field?
> Who would cast away his shield?—
>     Let him basely go:
> Who for Zion's King will stand?
> Who will join the faithful band?
> Let him come with heart and hand,
>     Let him face the foe
>
> By the mercies of our God?
> By Immanuel's streaming blood,
> When alone for us he stood,
>     Ne'er give up the strife:
> Ever, to the latest breath,
> Hark to what your Captain saith;—
> "Be thou faithful unto death;
>     "Take the crown of life."
>
> By the woes which rebels prove,
> By the bliss of holy love,
> Sinners, seek the joys above;
>     Sinners, turn and live!
> Here is *freedom* worth the name;
> Tyrant sin is put to shame;
> Grace inspires the hallow'd flame;
>     God the crown will give.[38]

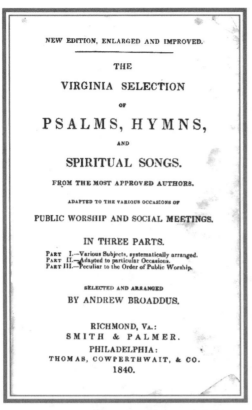

NEW EDITION, ENLARGED AND IMPROVED.

THE

VIRGINIA SELECTION

OF

PSALMS, HYMNS,

AND

SPIRITUAL SONGS.

FROM THE MOST APPROVED AUTHORS.

ADAPTED TO THE VARIOUS OCCASIONS OF

PUBLIC WORSHIP AND SOCIAL MEETINGS.

IN THREE PARTS.

PART    I.—Various Subjects, systematically arranged.
PART   II.—Adapted to particular Occasions.
PART III.—Peculiar to the Order of Public Worship.

SELECTED AND ARRANGED

BY ANDREW BROADDUS.

RICHMOND, VA.:
SMITH & PALMER.

PHILADELPHIA:
THOMAS, COWPERTHWAIT, & CO.
1840.

Title page from Andrew Broddus' *The Virginia Selection*,
Second edition (Richmond, 1840).

## The Virginia Selection

Even as *The Dover Selection* found a place among Virginia Baptists, its shortcomings and the aging of the standard hymn collections created a need for a new, more serviceable anthology. In a letter published in *Religious Herald* on October 25, 1833, Joseph Baker reviews the situation and announces that he will publish a new hymnal of some 800 entries the following January.[39] Two weeks later there is a response from Andrew Broaddus. He acknowledges the deficiencies of *The Dover Selection* (while recalling the limitations of its purpose) and advises that he, too, has been at work on a comprehensive hymnbook. He suggests that such a book, in order to receive wide usefulness and acceptance, should be reviewed by a committee. Further, he says that he does not wish to compare with Baker in the publication of a book.[40]

In this same November 8, 1833, issue, there is an item from the *Herald's* editor, William Sands. He mentions the letters of Baker and Broaddus and a personal note recently received from James Fife that also proposes that a new hymnal be prepared. Sands states that some of the members of the Book and Tract Society have also been considering a new collection. He suggests that the work might go forward under the Society, of which both Baker and Broaddus are members.[41]

Broaddus prepared his work and brought it to his colleagues in the Dover Association for their review in 1835. The minutes of that year record:

> *Resolved,* That a Committee be appointed to examine a collection of Hymns, now at this place, compiled by Elder A. Broaddus, and report to-morrow.

Brethren Ball, Keeling, Jeter, Montague, Northam, Mason, and Cornelius, were appointed the Committee.[42]

On the following day:

> Brother Ball, from the Committee appointed yesterday to examine a collection of Hymns, presented the following report:
> The Committee appointed to examine the Hymn-book recently compiled by Elder Andrew Broaddus, have bestowed as much attention upon it, as their limited time would permit, and although they could not enter into a minute examination of the whole volume, yet they have no hesitancy in saying, that they believe it to be an excellent selection of choice Hymns, well arranged, and well adapted to public and private worship. They cheerfully recommend it to ministers and congregations for public meetings, and for private devotion. As such a work as the above is much needed, the Committee ardently hope that its patronage will be as extensive as are its merits.
> E. Ball, Chairman[43]

The report was unanimously adopted, and the Committee discharged.

The examiners' public commendation was, apparently, accompanied by some private suggestions. A notice from Broaddus in the October 30, 1835, issue of *Religious Herald* states that the release of the book will be delayed so that additions recommended by the committee can be made.[44] A footnote in the association minutes had advised that "Several members of the Committee had previously examined this Compilation."[45]

*The Virginia Selection of Psalms, Hymns, and Spiritual Songs* came from the press in 1836. It was substantially enlarged in a second edition, Broaddus acknowledging in its preface that the first edition "has been found defective, in regard to the number and variety of Hymns for the common occasions of pulpit service."[46] It was this second edition (and a third with only minor changes) that was widely accepted, remaining in print as late as 1876.

This book had been designed to serve the needs of both "Public Worship and Social Meetings," as stated on the title page.[47] Thus it is a large anthology, with 710 texts disposed in three sections: "Various Subjects, systematically arranged," "Adapted to particular Occasions," and "Peculiar to the Order of Public Worship."[48] The hymns are further grouped under topical or functional headings within the three major sections. The model of Rippon for this type of organization is acknowledged.[49]

Regarding the continuing inclusion of the less formal songs, Broaddus observes that some of these "may not be capable of standing the test of a refined criticism."[50] He then turns a fine phrase to say that a hymnal editor must consider his public.[51]

> On this point, let it suffice to say, that as this book is designed for *popular* as well as for *pulpit* use, some allowance must be made for popular liking—some sacrifice at the altar of devotional feeling.

*The Virginia Selection* again shows growth not only in the number of hymns, but, more significantly, in the breadth of sources. Newly represented are Anne Steele, John Bowring, Timothy Dwight, and American Baptists Richard Furman, Adoniram Judson, and Samuel Smith. There is also growing sophistication. Most hymns are identified as to author or source, whereas none were so marked in the *Collection,* and only the appendix of *The Dover Selection* carried attributions.

*The Virginia Selection* includes a number of hymns used by Southern Baptists in the present era. *The Baptist Hymnal,* 1991, contains 30 of these texts, while 35 were in its predecessor, *Baptist Hymnal,* 1975. Among these are: "Go to dark Gethsemane," "How firm a foundation," and "I love thy kingdom, Lord."

Five hymns by Andrew Broaddus are in *The Virginia Selection.* In addition to the two published earlier, there are "Send thy blessing, Lord, we pray" (667):

> Send thy blessing, Lord, we pray,
>   On the labours of this day;
> Seal the truth and own thy word:
>   Pardon all our failings, Lord.
> May we in thy ways be found—
>   Faith grow stronger—love abound;
> Strike the careless soul with fear,
>   Wipe away the mourner's tear.
>
> Lord, unless thy Spirit move,
>   Vain will all our efforts prove;
> Paul might plant in vain, we know.
>   And Apollos water too:

O! do thou the increase give;
   Let us all thy grace receive;
Send thy blessing, Lord, we pray.
   On the labours of this day.[52]

and one titled "The Wandering Sinner" (708):

Restless thy spirit, poor wandering sinner.
   Restless and roving—O, come to thy home!
Return to the arms—to the bosom of mercy:
   The Saviour of sinners invites thee to come.

Darkness surrounds thee, and tempests are rising.
   Fearful and dangerous the path thou hast trod;
But mercy shines forth in the rainbow of promise.
   To welcome the wanderer home to his God.

Peace to the storm in thy soul shall be spoken,
   Guilt from thy bosom be banish'd away;
And heaven's sweet breezes, o'er death's tolling billows
   Shall waft thee at last to the regions of day.

But, oh! if regardless of God's gracious warning,
   Afar from his favour your soul must remove;
May you never hear—never feel the dread sentence;
   But live to his glory, and die in his love.[53]

The handwritten original of this last text is in the archives of the Virginia Baptist Historical Society. It accompanies a letter, dated July 4, 1836, to James Thomas, Junior, of Richmond, which indicates that the poem was written at Thomas' request. Both the letter and the hymnal indicate that "The Wandering Sinner" is sung to the same air as Burns' "Wandering Willie."[54]

## Broaddus' Use of Hymns

There are scattered quotations in Broaddus' *Sermons and Other Writings* that suggest the way in which he used hymnic literature in his preaching and writing. That he was not uncritical in his borrowing is confirmed by a note to his essay on "The Exhibition of the Gospel" in which he recalls altering a text for inclusion in *The Virginia Selection* in order to align it with his theological stance.[55]

Broaddus' feeling for a broader view of music than was common among Baptists of his time may be gathered from his choice of metaphor in a sermon recounted by Jeter.

> Many years ago, in a sermon at the Dover Association, he produced a thrilling effect, by comparing the departed ministers of the Association to a band of musicians. Ford, Noell [*sic*], Lunsford, Straughton, Toler, Courtney and others, were skillfully arranged in the band, according to their varied gifts: one sounded the silver trumpet, another played on the viol, a third on the bassoon, and so on.[56]

Broaddus' most thorough treatment of the place of hymn singing in the church's worship is in the circular letter prepared for the 1839 meeting of the Dover Association. At the 1838 session, he was directed to prepare an essay "with liberty to choose the subject."[57] This in itself was unusual, as the motion to choose the writer of the annual letter usually designated the topic. Broaddus selected the subject "Singing the Praises of the Most High."[58]

The letter opens with the statement that this is a matter deserving of serious attention and an area in which "there is a sad defect among many of the churches."[59] An outline of seven points is then pursued.

With citations of Matthew 26:30, Ephesians 5:19, Colossians 3:16, and 1 Corinthians 14:15, Broaddus asserts that "singing the praises of God is *an ordinance of divine worship.*"[60] Second, he says that all should sing, "that singing the praises of God in the churches is a *Christian duty.*"[61] Next, he admonishes those who do not sing, that their dormant talent should be developed. Then, to those who sing only when it pleases them, he quotes Paul, that "God loveth a cheerful giver," not only of material goods, but of self.[62]

His fifth point is the need for attention to "method and correctness."[63] He advocates the use of singing schools, provided they are directed to the improvement of music for worship, and recommends that *"among those who are best qualified, some brother ought to be considered and looked to, as a leader in the exercise of singing."*[64]

In the sixth place, Broaddus states that while he is not opposed to "free singing" (evidently the same as the social singing of "spiritual songs"), he is focusing his remarks about "the science of vocal music" on "the pulpit service."

An improvement in this respect, both as it regards a greater variety of suitable tunes, and a more correct and harmonious method of performing the service, appears to us to be highly desirable.[65]

Before moving to his final point, Broaddus apologizes for the detail into which he has gone, but avers that it is necessary for the proper address of the subject, that the churches be edified.[66]

His final point is devotional: "that the voice should be but the echo of the heart."[67] He closes with the prayer

> that with hearts and voices better tuned, we may all unite at last in the general chorus of "Blessing, and honor, and glory, and power, unto Him that sitteth on the throne, and unto the Lamb for ever and ever."[68]

## Conclusion

Hymn singing was not a new activity among Virginia Baptists in the time of Andrew Broaddus. It had, however, been reinvigorated by the Great Revival of the 1780s and was a common element in the worship and social activities of the churches. Broaddus gave direction to this aspect of the churches' lives through the enunciation of a theological rationale, through the provision of good models of hymn usage in preaching, and, most importantly, through the production of serviceable and influential collections of hymn texts for varied types of Christian gatherings.

[1]Garnett Ryland, *The Baptists of Virginia, 1699–1926* (Richmond, 1955), 171.
[2]W. B. Hackley, *Faces on the Wall* (Richmond, 1972), 7.
[3]Andrew Broaddus, *Sermons and Other Writings with a Memoir of His Life,* by J. B. Jeter (New York, 1852), 4.
[4]Ibid., 12.
[5]Ibid.
[6]Ibid.
[7]R. B. Semple, *A History of the Rise and Progress of the Baptists in Virginia* (Revised and Extended by Beale, Richmond,1894), 160.
[8]W. L. Lumpkin, *A Chronicle of Christian Heritage: Dover Baptist Association 1783-1983* (Richmond: Skipworth Press, 1983), 15.
[9]Ibid., 40.
[10]Broaddus, *Sermons,* 121.
[11]Ibid., 15.
[12]Richard Broaddus and Andrew Broaddus, *Collection of Sacred Ballads* ([n.p.] 1790).
[13]A[ndrew] Broaddus, *A History of the Broaddus Family* (St. Louis, 1888), 56.
[14]Broaddus and Broaddus, *Collection,* 3.
[15]Lumpkin, *A Chronicle,* 15.
[16]Wesley L. Forbis, editor, *The Baptist Hymnal* (Nashville: Convention Press, 1991).
[17]William J. Reynolds, general editor, *Baptist Hymnal* (Nashville: Convention Press, 1975).
[18]There are a few leaves missing and a few leaves displaced in the manuscript. Also, the manuscript contains additional hymns. While the published version's last hymn is number 107, the manuscript has texts numbered 108, 109, 110, 118, and 119 (numbers 112-117 being, presumably, on missing leaves).

[19]Andrew Broaddus, *The Dover Selection of Spiritual Songs with an Appendix of Chorus Hymns, on Various Occasions: Compiled by the Recommendation of the Dover Association*, 2d. ed. (Richmond, 1829), iii.

[20]Broaddus, *Sermons*, 22.

[21]*Minutes of the Dover Association*, 1827, 6.

[22]Hackley, *Faces*, 7.

[23]Broaddus, *The Dover Selection*, iv.

[24]In the 1827 *Minutes of the Dover Association*, 3, Todd is listed as pastor of the Lower King and Queen Church; Spencer as pastor of Pocatoane Church.

[25]*Minutes of the Dover Association*, 1828, 6.

[26]Lumpkin, *A Chronicle*, 20.

[27]Ibid., 59.

[28]Broaddus, *The Dover Selection*, ix.

[29]Ibid., 11.

[30]Ibid., 323.

[31]Ibid., iii.

[32]Ibid.

[33]Ibid., v.

[34]Ibid., vii.

[35]Ibid., v.

[36]Ibid., 302.

[37]Ibid., 291.

[38]Ibid., 240-41. William Walker included all four stanzas of this text in *The Southern Harmony and Musical Companion* (Philadelphia, 1835). It appears on p. 132, set to the tune BRUCE'S ADDRESS. Walker's attribution cites *"Dover Sel. p. 152."* I am indebted to Harry Eskew for calling this to my attention.

[39]*Religious Herald*, Oct. 25, 1833, 1.

[40]*Religious Herald*, Nov. 8, 1833, 1.

[41]Ibid., 2.

[42]*Minutes of the Dover Association*, 1835, 5.

[43]Ibid., 54.

[44]*Religious Herald*, Oct. 30, 1835, 4.

[45]*Minutes of the Dover Association*, 1835, 6.

[46]Andrew Broaddus, *The Virginia Selection of Psalms, Hymns, and Spiritual Songs From the Most Approved Authors. Adapted to the Various Occasions of Public Worship and Social Meetings.* New edition, enlarged and improved. (Richmond, 1840), vi ff.

[47]Ibid., iii.

[48]Ibid.

[49]Ibid., vi.

[50]Ibid., vii.

[51]Ibid.

[52]Ibid., hymn no. 667.

[53]Ibid., hymn no. 708.

[54]Letter from Andrew Broaddus to James Thomas, Jr., July 4, 1836.

[55]Broaddus, *Sermons*, 364.

[56]Ibid., 55ff.

[57]*Minutes of the Dover Association*, 1838, 7.

[58]*Minutes of the Dover Association*, 1839, 11.

[59]Ibid.

[60]Ibid.

[61]Ibid.

[62]Ibid., 12.

[63]Ibid., 13.

[64]Ibid.

[65]Ibid.

[66]Ibid.

[67]Ibid., 14.

[68]Ibid.

# ELEAZAR CLAY'S
# *Hymns and Spiritual Songs* (1793)
## Paul A. Richardson

Reprinted, with revisions, from *The Virginia Baptist Register,* 1990. Used by permission.

> Your committee has examined the said collection, and do approve of the
> same as laudable, and hope the said book may be a benefit to the pop-
> ulace in general, and to the church of Christ in particular.[1]

B Y RECEIVING AND ADOPT-
ING this evaluation, the
Baptist General Commit-
tee of Virginia, on May 14, 1792,
gave its blessing to a hymnal
assembled by one of its leading
members. Both the book itself
and its endorsement by this
body were notable developments in the early course of
hymnody among Baptists in
America.

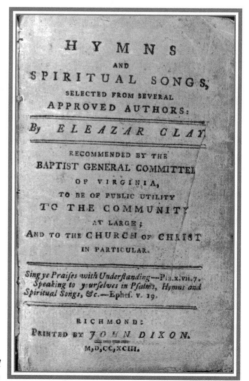

### Eleazar Clay

The compiler of *Hymns and
Spiritual Songs*[2] was Eleazar
Clay,[3] a man characterized by his
friend, Isaac Backus, as "a

Title page from Eleazar Clay's *Hymns and
Spiritual Songs* (Richmond, 1793).

wealthy and most agreeable Christian."[4] An extensive biography will not be attempted here, that having been accomplished in an article by John Edens[5] and in an unpublished paper by Dennis Nofsinger.[6] A brief consideration of his life will, however, help to establish the context of his work. Clay's tombstone provides the essentials:

In
Memory of
REV'D E. CLAY
Born Augt 4th 1744
Went into the French and
Indian War in March, 1758.
Made a profession of the
Christian Religion in Augt
1771, became a member of the
Baptist Church & Commenced
Preaching the everlasting Gospel
of JESUS CHRIST the same year.
And continued as is believed an
Humble follower of Jesus to his
Death which was 2nd May 1836.
Aged 91 Years 8 Mo & 28 Days.[7]

The epitaph features two prominent aspects of Clay's life between the records of his birth and death. First is his service in the French and Indian War (at the age of 13!). This is evidence of his patriotism and bravery—important traits of the Clay family. Eleazar was a great-great-grandson of "Captain" John Clay, one of the early settlers of Jamestown.[8] The family annals document the significant service to country, church, and society that characterized the line. Its most prominent figure was the statesman Henry Clay, the son of Eleazar's first cousin.

Eleazar Clay was the second of 11 children and the eldest of 6 sons.[9] Each of the brothers left his mark. Charles was an Episcopal minister, a friend of Thomas Jefferson, and a patriot.[10] Henry lost his life at Trenton in the Revolutionary War.[11] Thomas was also a soldier in that conflict and was a member of the first constitutional convention of Kentucky.[12] Matthew, likewise, fought in the Revolution and served in the congress of the United States.[13] Green was a delegate to the Virginia convention that ratified the U. S. constitution, a state legislator in both Virginia and Kentucky, and speaker of the Kentucky senate. He so distinguished himself as a general in the War of 1812 that a county in Kentucky was named for him.[14]

Eleazar apparently did not possess the wanderlust of the others. After his youthful service in the military, he settled on the family's land, expanded it, and amassed a considerable estate.[15] He also reared a large family, fathering at least 11 children in the first and second of his three marriages.[16] He seems to have been less active in politics than his brothers, but just as willing to champion unpopular causes when he thought they had merit.

One of these unpopular causes was that of the Baptists. The legend on his gravestone devotes most of its words to his conversion, his Baptist identity, and his long, faithful service in the cause of Christ.

Clay's identification with the Baptist position came at a difficult time in the story of Baptists in the commonwealth. The early 1770s marked the height of persecution of Baptist preachers in Chesterfield county. Though he had apparently been exposed to the Baptist view of the gospel early in his life, Clay was quickened to it during the imprisonment of Baptist preachers in the Chesterfield jail in 1770-71.[17] According to Taylor, it was "an intimate friend of Elder Clay," converted through the preaching from jail of William Webber and Joseph Anthony, who visited Clay and helped lead him to a profession of faith.[18] He was baptized on the first Sunday of August, 1771,[19] and began immediately to preach. By his own record, as recalled by W. J. Morrissett, Clay preached three times on that very day![20]

Clay not only preached, but he lent his considerable wealth and influence to the Baptist cause. He sent beds and provisions to those who were jailed for their preaching.[21] An incident conveyed by Morrissett has been a favorite in the sketching of Clay portraits:

> One of the prisoners being sick on one occasion, and needing a little stimulant, Elder Clay bought a "jug" of wine and carried it to the jail. The jailer told him it was against orders for the prisoners to have wine. Elder Clay writes, "I greased his paw and got it in."[22]

Clay's position in the community, so different from that of other Baptists who were, for the most part, poor and without influence, apparently protected him from prosecution.[23] As William Lumpkin observed, Chesterfield was the focus of Baptist persecution before the revolution, but a center of Baptist strength thereafter.[24] Eleazar Clay played no small role in this transformation.

When the Chesterfield church was constituted on August 22, 1773, the service took place in Clay's barn, with Eleazar and his wife, Jane, among those dismissed from the Cumberland church for that purpose.[25] He was selected as the congregation's delegate to the General Association the following May.[26] Subsequent entries in the church's minute book note that he was ordained as "Teachin Eldor" on January 1, 1775,[27] and that he "acted as our Deacon."[28] Later that year, on "May 27 & 28 at a great Meeting," Clay was ordained the congregation's first pastor.[29] He held this position until his death 61 years later. During those years he also helped to start two other congregations, Second Branch and Salem.[30]

Clay was also a force in larger arenas of Baptist life. As Edens shows in his article, Clay was the dominant figure in the Middle District Association from its founding in 1784. He was also prominent in the Baptist General Committee, the body that acted on his hymnal.

### The General Committee

The General Committee was designed in 1783 when its predecessor, the General Association, disbanded in favor of four district associations, of which Middle District was one.[31] It first met on October 9, 1784.[32] The General Committee was a representative body composed of four persons from each district association. Its stated purpose was to "consider all the political grievances of the whole Baptist society in Virginia, and all references from the district associations, respecting matters which concern the Baptist society at large."[33]

Clay's first involvement in this group cannot be documented, as the Committee's records prior to 1790 have been lost, but Semple records that he served on a committee appointed at its March 7, 1788, meeting to draft a memorial to the General Assembly petitioning for the sale of glebe lands.[34] He also reports that at the next meeting, on August 11, 1788, Clay was again on the committee for the memorial and that he was appointed to a committee for a "seminary of learning."[35] The extant minutes (1790, 91, 92, 93, and 99) all list Clay as a member of the General Committee and cite his work in a variety of roles.[36]

It was to this body, gathered on May 12, 1792, at the Tomahawk meeting house,[37] that Clay presented his collection of hymns. Semple provides the rationale for this action:

> At this session several books designed for publication, were offered to the general committee, in order to obtain their sanction. This was granted. This is one, of many ways, in which such a meeting might be

useful. To bring a book, designed for publication, immediately before a public assembly, in order to gain their approbation, would be impracticable; but a general meeting might be useful, by appointing a standing committee, for the purpose of examining anything intended for the press, which directly concerns the honour and interests of the Baptists. This select committee might make a report, stating the outlines of the book, according to which the general meeting could properly give, or withhold their recommendation; this would probably, on the one hand, give currency to such tracts as possess merit; while, on the other hand, it might happily suppress such, as would do injury to the cause of God and truth.[38]

The minutes record that "On motion... Messrs. Thomas, Waller and Toler be appointed to examine the Collection of Hymns by Brother Clay and make their report."[39] Two days later, on May 14, "The Report of the Committee appointed to examine a Collection of Hymns prepared by the Rev. Eleazar Clay, was reveived [*sic*] and agreed to as follows: [here is entered the sentence that appears at the head of this article]."[40]

This procedure seems to have been an innovation. The Philadelphia Association had approved a hymnal in 1790, but the association itself had commissioned the work two years before.[41] This action on Clay's book seems to be the first record of a prepublication review of an unsolicited hymnal by an American Baptist body. The practice came to be of some importance. Andrew Broaddus' two later collections, *The Dover Selection* (1828) and *The Virginia Selection* (1836) were both evaluated in this manner.[42]

## The Collection

Having gotten the blessing of his peers, Clay proceeded to publish. The book is small, measuring 4½ by 3 inches. The copy at the Virginia Baptist Historical Society, inscribed with the name A. M. Garnett, is in very poor condition. Its leatherlike board cover is separated from the pages, which are themselves loose. Several pages are lost, though their contents can be established through the index of first lines, which is intact. The leaves are spotted and stained.

The title page contains information typical of the period. At the head are the full title and the author's name: "Hymns and Spiritual Songs, Selected from Several Approved Authors: by Eleazar Clay." Next comes the endorsement, its language slightly altered: "Recommended by the Baptist General Committee of Virginia, to be of public utility to the community at large; and to the Church of Christ in particular." Two scriptural quotations follow: "Sing ye Praises with Understanding—Psa. xlvii.7. Speaking to yourselves in Psalms, Hymns and Spiritual Songs, &c.—Ephes. v.19." The last item provides the publication information: "Richmond: Printed by John Dixon, M,D,CC,XCIII."

The reason for the delay of at least eight months before publication, resulting in a date on the book of 1793, is not known. It is possible that the version shown to the committee was in manuscript and that the process of typesetting was time consuming. It could also be that revisions were made (perhaps at the suggestion of the reviewers) or that the printer encountered logistical problems. Any attempt at explanation, however, is an argument from silence.

The page following the title is blank. There being no preface or other introductory material, the book proceeds directly to the hymns themselves, with the first page of texts headed "HYMNS, &c." Portions of the book are arranged under topical subheads. "Morning" appears before the first text, "Evening" before the sixth, "Morning or Evening" before number X, and "The Lord's Day" prior to XII. This plan must have been forgotten or abandoned because headings do not reappear until "Baptism" (before CCLVI) and "Supper" (at CCLXI). The last three entries only have descriptive titles: "A Parting Blessing" (first line: "Jesus, grant us all a blessing"); "The Slow Traveller" ("O happy souls how fast you go"); and "The Complainer" ("I set myself against the Lord").

Beginning with the second page of hymns (page 4), each page is numbered at the top. The 280 hymns, plus 13 single stanzas for baptism, occupy 261 pages. Each text is headed with a Roman numeral, for example, "HYMN XCVII." The texts are displayed in poetic form, with each stanza numbered by an Arabic numeral. Some have stanzas bracketed, perhaps to suggest possible omissions. No authors are identified within the collection.

At the end of the book is "A Table to find any Hymn by the Page," an index of first lines.

## Context and Content

The motivation prompting Clay's preparation of a hymnal and the circumstances surrounding the project are unknown. Many collections of the period provide a statement of objectives in a preface, but such is omitted here. Perhaps his lost diary might have shed some light on this.[43] We are also without help from church records, as the early minutes book of Chesterfield church ends in 1788, with no indication that hymn singing or hymn selection was a matter of concern.

We do not know anything of Clay's education, but there is nothing to suggest that he received any special training for ministry, let alone any direction in the as-yet-undeveloped area of hymnology. Among the items put up for auction after his death were a family Bible, *Cruden's Concordance*, Benedict's *History of the Baptists*, and other unnamed books.[44] Whether any hymnals were among these cannot be proved, though a consideration of the contents of *Hymns and Spiritual Songs* suggests his familiarity with at least three specific collections.

The most significant accomplishment in the compilation of Baptist hymnals to this time was John Rippon's *A Selection of Hymns*, published in London in 1787.[45] Two American printers issued the book in 1792.[46] These would have been too late to influence Clay's work, but the availability in the United States of copies printed in England[47] supports the supposition that Clay had access to this material.

Baptists in America had published more than a dozen hymnals before Clay presented his book to the General Committee. The first of these was a 1762 Boston reprint of Benjamin Wallin's *Evangelical Hymns and Songs*,[48] with added hymns of Watts and Joseph Stennett. This book had been published in London in 1750. The first Baptist hymnal edited on these shores was *Hymns and Spiritual Songs*, published in Newport, Rhode Island, in 1766.[49] Several scholars refer to a reprinting of this hymnal in Williamsburg in 1773, but no copies are known to be extant.[50] In 1784, Enoch Story, Jr., issued *A Choice Collection of Hymns*.[51] *A Selection of Psalms and Hymns*, the hymnal commissioned by the Philadelphia Association, was compiled by Samuel Jones and Burgis Allison and released in 1790.[52] In that same year, Virginians Richard and Andrew Broaddus issued *Collection of Sacred Ballads*.[53] In 1791 or before, Joshua Smith published the first of several editions of *Divine Hymns, or Spiritual Songs*.[54]

The contents of *Hymns and Spiritual Songs* strongly suggest that Clay was familiar with Rippon's *Selection*. A significant amount of the material in Clay had been included in Rippon. This is particularly evident in the realm of hymnody by Baptist authors. Thirty-eight of the 43 hymns by Baptists that appear in Clay's book had been included in Rippon's. Of the five not in Rippon, four are by John Leland, who spent much of his ministry in Virginia.

Similar dependence is suggested on the work by the Broadduses. Twenty-three texts that Clay included had made their first American appearance in the *Collection of Sacred Ballads*. Among these are two of the Leland hymns and 14 whose authors are still unknown. These anonymous hymns are predominantly of the ballad or "social" type, with language pressing the welcome of the gospel. This is evident even in the first lines of such examples as "Come all ye saints and sinners near," "Come brethren and sisters that love my dear Lord," and "Come guilty souls and flee away."

Another source that may be inferred from the contents is *Olney Hymns*.[55] This collection, published in London in 1779, is the collaboration of two authors, John Newton and William Cowper. It was printed in New York as early as 1790. There are 40 texts by Newton in *Hymns and Spiritual Songs*. This far exceeds the number of his hymns included in any earlier Baptist hymnal, British or American. The quantity of Newton texts is exceptional for non-Baptist books as well. According to the files of the *Dictionary of American Hymnology*,[56] 22 of the Newton hymns made their first American appearance in *Hymns and Spiritual Songs*. Clay's inclusion of so many indicates that he had access to a copy of *Olney Hymns* and that he resonated strongly with Newton's style.

A similar pattern, but in much smaller numbers, is true for Cowper's hymns. Of the seven texts by this author that are included, three were making their American debut in Clay's book.

The most prominent author in *Hymns and Spiritual Songs* is Isaac Watts, with 80 hymns. Such domination reflects his position in the hymn-singing practices of Baptists of this period.[57]

The leading Baptist contributor to this book is Anne Steele, with 11 texts. John Fawcett and Samuel Stennett each have seven inclusions. All of their hymns in this collection had previously been included by Rippon. The sole American, John Leland, has four; Benjamin Beddome, three; and John Fellows, two. Those who are represented by a single text are John Adams, Charles Cole, Benjamin Francis, Joseph Grigg, Samuel Medley, James Newton, and Robert Robinson. Counted as Baptist hymns in this census are "All hail the power of Jesus' name," in Rippon's revision, and "How firm a foundation," which appeared first in Rippon's *Selection*, attributed to the mysterious "K."

Not included in these figures are 13 single stanzas on baptism. Four of these are by Beddome; three by "H. F."; two by Joseph Stennett; one, each, by "G." and "H."; and two are without any indication of authorship. The fact that these are identical to a set in Rippon's *Selection* is further evidence of Clay's dependence on that volume.

The contributions of all authors with more than a single text are as follows:

80   Isaac Watts
     [43 Total by Baptist authors]
40   John Newton
23   Philip Doddridge
18   Joseph Hart
11   Anne Steele (Baptist)
 9   Charles Wesley
 7   William Cowper
 7   John Fawcett (Baptist)
 7   Samuel Stennett (Baptist)
 4    John Leland (Baptist)
 3   Benjamin Beddome (Baptist)
 3   John Cennick
 3   John Mason
 3   Thomas Toplady
 2   John Fellows (Baptist)
 2   Joseph Humphreys

There are 24 other authors or sources represented by one hymn each. The writers of 34 hymns are not known.

## Influence

Much remains to be learned about the whole area of 18th-century Baptist hymnody in America before the direct influence of Clay's work as a hymnal compiler can be evaluated accurately. The extent to which *Hymns and Spiritual Songs* was sold and used has not been established. Its possible study by other compilers in the immediate geographical area, such as John Courtney[58] and Andrew Broaddus, has not yet been explored.

It was, perhaps, in his inclusion of texts from John Newton that Clay made his most significant contribution. He was not the first American to print Newton's hymns, but, as noted above, his use of them far outstripped his predecessors. Baptists would certainly give Clay a place of honor for being the first of his denomination in America to publish "Amazing grace! How sweet the sound." He performed the same service for "How sweet the name of Jesus sounds" and was the first of all American compilers to publish "Come, my soul, thy suit prepare." Among American Baptists, he was also first to include "I'm not ashamed to own my Lord" (Watts) and "While shepherds watch [sic] their flocks by night" (Nahum Tate).[59]

*The Baptist Hymnal,* 1991,[60] includes 12 of the 280 hymns that Clay selected for *Hymns and Spiritual Songs*. Five others were in *Baptist Hymnal,* 1975.[61] These show the endurance of the hymns of the two leading figures, Watts and Newton, and of three Baptist hymns that have gained something like universal use. Three Watts texts endure to the present: "Alas, and did my Savior bleed," "Am I a soldier of the cross," and "Come, we that love the Lord." Two of the hymns that are still sung come from Newton: "Amazing grace! How sweet the sound" and "How sweet the name of Jesus sounds." The Baptist hymns that have lasted are "All hail the power of Jesus' name" (in Rippon's version), "Come, Thou fount of every blessing" (Robinson), and "How firm a foundation" ("K"). The others that survive among Southern Baptists are "Come, ye sinners, poor and needy " (Joseph Hart), "Jerusalem, my happy home" (anonymous), "Lo, He comes with clouds descending" (Charles Wesley), and "Rejoice, the Lord is King" (Wesley).

## Conclusion

Though we know little about the circumstances surrounding Clay's compilation or of his background for this work, we admire his accomplishment. We appreciate his resourcefulness and taste as they are apparent in his selection of sources: the finest Baptist (many would say, finest English) collection of the time (Rippon); the only locally-edited Baptist hymnal (Broaddus and Broaddus); and the trend-defining poetry of Anglican evangelicalism[62] (Newton and Cowper). We value his example of consultation in the process of providing for the needs of Baptists at worship. We applaud this further evidence of his willingness to devote his energy and resources to the advancement of Baptists in Virginia.

[1]Minutes of the Baptist General Committee of Virginia, May 14, 1792. At the Virginia Baptist Historical Society.
[2] Eleazar Clay, *Hymns and Spiritual Songs, Selected from Several Approved Authors* (Richmond: John Dixon, 1793).
[3]This seems to be the preferred spelling of Clay's first name, though it often appears as Eleazer or, abbreviated, as Eli.
[4]Alvah Hovey, *A Memoir of the Life and Times of the Rev. Isaac Backus, A.M.* (Boston, 1859), 294.
[5]John D. Edens, "The Role of Eleazar Clay in the Middle District Association," *The Virginia Baptist Register*, 9 (1970), 407-24.
[6]Dennis Nofsinger, Jr., "Eleazar Clay, First Baptist Minister of Chesterfield County, Virginia," unpublished paper, June 12, 1961. A copy is on file at the Virginia Baptist Historical Society.
[7]Ibid, photograph. Clay is buried in the family cemetery, near Swift Creek, on the property he owned in Chesterfield County, Virginia.
[8]Zachary F. Smith and Mary Rogers Clay, *The Clay Family* (Louisville: Filson Club Publications, No. 14, 1899), 63.

[9]Ibid., 77.

[10]Ibid., 84-85.

[11]Ibid., 77.

[12]Ibid., 86.

[13]Ibid.

[14]Ibid., 87-88.

[15]Carefully documented by Edens, "The Role," 407-24.

[16]Smith and Clay, *The Clay Family*, 83-84.

[17]James B. Taylor, *Lives of Virginia Baptist Ministers* (Richmond, 1837), 178-79.

[18]Ibid., 179.

[19]*The Richmond Enquirer*, May 17, 1836, p. 3, col. 6, as cited in Edens, "The Role," 408.

[20]*Religious Herald*, August 29, 1872, p. 1, col. 4., carries a letter from W. J. Morrissett, in which he relates that he once possessed Clay's diary, but that it was destroyed in a fire before the Civil War. A copy, lent to George B. Taylor, was also apparently lost. He recalls several incidents about which Clay wrote. Other letters from Morrissett concerning Clay appeared in *Religious Herald* on March 4, 1858, and September 5, 1872.

[21]Ibid.

[22]Ibid.

[23]Ibid. Morrissett reports that "Colonel Cary, the chief magistrate of the county, was asked, on one occasion, why he permitted Elder Clay to preach unmolested, whilst he had others arrested, lodged in jail and punished. Col. Cary replied, 'Mr. Clay had a livelihood, but these others are taken up under the vagrant law.' " Taylor asserts that "He was a man of dauntless spirit, and the opposers feared to maltreat him."

[24]William L. Lumpkin, *A History of the Middle District Baptist Association of Virginia, 1784-1984* (Richmond, 1984), 9.

[25]*Chesterfield Baptist Church Minutes, 1773-1788* [title on modern cover], 1. At the Virginia Baptist Historical Society.

[26]Ibid., 2.

[27]Ibid., 7.

[28]Ibid.

[29]Ibid., 8.

[30]L. W. Moore, *A History of the Middle District Baptist Association* (Richmond, 1886), 50-51.

[31]Robert B. Semple, *A History of the Rise and Progress of the Baptists in Virginia* (Richmond, 1810), 67-68.

[32]Ibid., 69.

[33]Ibid., 70.

[34]Ibid., 76-77. Semple gives the year as 1778, but only 1788 fits his chronology.

[35]Ibid., 77-78.

[36]Minutes of the Baptist General Committee of Virginia, *passim*. Among the tasks mentioned are examining the funds of the Committee; representing the Committee to the General Assembly, the Methodist conference, and the Presbytery; and serving on the Select Committee [one from each association] to prepare the agenda for the meetings.

[37]Ibid., May 12, 1792.

[38]Semple, 84-85.

[39]Minutes of the Baptist General Committee of Virginia, May 12, 1792.

[40]Ibid., May 14, 1792.

[41]Henry S. Burrage, *Baptist Hymn Writers and Their Hymns* (Portland: ME, 1888), 641.

[42]See "Andrew Broaddus and Hymnody," in Part II of this volume.

[43]See note 20.

[44]Nofsinger, "Eleazar Clay," 10.

[45]John Rippon, *A Selection of Hymns from the Best Authors* (London, 1787).

[46]New York, New York, and Elizabeth-Town, New Jersey.

[47]"Of the first six thousand copies printed, about eight hundred went across the Atlantic," according to Kenneth R. Manley, "John Rippon and American Baptists," *The Quarterly Review*, Vol. 41, No. 1 (Oct-Nov-Dec., 1980), 59. Manley cites a letter from Rippon to James Manning, dated September 21, 1789, which is now at Brown University.

[48]Benjamin Wallin, *Evangelical Hymns and Songs* (Boston, 1762).

[49]*Hymns and Spiritual Songs* (Newport: RI, 1766).

[50]*Hymns and Spiritual Songs* (Williamsburg, 1773). This is listed in Charles Evans' *American*

*Bibliography*, rpt., New York, 1941, vol. 4, p. 347, as no. 12660. Arthur L. Stevenson, in *The Story of Southern Hymnology* (Salem: VA, 1931), 1, reports that he saw this book "in the Library of the Virginia Baptist Historical Association at the University of Richmond." Edward Starr's *A Baptist Bibliography* (Rochester, 1966), Vol. 11, 194, lists the work as H 6691, citing Evans and Stevenson. In *The Baptists of Virginia, 1699-1926* (Richmond, 1955), 86, Garnett Ryland mentions the book without stating whether he has viewed it.

[51]*A Collection of Hymns, from Various Authors* (Philadelphia: Enoch Story, jun., 1784).

[52]Samuel Jones and Burgis Allison, *A Selection of Psalms and Hymns, Done under the Appointment of the Philadelphian Association* (Philadelphia, 1790).

[53]Richard Broaddus and Andrew Broaddus, *Collection of Sacred Ballads*, ([n.p.] 1790).

[54]Joshua Smith, *Divine Hymns, or Spiritual Songs*, 3d. ed. (Exeter: NH, 1791). The oldest extant edition is 1793. It has been suggested that the first edition may have been as early as 1784.

[55]John Newton, *Olney Hymns* (London, 1779).

[56]Leonard Ellinwood, *Dictionary of American Hymnology: First-line Index* (New York, 1984).

[57]Louis F. Benson, *The English Hymn* (Philadelphia, 1915), 360-62.

[58]Courtney, who had served with Clay on the General Committee, edited *The Christian's Pocket Companion* (Richmond, 1805).

[59]These conclusions are based on the *Dictionary of American Hymnology*. See note 56.

[60]Wesley L. Forbis, editor, *The Baptist Hymnal* (Nashville: Convention Press, 1991).

[61]William J. Reynolds, general editor, *Baptist Hymnal* (Nashville: Convention Press, 1975).

[62]This is the judgment of Donald E. Demaray in his *The Innovation of John Newton (1725-1807)* (Lewiston: NY, 1988), 261.

# STARKE DUPUY:
# Early Baptist Hymnal Compiler
## David W. Music

THE FULL STORY OF BAPTIST hymnody in the southern United States has yet to be written. A number of excellent surveys have sketched the broad outlines of this fruitful field of investigation. However, several important hymnals and tunebooks have never been studied in depth, and the lives of many Southern Baptist compilers, authors, and composers of hymns are in need of serious research. Until these works and their authors have been investigated more thoroughly, the history and present course of Southern Baptist church music cannot be fully understood.

One of the earliest and most popular of these Baptist hymnals was Starke Dupuy's *Hymns and Spiritual Songs.* This article seeks to add to the current small store of information about this compiler and his significant collection, with the hope that a more comprehensive understanding of Baptist hymnic heritage will result.

### Dupuy's Life

Little is known about Dupuy's life.[1] He was born sometime during the month of November 1779, in Powhatan County, Virginia. His father, James Dupuy, was one of Powhatan County's early Baptist preachers. Starke's unusual first name was derived from the maiden name of his mother (Anne Starke).

The Dupuys moved to Woodford County, Kentucky, about 1788, where they apparently joined the Clear Creek Baptist Church. James Dupuy later helped constitute a church at Buck Run, but "after a while faction tore out the bowels of this church, and it died a natural death."[2] About 1797 the Dupuys moved to Shelby County, Kentucky, where the elder Dupuy probably led in founding the Tick Creek (later called Bethel) Baptist Church, located about five miles east of Shelbyville. Here young Starke Dupuy was called to preach.

J. S. Spencer described Dupuy as "a young man of fine energy and public spirit" and "a young preacher of ardent zeal and excellent promise."[3] Spencer also noted that he received a good English education for that time and place,[4] though he was later characterized as "not a learned man."[5]

The date and place of Dupuy's marriage are not known. His wife was named Anne Webber; five boys and one girl were born of this union.

Dupuy's first publication was *A Selection of Hymns and Spiritual Songs* (Frankfort: William Gerard, 1811). In 1812 he founded *The Kentucky Missionary and Theological Magazine,* the first Baptist periodical published in Kentucky. Unfortunately, it appears from the only surviving issue (May 1812) that Dupuy had difficulty securing subscribers for the magazine, a situation which worsened with the advent of the War of 1812. The editor suspended publication of the magazine after the fourth issue (February 1813), promising to revive it again after the cessation of hostilities. At the conclusion of the war, however, competition from Silas M. Noel's *The Gospel Herald* (founded in 1813) made such a venture impractical, and Dupuy never fulfilled his intentions.

According to an entry in the journal of Luther Rice (November 24, 1815), Dupuy was still living "near Shelbyville" when he was elected corresponding secretary of "The Shelbyville Society Auxiliary to the Baptist Board of Foreign Missions." His whereabouts following 1815 are not known. He is said to have served as a missionary to the Choctaw Indians for a short time, though it is not known when this occurred.[6] According to Spencer, Dupuy's health failed soon after he began to preach, and he traveled the southern states in search of a mild climate.[7]

At any rate, by 1825 Dupuy appears to have settled in West Tennessee. On May 28, 1825, *The Jackson* (Tennessee) *Gazette* advertised the opening of Mount Pinson Academy, with Dupuy serving as one of two superintendents and having responsibility for the "English Department." An advertisement in the *Gazette* of June 25, 1825, called for a meeting of Baptists interested in forming an association. Dupuy was elected moderator and Josiah W. Fort was elected secretary of the preliminary meeting, held late in July. The formal organization of the Forked Deer Baptist Association took place on October 1-3, with Dupuy and Fort being reelected to their respective posts.[8] According to the associational minutes, Dupuy was pastor of the Middle Fork Baptist Church, which reported a total of 37 members. At the September 2, 1826, meeting of the association, Dupuy was again elected moderator; his church reported 34 members.[9]

Sometime after the 1826 associational meeting, Dupuy appears to have left the Jackson area. The Forked Deer Association minutes for 1827 do not name Dupuy among the messengers; Aaron Compton is listed as pastor of the Middle Fork Church.

The 1830 census of Tennessee located Dupuy's residence in Fayette County. However, in the same year, Dupuy was listed as a messenger from Shelby County's Providence Baptist Church to the Big Hatchie Baptist Association. Unfortunately, the 1831 and 1832 minutes of the Big Hatchie Association were unavailable for this study. The minutes for 1833 and 1835 do not list Dupuy nor Providence Church. Since the church reported only 19 members in 1830, it is possible that it had folded by 1833.[10]

Dupuy's listing in the 1830 census and Big Hatchie Association minutes are the last known records of his activities or whereabouts. He probably died about 1840. His name did not appear in the Tennessee census for that year, though his son (also named Starke Dupuy) was listed as a resident of Fayette County. According to Spencer, Dupuy died of "that fatal malady, popularly known as consumption of the lungs."[11]

### Significance of Dupuy's *Selection of Hymns and Spiritual Songs*

Dupuy's *Selection of Hymns and Spiritual Songs* proved to be one of the most widely used Baptist hymnals of its time. Dupuy himself revised the hymnal twice, and it was published in 22 editions. According to B. H. Dupuy, more than 100,000 copies were put into circulation.[12] The following issues of the hymnal have been noted, most of them under the title *Hymns and Spiritual Songs:* 1811 (1st ed., Frankfort); 1812 (2nd ed., Frankfort); 1818 (3rd ed., Frankfort); 1825 (5th ed., Nashville); 1832 (7th ed., Louisville); 1841 (22nd ed., Louisville?); and 1843 (rev. by J. M. Peck, Louisville). Dupuy's hymnal seems to have been especially popular in Kentucky and Tennessee, but it penetrated the northern states as well. Indeed, the book was in use at the Pigeon Creek (Primitive) Baptist Church in Illinois where young Abraham Lincoln was an occasional attender.[13]

Dupuy's collection was characterized by some 19th- and early 20th-century writers as "doggerel," "emotional," and "illiterate." Viewed as religious poetry, many of the hymns in Dupuy's book can lay little claim to literary greatness.

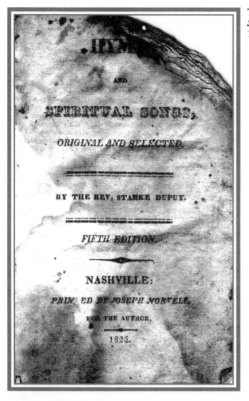

Title page from Starke Dupuy's *Hymns and Spiritual Songs* (Nashville, Tennessee, 1825).

However, in 1933, George Pullen Jackson published the first of his five major studies of the American spiritual folk song, also called the "folk hymn." This book, *White Spirituals in the Southern Uplands* (Chapel Hill: University of North Carolina Press, 1933), brought this hitherto almost-forgotten folk heritage to light. At first Jackson's attention was drawn primarily to the tunes of the folk-hymn tradition; later, however, he was led to study the texts to which these tunes were set. Dupuy's book contained a number of hymns of the type he was investigating. Jackson's sympathetic outlook on American folk hymnody was reflected in his characterization of Dupuy's book as a "notable Baptist collection." What had seemed to be emotional, illiterate doggerel to earlier writers was now viewed as a "comprehensive mass of folky hymns."[14] This, after all, was a valid and valuable part of American folk tradition.

The third edition of Dupuy's book—the one used for this study—opens with a preface addressed to the "Christian Reader." The reader is informed that the book "contains not only the chief of those Hymns in the two former [editions], but likewise a number selected from the most celebrated Authors, together with several which have not hitherto appeared in print." Dupuy expressed his disapproval of the common practice of altering hymns by "celebrated authors." However, he also felt it was his "privilege and duty" to alter "such modern songs as are neither orthodox nor correct."

Dupuy's collection contained 286 hymns arranged under 23 subject headings. For the most part, the subject headings were those still used in hymnals today (e.g., God, Creation, Salvation, and so forth). Two unusual headings were "[Hymns] Used in Psalmody" and "Spiritual Songs." The former provided texts for use with the music of the singing school, while the latter contained folk-like hymns of the camp-meeting variety.

Many of the hymns in Dupuy's collection were not literary masterpieces; however, quite a few were the products of well-known English writers. The name encountered most frequently in *Hymns and Spiritual Songs* was that of Isaac Watts. Other well-known hymnists whose works appeared in the book were William Cowper, Philip Doddridge, John Fawcett, Joseph Hart, Samuel Medley, John Needham, John Newton, Anne Steele, and Joseph and Samuel Stennett.

Also significant is that a number of texts found in *Hymns and Spiritual Songs* are still in use in Baptist churches today. In fact, over 30 hymns from Dupuy's collection are included in the 1956 and 1975 editions of *Baptist Hymnal,* and the 1991 edition of *The Baptist Hymnal.* Among these are such familiar hymns as "Alas, and did my Savior bleed," "Amazing grace! How sweet the sound," "Come, thou fount of every blessing," "Hark! The herald angels sing," "There is a fountain," and "When I survey the wondrous cross." Thus, Dupuy's book is not as ephemeral as it is sometimes thought to be.

Nevertheless, the most interesting feature of the book is its heavy reliance upon folk-hymn materials. These hymns frequently feature a ballad-like form with a "come" or "come all ye" emphasis in the first line. The literary polish of the English hymn writers named above is conspicuously absent from these homespun verses. In the main, these folk hymns were written by unlettered men for unlettered congregations.

As might be expected, the largest mass of folk hymns appeared in the "Spiritual Songs" section of Dupuy's hymnal, but songs of the folk variety are found

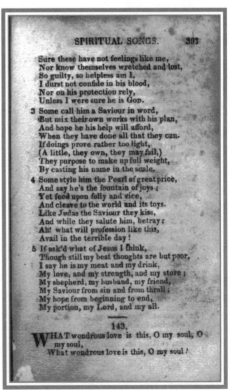

"Wondrous Love " from Starke Dupuy's *Hymns and Spiritual Songs* (Frankfort, Kentucky, 1811).

scattered throughout the collection. Most of these folk hymns have long since passed out of use. Their literary crudeness and polemical nature make many of them unfit vehicles for today's worship. An example is the hymn, "Go Read the Third [Chapter] of Matthew," which criticized infant baptism and sprinkling in no uncertain terms. A sequel to this hymn, "You've Read the Third of Matthew," contains the following remarkable stanza:

> John was a baptist preacher,
>   when he baptiz'd the Lamb,
> Then Jesus was a baptist,
>   and thus the baptists came;
> If you would follow Jesus,
>   as christians ought to do,
> You'd come and be immersed
>   and be a baptist too.

Most Baptist congregations today would have difficulty singing those lines.

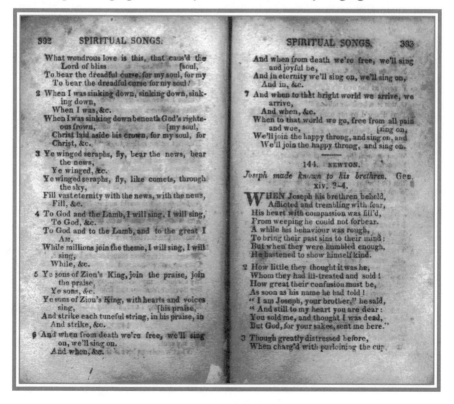

At least one folk hymn in Dupuy's *Hymns and Spiritual Songs* has achieved the status of a "classic"; this is "What wondrous love is this," which apparently received its first printing in either the first edition of Dupuy's book or  Stith Mead's *Hymns and Spiritual Songs* (1811).[15]

Dupuy's *Hymns and Spiritual Songs* was a words-only hymnal; no tunes were included. However, in the section titled "Used in Psalmody," a suggested tune was named for each hymn. Many of these tunes originated in the northern United States during the late 18th century, but a number were of more recent origin. The newer tunes demonstrate that Dupuy was familiar with several of the more popular shape-note tunebooks used in the South during the early 19th century. These tunebooks almost invariably contained a selection of folk-hymn tunes.

At least six tunes mentioned by Dupuy were first printed in John Wyeth's *Repository of Sacred Music, Part Second* (Harrisburg, PA, 1813), a book which was to be quite influential in the development of folk hymnody in the South.[16] Two tunes, TRIBULATION and JUDGMENT, first appeared in Ananias Davisson's *Kentucky Harmony* (Harrisonburg, VA, 1816), the earliest shape-note tunebook published in the South.

Of special interest is the fact that one folk-hymn tune mentioned by Dupuy, OLNEY, had been published for the first time in the same year the third edition of *Hymns and Spiritual Songs* was issued. Significantly, the book in which OLNEY appeared was the product of a Middle Tennesseean, Alexander Johnson, whose *Tennessee Harmony* (Cincinnati, 1818) was the first tunebook published by a Tennessee compiler. Dupuy's mention of the tune OLNEY almost certainly means that he was personally acquainted with *Tennessee Harmony* and even perhaps with its compiler.[17]

Though tune names are not given for the hymns in other sections of Dupuy's book, one may safely assume that in actual practice the majority of the texts in *Hymns and Spiritual Songs* were sung to folk-hymn tunes. While the hymns by English authors, such as Watts and Cowper, had more literary grace than did their country cousins (the "spiritual songs"), folk-hymn tunes were still set to both types of text. Indeed, some of the texts by the great English hymn writers are familiar to Baptists today chiefly through their association with American folk-hymn tunes (e.g., "Amazing grace! how sweet the sound," "Come, Thou fount of every blessing," and "On Jordan's stormy banks"). Thus one may surmise that when a group of Baptists used Dupuy's hymnal, they sang the text to some old folk-hymn tune in an appropriate meter.

*Hymns and Spiritual Songs* cannot lay claim to greatness as a compendium of religious poetry; it also cannot boast the inclusion of an original hymn which is in common use today. However, because of its once great popularity, it provides an accurate record of Baptist tastes in worship music during the early 19th century and serves as an interesting repository of folk hymns from a fascinating and vigorous period of American religious culture.

[1]The chief biographical sources on Dupuy are B. H. Dupuy, *The Huguenot Bartholomew Dupuy and His Descendants* (Louisville: Courier-Journal Job Printing Co., 1908), 357-58; and J. H. Spencer, *A History of Kentucky Baptists,* I (Cincinnati: J. H. Spencer, 1886), 169-70, 346-48.

[2]John Taylor, *A History of Ten Baptist Churches* (Frankfort, KY, 1823; reprinted, Cincinnati: Art Guild Reprints, Inc., 1968), 61.

[3]Spencer, *A History,* 347, 170.

[4]Ibid., 347.

[5]B. H. Dupuy, *The Huguenot Bartholomew Dupuy,* 357.

[6]Larry Douglas Smith, "The Rise of the Missionary Spirit Among Kentucky Baptists," *The Quarterly Review*, 40:75, April-June, 1980.

[7]Spencer, *A History,* 170.

[8]Samuel Cole Williams, *Beginnings of West Tennessee* (Johnson City, TN: Watauga Press, 1930), 188-89.

[9]Smith Hansbrough, *A History of the Forked Deer Baptist Association* (Memphis: M'Mahon, Moseley and Dooley, 1845), 5-6, 13-14.

[10]The writer is indebted to Lynn E. May, Jr., of the Southern Baptist Historical Commission for the information from the Big Hatchie Association minutes.

[11]Spencer, *A History,* 348.

[12]B. H. Dupuy, *The Huguenot Bartholomew Dupuy,* 357.

[13]Albert J. Beveridge, *Abraham Lincoln, 1809-1858,* I (Boston: Houghton Mifflin Co., 1928), 72.

[14]George Pullen Jackson, *White and Negro Spirituals* (New York: J. J. Augustin, 1943), 61.

[15]Leonard Ellinwood, ed., *Dictionary of American Hymnology: First-Line Index* (New York: University Music Editions, 1984). Cf. *The Baptist Hymnal,* 1991, No. 143.

[16]The six tunes were FIDUCIA, NINETY-FIFTH, NINETY-THIRD, TWENTY-FOURTH (cf. *Baptist Hymnal*, 1975, No. 504), NEW MONMOUTH, and VERNON. On the role of Wyeth's *Repository, Part Second* in the development of American folk hymnody, see Irving Lowens' introduction to *Wyeth's Repository of Sacred Music, Part Second* (Harrisburg: John Wyeth, 1820; reprinted, New York: Da Capo Press, 1964), v-xiv.

[17]For more information on Johnson and his tunebook, see David W. Music, "Alexander Johnson and the *Tennessee Harmony*," *Current Musicology* 37/38 (1986), 59-73.

# The Hymns of
# RICHARD FURMAN

## David W. Music

Reprinted, with revisions, from *Journal of the South Carolina Baptist Historical Society*, November 1990. Used by permission.

R ICHARD FURMAN IS FAMILIAR to Baptist historians as a preacher, pastor, patriot, pioneer of theological education, supporter of early Baptist missions movements, and a founding member of the Triennial and South Carolina Baptist Conventions. Less well known are his contributions to hymnody, which, though few in number and but a sidelight to his other activities, are interesting as examples of the poetic workings of Furman's mind and for what they reveal of early Baptist hymn writing in the South.

Furman's known contributions to the repertory of hymnody were three in number.[1] The three hymns in question, "Sovereign of all the worlds above," "Ye ransom'd people join," and "We hail the glad day," all received their first printing in Furman's *America's Deliverance and Duty. A Sermon, Preached at the Baptist Church, in Charleston, South-Carolina, on the Fourth Day of July, 1802, Before the State Society of the Cincinnati, the American Revolution Society; and the Congregation which Usually Attends Divine Service in the Said Church* (Charleston: W. P. Young, 1802). The hymns were appended to the end of the printed text of the sermon. That the hymns were "occasional" works—written to accompany the sermon on this specific occasion—is implied by the heading they received in this initial publication: *"HYMNS Composed for the Twenty-sixth Anniversary of Amer-*

Portrait of Richard Furman
1755-1825

*ican Independence"* (p.[23]). It is likely that the hymns date from the same year as their first publication (1802).

*America's Deliverance and Duty* did not specifically attribute the hymns to Furman. However, if hymns by someone else had been printed in conjunction with a sermon by Furman, surely the publication would have revealed that fact. Furthermore, the texts were attributed to Furman in later hymn collections. There can be little doubt that the hymns were written by the famous preacher.

## The Hymn Texts

Following are the complete texts of the three hymns.

### Hymn I (L.M.)

Sovereign of all the worlds above;
    Thy glory, with unclouded rays,
Shines through the realms of light and love,
    Inspiring angels with thy praise.

Thy power we own, thy grace adore:
    Thou deign'st to visit man below!
And in affliction's darkest hour,
    The humble shall thy mercy know.

These western states, at thy command,
    Rose from dependence and distress;
Prosperity now crowns the land,
    And millions join thy name to bless.

Oppression shook his iron rod,
    And slavr'y clank'd her galling chain;
We sought protection from our God,
    And he did freedom's cause maintain.

For statesmen wise, for gen'rals brave,
    For all the valiant, patriot host,
By whom thou didst our country save,
    Thy praise shall sound from coast to coast.

Praise is thy due, eternal king!
   We'll speak the wonders of thy love;
With grateful hearts our tribute bring,
   And emulate the hosts above.

O! be thou still our guardian God;
   Preserve these States from ev'ry foe;
From party rage, from scenes of blood,
   From sin, and ev'ry cause of woe.

Here may the great Redeemer reign,
   Display his grace and saving pow'r!
Here liberty and truth maintain,
   'Till empires fall, to rise no more!

**Hymn II (S.M.)**
Ye ransom'd people join,
   To sing Jehovah's praise!
While faithfulness and love divine,
   Invite us near his face.

He sav'd us in the hour
   When huge affliction rose;
For us display'd deliv'ring pow'r,
   And triumph'd o'er our foes!

O! be his love *your* theme,
   In high seraphic lays:
Render to him *your* love supreme,
   And speak aloud his praise!

**Hymn III (P.M.)**
We hail the glad day
   When this empire rose!
God thunder'd from heav'n,
   And frown'd on our foes:
Dismay seiz'd the armies
   Which compass'd us round;

Our fears were all banish'd;
  Our wishes were crown'd:

The storms of distress
  Thus hush'd by thy word,
And blessings of peace,
  From thee, mighty Lord!
O'erspreading the nation
  Which thou didst redeem,
We shout thy salvation,
  And bless thee supreme.

By God's high decree,
  Here freedom resides;
The *Conscience* is free,
  And justice presides:
Religion is honor'd,
  And Science prevails;
The Arts spread their banners,
  And Commerce her sails.

The Gospel here shines,
  Diffusing abroad
The life-giving hope
  Of mercy from God:
Here the Saviour is known,
  His churches he cheers,
His smiles bless the land, and
  His glory appears.

The Nation how blest
  Thus favor'd by heav'n!
Be joy then express'd
  And gratitude giv'n:
But most for redemption
  Through Jesus's blood,
High praise we would render,
  And love to our God.

**Gloria Patri**

To Father and Son
  And Spirit of Grace,
The great Three-in-One,
  Be glory and praise!
Unite all ye nations!
  The notes to prolong;
Ye choirs of blest angels!
  Re-cho [sic: "Re-echo"] the song.

It is worthy of note that Furman chose to cast each of these patriotic texts in a different hymnic meter. "Sovereign of all the worlds above" is in Long Meter (L. M.); that is, each stanza has four lines of eight syllables each. "Ye ransom'd people join" also contains four-line stanzas; the first, second, and fourth lines have six syllables, while the third line has eight. This is known as Short Meter (S. M.). Both Long Meter and Short Meter were (and are) of frequent occurrence in hymnody. "We hail the glad day" is in Particular Meter (P. M.), meaning that it does not fall into one of the more common hymnic patterns. In this case, the stanzas contain eight lines, with the following syllable structure: 5.5.5.5.6.5.6.5.

Since Furman was not a professional hymn writer, it is perhaps not surprising to hear echoes of texts by other authors in certain lines from these poems. The first line of "Sovereign of all the worlds above" has parallels in a number of earlier hymns, including Philip Doddridge's "Sovereign of all the worlds on high," John Ryland's "Sovereign ruler of the skies," and Isaac Watts' "Lord of the worlds above." Furman's familiarity with the works of Isaac Watts may be taken as a matter of course, since "Watts entire" formed the core congregational repertory for many Baptist churches of the time.[2]

Several other passages from Furman's hymns also seem to parallel lines from the poems of Watts. "Sovereign of all the worlds above" contains a number of incidental similarities to Watts' familiar "Jesus shall reign where'er the sun," as may be seen in the following comparisons.

Thy praise shall sound from coast to coast (Furman)
His kingdom stretch from shore to shore (Watts)

Here may the great Redeemer reign (Furman)
Jesus shall reign where'er the sun (Watts)

Till empires fall, to rise no more! (Furman)
Till moons shall wax and wane no more (Watts).

The first four lines of another hymn by Watts might have given Furman the idea for stanza one of "Ye ransom'd people join."

Ye tribes of Adam join
    With heaven and earth and seas,
And offer notes divine
    To your creator's praise,[3]

Obviously the similarities pointed out here are relatively minor. Perhaps they are merely coincidental; it is more likely that Furman's lines were subconscious echoes of works he knew by Watts.

Of more certain derivation is the fourth stanza of "Sovereign of all the worlds above." This is an adaptation of a stanza by William Billings, a New England composer, singing-school teacher, and tanner, who published six tunebooks in Boston between 1770 and 1794. Billings' first collection, *The New-England Psalm-Singer* (1770), included a tune named CHESTER, set to the following text:

Let tyrants shake their iron rod
    And slavery clank her galling chains,
We fear them not, we trust in God,
    New-England's God forever reigns.

Authorities are generally agreed that, though the text appeared without attribution in Billings' tunebook, the words were the work of the compiler himself.[4] Billings later reprinted the music and text—with additional stanzas—in his *Singing Master's Assistant* (1778). CHESTER became quite popular as a rallying cry for Americans during and after the Revolutionary War, and—given Furman's patriotic activities—it is inconceivable that he would not have known Billings' text. The conclusion that Furman's stanza is a purposeful adaptation of Billings' verses is inescapable.

*America's Deliverance and Duty* gave no indication of the tunes that might have been sung with Furman's words on July 4, 1802. "Sovereign of all the worlds above" could have been sung to any of a number of popular Long Meter tunes, including OLD 100TH (the "Doxology"), though it is tempting to speculate on the possible use of Billings' CHESTER, given Furman's quotation from its text. "Ye ransom'd people join" would have fit well with ST. THOMAS (usually sung today to "I love thy kingdom, Lord"). OLD 100TH and ST. THOMAS were both familiar tunes among American churchgoers in the late 18th and early 19th centuries. The possibilities for "We hail the glad day" were more limited, due to the unusual meter of the words. This text was almost certainly sung to the tune HANOVER (also known in the 18th century as Psalm 149). HANOVER was one of the very few contemporary tunes in this meter to achieve widespread use in America.[5]

## Subsequent Use of Furman's Hymns

Unfortunately Furman's three hymns do not appear to have met with widespread acceptance. "We hail the glad day" seemingly received no hymnal publication after its appearance in *America's Deliverance and Duty*. According to the *Dictionary of American Hymnology,*[6] "Sovereign of all the worlds above" and "Ye ransom'd people join" were both reprinted in William P. Biddle and William J. Newborn's *The Baptist Hymn Book* (Washington, 1825). No subsequent publications of "Ye ransom'd people join" are recorded.

"Sovereign of all the worlds above" proved to be the most durable of the three hymns, appearing in at least seven collections besides the Biddle/Newborn book noted above. The hymn was included in two of the more popular hymnals by Baptist compilers—Andrew Broaddus's *Virginia Selection* (Richmond, 1836 and 1840 [2nd edition] ) and Basil Manly and Basil Manly, Jr's., *Baptist Psalmody* (Charleston, 1850). Use of the hymn was not restricted to Baptists, for it also appeared in two Presbyterian hymnals and one Methodist book during the 19th century. None of Furman's hymns appear to have been used in 20th-century hymnals.

Nine years before he wrote and published these three hymns, Richard Furman observed in a letter that he "considered singing an important part of Divine Worship and have also considered it my Duty properly to attempt its promotion."[7] His leadership of the singing at his own church[8] and his attempt to provide actual materials for congregational singing attest to the genuineness of these sentiments. If Richard Furman cannot be numbered among the great hymn writers, his hymns are nevertheless suitable for occasional use and serve as interesting specimens of early hymn writing among Southern Baptists.[9]

[1]William L. Hooper, in his *Church Music in Transition* (Nashville: Broadman Press, 1963), 116, observed that Furman "was the author of *Pleasure of Piety and Other Poems,* which included some of his hymns." However, while this collection of poems was indeed written by a Richard Furman, it was not the Richard Furman of this study, but his grandson (1816-1886).

[2]William J. Reynolds, *Companion to Baptist Hymnal* (Nashville: Broadman Press, 1976), 9, 11-12.

[3]The Watts passages quoted above are all from his *Psalms of David Imitated in the Language of the New Testament,* first published in 1719. The selections are from his paraphrases of Psalms 84, 72 (Part II), and 148.

[4]Cf. David P. McKay and Richard Crawford, *William Billings of Boston* (Princeton: Princeton University Press, 1975), 118.

[5]The popularity of OLD 100TH, ST. THOMAS, and HANOVER/PSALM 149 at the turn of the 19th century is attested by the large number of printings they received in early American tunebooks. See Richard Crawford, ed., *The Core Repertory of Early American Psalmody,* Vols. XI and XII of *Recent Researches in American Music* (Madison: A-R Editions, Inc., 1984), Nos. 68, 83, and 72. For an easily accessible printing of these three tunes see *Baptist Hymnal,* 1975, Nos. 6, 240, and 292.

[6]Leonard Ellinwood, ed., *Dictionary of American Hymnology: First-Line Index* (New York: University Music Editions, 1984).

[7]Richard Furman to Edmund Botsford, June 11, 1793, quoted in James A. Rogers, *Richard Furman: Life and Legacy* (Macon: Mercer University Press, 1985), 216-17.

[8]Cf. the recollection of Furman's hymn leadership by Eliza Yoer Tupper quoted in Rogers, 206.

[9]For general (i.e., other than patriotic) use, "Ye Ransomed People Join" can be sung today as originally written by Furman. "Sovereign Ruler of all the Worlds Above" can be turned into a universal hymn of praise by singing stanzas one, two, six, and eight, or any combination of these stanzas. The hymns may be sung to the tunes mentioned above or to others in the same hymnic and poetic meters.

# PART II:
## PASTOR–HYMNISTS OF THE 19TH-CENTURY SOUTH

# BASIL MANLY, JR.:
# Southern Baptist Pioneer in Hymnody
## Paul A. Richardson

Reprinted, with revisions, by permission of the Historical Commission of the Southern Baptist Convention. This article first appeared in the April, 1992, issue of *Baptist History and Heritage*.

UPON HIS DEATH A CENTURY AGO, Basil Manly, Jr., was eulogized by his long-time co-laborer, John A. Broadus, as "the most versatile man I ever met."[1] Manly's accomplishments as preacher and pastor, teacher and administrator, and Sunday School leader in the formative years of the Southern Baptist Convention are widely appreciated. Less well known are the contributions he made as hymnist and hymnologist.

Manly's interest in the church's song spanned his life. As an adult he recalled the influence of a particular song on his spiritual awakening. On his deathbed he not only turned to hymns for comfort and assurance, but edited the proofsheets of his last collection of hymns.[2]

### Biographical Sketch

Basil Manly, Jr., was born in Edgefield County, South Carolina, on December 19, 1825, to Basil and Sarah Murray Rudolph Manly. When he was less than a year old, the family moved to Charleston, where his father had accepted the pastorate of First Baptist Church. In 1837, the elder Manly became president of the University of Alabama, and the family settled in Tuscaloosa. Basil, Jr., made his statement of faith before the congregation of the First Baptist Church of Tuscaloosa in 1840 and entered the university in

Portrait of Basil Manly, Jr.
1825–1892

that same year. He graduated with his B.A. degree as valedictorian in December 1843.[3]

The 19-year-old college graduate was licensed to preach in May 1844 and entered Newton Theological Institution that fall. Upon the separation of Baptists in the South from those in the North (an event in which his father played a leading role), he left Newton,[4] enrolled at Princeton Theological Seminary, and completed his studies there in 1847. Following his graduation from Princeton, he accepted the call of Providence Baptist Church in Sumter County, Alabama, and was subsequently ordained by First Baptist Church, Tuscaloosa. He simultaneously served three churches: Providence; Sumterville, also in Sumter County; and Shiloh, in Noxubee County, Mississippi. The burden of these responsibilities took their toll on his health, and he resigned the churches within a year. While recovering his strength, he served as stated supply of the Tuscaloosa congregation.

In 1850, Manly was called to the pastorate of First Baptist Church, Richmond, Virginia. He served there for four years, resigning to become the founding president of the Richmond Female Institute.

Manly had been among those advocating the establishment of a theological seminary for Baptists in the South; when The Southern Baptist Theological Seminary was founded in Greenville, South Carolina, in 1859, he became one of its first professors. While the seminary was inactive because of the Civil War, Manly focused his energies on the fledgling Sunday School Board, of which he was president. In 1865, when the seminary resumed classes, he again took up his work in the classroom.

In 1871, Manly moved to Georgetown, Kentucky, to become president of Georgetown College. He served there until 1879, when he rejoined the faculty of Southern Seminary, by that time located in Louisville. He taught at the seminary until his death on January 31, 1892.

### Early Interest in Hymnody

As the son of a pastor, Manly heard hymn singing regularly. His father's sermon manuscripts (many of which the son preached later) are marked with numbers of appropriate hymns.[5] Thus, a thoughtful approach to hymn selection would have been the example offered from his childhood. In a reminiscence of his spiritual development, Manly wrote: "I can remember some feelings when I must have been 8 or 9—in connection with the singing of the chorus 'I'm on my journey home, etc.' "[6]

Manly apparently had some skill and training in music. Several letters during his years away from home contain references to this. His father, writing to the first-year student at Newton, inquired:

> Do you wish your violin sent you? I think you should cultivate music. If it would not be against the rules of the Institution, you might hire a piano by the year; or possibly you might get the use of a chamber organ, in a cheap way, to keep in your room & practice on.[7]

According to the family biographer, Louise Manly, he became proficient on the violin, but later gave it up, so as not to offend those who perceived it as an instrument for dance music. At Princeton he sang in the student choral society, which performed oratorios.[8]

The correspondence between father and son also dealt specifically with hymnody. In one letter, Manly, Sr., wrote to his son about two hymns he had heard: "Jesus, my all to heaven is gone" and "O when shall I see Jesus." The subject was of such interest that not only were nine stanzas of the second hymn written in poetic form, but both tunes were notated on hand-drawn staves.[9] The level of their discourse reveals both knowledge and concern, as in this excerpt from son to father:

> By the bye, when you set about compiling *That Hymn Book*—which you know Daddy Hood was recommending you to do—(& if you can only secure his impress & certificate to the book it will crown it with success among all the *literary* world) it would be well to look over some of Toplady's pieces that do not appear in any of the Hymn Books. Though of inferior merit to "Rock of Ages" & "Oh thou that hear'st the prayer of faith," &c. they would some of them have a powerful *effect*, and that, as you remark, is the criterion. In the mean time however, do not we Southern folks need a Hymn Book "better suited to the wants of the denomination" than the *Psalmist* itself? Shall Dossey & Mercer still continue to be the sole ornament of Baptist Lyrical Literature at the South? The Psalmist don't [*sic*] suit *us*, that is clear. ...Sears thinks the Psalmist preferable to Winchell's Watts—& so do I. *But* he says the Psalmist is a beautifully got up collection of tasteful, & elegant sacred poetry, but thinks it lacks fervor-point-energy—that which makes a thing stick & take hold. The fact is Smith did a foolish thing in inserting so many of his own hymns. I wonder, in all the by no means partial reviews that Baker & Buck have given the book, that they never hit him hard on this point.[10]

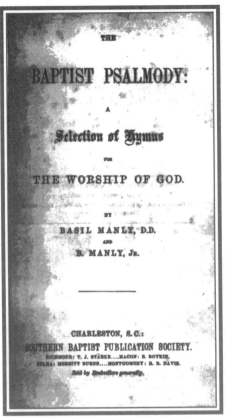

THE

# BAPTIST PSALMODY:

A

## Selection of Hymns

FOR

### THE WORSHIP OF GOD.

BY

BASIL MANLY, D.D.

AND

B. MANLY, Jr.

CHARLESTON, S. C.:

SOUTHERN BAPTIST PUBLICATION SOCIETY.

RICHMOND: T. J. STARKE....MACON: S. BOYKIN.
SELMA: MERRITT BURNS....MONTGOMERY: B. B. DAVIS.

*Sold by Booksellers generally.*

Title page from Basil Manly and Basil Manly, Jr.'s,
*The Baptist Psalmody* (Charleston, 1850).

This letter not only shows that both Manlys were informed about hymnody, it establishes the context out of which would come *The Baptist Psalmody*,[11] Southern Baptists' first hymnbook.

## The Baptist Psalmody

Cited several times in this letter is *The Psalmist*,[12] a hymnal edited by Boston pastors Baron Stow and Samuel F. Smith (author of "My country, 'tis of thee" and other hymns). *The Psalmist* was published in Boston in 1843 by Gould, Kendall, and Lincoln, with the imprimatur of the American Baptist Publication and Sunday School Society. It set a new standard for Baptist collections in America and was widely accepted in the North. Its success in the South was more limited, owing to its omission of several hymns that were favorites in the region, its somewhat heavy-handed emendation of texts, and the growing sense of sectionalism that made Northern products suspect.

Southern congregations at this time used a variety of hymnbooks, none of which had the size, topical breadth, or literary quality of *The Psalmist*. Among these were Jesse Mercer's *Cluster*[13] and William Dossey's *The Choice*,[14] both mentioned disparagingly in the letter above. The Manlys and others perceived the need for a comprehensive, carefully-edited collection to serve churches in the South.

As the letter indicates, Manly, Sr., had been urged to prepare such a book as early as 1845. Other matters caused this project to be put aside for four years, but on October 31, 1849, *The Alabama Baptist* carried a letter signed by both Manlys announcing that a hymnbook was in preparation:

In accordance with a request of the Tuscaloosa Association, at its late session, the undersigned propose to publish a Hymn Book adapted to the use of Baptist Churches in the South. We design it to contain unaltered, *the old hymns*, precious to the children of God by long use, and familiarized to them in many a season of perplexity and temptation as well as spiritual joy. We shall also add such other hymns of more recent date as seem worthy to be associated with the former, in order to make a complete Hymn Book for public and private worship.[15]

Without naming other collections, this public letter echoed the criticisms of the earlier private one: that some hymnals (that is, *The Psalmist*) made personal taste the only standard, without considering the wants and traditions of the churches, while others (for example, those of Dossey and Mercer) merely included favorites, without regard to taste or doctrine.

The new hymnbook was to have been published by M. D. J. Slade, a Tuscaloosa printer, but, after several letters of negotiation, the task was turned over to the Southern Baptist Publication Society,[16] which had been urged since its founding to produce such a volume.[17] As A. M. Poindexter, secretary of the society, wrote, the need was being felt keenly: "The urgent solicitations of friends seem to render it imperative upon us to get out a Hymn Book."[18] The freedom of Manly, Jr., from pastoral responsibilities permitted him to proceed quickly, as he was able to advise Poindexter on January 21, 1850:

The work is still in process of preparation, & if no unforeseen interruption arises may be ready for the press in something like six weeks perhaps. But as to this, I would not be too confident. We are bestowing a good deal of pains on the arrangement of the hymns in a systematic textual order & in the provision of complete indexes both of subjects & Scriptures, especially the latter.[19]

*The Baptist Psalmody*, described in its subtitle as "A Selection of Hymns for the Worship of God," is the largest hymnbook ever produced by Southern Baptists. It contains 1,294 hymns, 9 single stanzas for baptism, and 16 doxologies. The size of the book reflects the intent that it supply hymns for any liturgical function and on any Scripture or topic that a preacher might address. Toward that end, it is, as Manly had noted, carefully organized and equipped with detailed indices to both topics and Scriptures. A six-page "Syllabus of the Arrangement" shows the topical arrangement of the contents.

The listing of Scriptures to which hymns are related occupies 14 pages. Though the wisdom and experience of his father undoubtedly helped to shape the book, the bulk of the work was done by Basil, Jr.[20]

About half the texts in *The Baptist Psalmody* are by Isaac Watts, whose hymns and paraphrased Psalms had formed the core of Baptist hymnody for a century. Other major contributors include Philip Doddridge, Charles Wesley, John Newton, and James Montgomery. The leading Baptist contributors are Anne Steele, with more than 50 texts, and Benjamin Beddome. There are three hymns by Samuel F. Smith, who granted Manly permission and advised him how to avoid the objections of the publishers of *The Psalmist*,[21] who were understandably reluctant to cooperate.[22] The diversity of sources, including many collections prepared for the use of other denominations, shows the breadth of the hymnological knowledge of the Manlys.

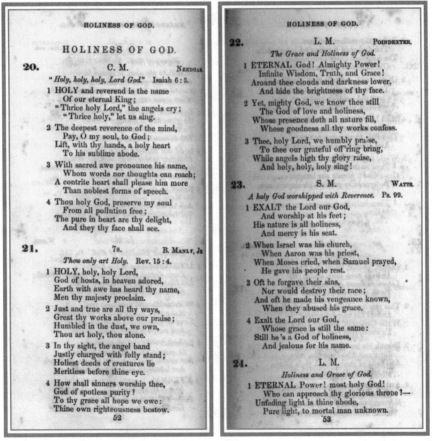

Pages from *The Baptist Psalmody* (Charleston, 1850), including "Holy, holy, holy Lord," by Basil Manly, Jr., and "Eternal God! Almighty Power," by Abram M. Poindexter.

Among the inclusions in *The Baptist Psalmist* are nine texts by Basil Manly, Jr.: "Before the pool a sufferer lay" (460);"God of the seas, whose ruling voice" (709); "God with us, O glorious name" (138); "Holy, holy, holy Lord" (21); "In doubt's dim twilight here I stay" (539); "Jesus, my Lord, I own thee God" (136); "Lord, I deserve thy deepest wrath" (445); "Our God invites the wanderers home" (345); and "There is a light which shines from heaven" (1023). While the occasion of writing for all of these is not known, the first, fifth, sixth, and eighth were composed between June 5 and June 10, 1850, while Manly was in Charleston editing the hymnbook. They appear in his journal, "Fragments of Thoughts, No. 19," along with five other hymns that were not published.[23]

None of these is a great hymn, yet all are polished and meet or surpass the standard of much hymnody of the time. Perhaps the most effective writing occurred when Manly adopted the homiletical style of his Baptist forebears, as in "Before the pool a sufferer lay." After three stanzas relating the story of John 5:1-9, he draws a conclusion and offers a prayer:

> To sin-sick souls he offers grace,
> Confined to neither time nor place;
> Where'er is offered heartfelt prayer,
> The fount of life is open there.
>
> Thou loving, gracious, healing Lord,
> Speak to my soul the pardoning word;
> My sins remove, new strength impart;
> O cleanse, and dwell within my heart.[24]

Two of these texts were reprinted in collections by other Baptists: "God with us," in *The Baptist Praise Book* (275);[25] and "Holy, holy, holy Lord," in both *The Baptist Hymn Book* (133)[26] and Spurgeon's *Our Own Hymn-Book* (189).[27]

It is with *The Baptist Psalmody* that one can begin to speak of Southern Baptist identity in a hymnbook. Though its compilation was not initiated by the Southern Baptist Convention or the Publication Society, the Convention gave its endorsement at the 1851 annual session.[28] *The Baptist Psalmody* gave Southern churches a collection worthy to compete with *The Psalmist*—and it did, sometimes as the subject of heated debate, as the denominational press of the day chronicled.[29] It appealed to Southern ministers and congregations by being more faithful to the original versions of texts and by including many regional favorites that had not been deemed up to the standards of *The Psalmist* or its *Supplement*.[30] *The Baptist Psalmody* was a successful book, reprinted as late as 1870,[31] with sales estimated at more than 50,000.[32]

## Baptist Chorals

Soon after the release of *The Baptist Psalmody*, Manly moved to Richmond. There he would have become better acquainted with the hymn collections of Andrew Broaddus[33] and John Courtney,[34] both of whom had served First Baptist Church. The next evidence of specific interest in hymnody is found in a letter to his parents of April 10, 1857, in which he proposed compiling a new book:

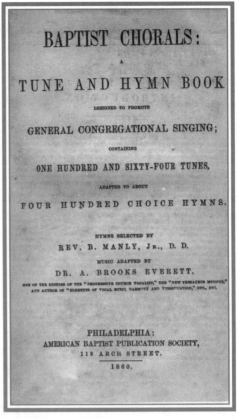

Title page from Basil Manly, Jr., and A. Brooks Everett's *Baptist Chorals* (Philadelphia, 1860).

> I think it w[ould] pay and it w[ould] not take me long neither [*sic*]. How w[ould] it answer to gather up out [of] old collecs. [of] ch. music the *best* of our old favorites and publish them with such a title as this 'Good Old Tunes—a Collection of ~~Sacred Music~~ The favorites ~~melodies~~ of our fathers; selected & arranged by B. M. Jr.' W[ould] that not go? I have a great mind to do it anyhow.[35]

The idea of a tunebook evolved, as he informed his father in a letter of January 4, 1859:

> I have written to my Petersburg Music man, Mr. Everett, agreeing to join with him. I must go to work soon, so as to fulfill my part of the contract, which is to furnish a selection of Hymns. I sh[ould] not need,

however, to spend much time on t[his], as he proposes t[o] select st[andard] h[ymns] confined to hymns wh[ich] [a]r[e] common to t[he] Ps[almist] & t[he] Ps[almo]dy so t[hat] our book can be used in conjunc. w. either.[36]

Manly's collaborator in *Baptist Chorals*[37] was A. Brooks Everett, a composer, arranger, and singing-school teacher who was already known for his writing and editing. The purpose and approach of the book were explained in the sub-title: "A Tune and Hymn Book Designed to Promote General Congregational Singing; Containing One Hundred and Sixty-four Tunes, Adapted to about Four Hundred Choice Hymns." The format was ingenious: On facing pages were two tunes, one traditional and one newly composed, with the same metric structure; below, across both pages, were three or more texts in the same meter (thus fitting either tune). The texts, with two exceptions, were selected from *The Psalmist* and *The Baptist Psalmody* and were, in most cases, common to both books. Thus, *Baptist Chorals* could be used as a tunebook for either of the major Baptist hymnbooks of the day or as a small self-contained hymnal.

Pages from *Baptist Chorals* (Philadelphia, 1860), showing the format, with a traditional tune on left and a new tune (in this case by Basil Manly, Jr.) on the right.

Manly's contributions were principally to select the texts, to write a preface, and to provide a condensed index of subjects. He included two of his own texts from *The Baptist Psalmody*: "Jesus, my Lord, I own thee God" (86), and "Our God invites the wanderers home" (10). He also composed two of the new tunes, REMISSION (141) and REALMS OF THE BLEST (158). Two other tunes seem to be tributes to him: BASIL (59), by R. M. McIntosh; and MANLY (54), by an unidentified composer (perhaps Everett).

More significant than the texts and tunes that Manly contributed to *Baptist Chorals* was the introduction that he wrote. This was his first published essay on the nature and purpose of congregational song. He made several points effectively: "that the Bible distinctly commands singing," that singing is effective in "promoting Christian emotion," and that it is "a powerful auxiliary to preaching."[38] He admonished with fervor:

> If churches everywhere would cease to regard sacred music either with indifference or as a matter of mere taste; if they would commence with the young, training their ears while they are sensitive, and their voices while they are flexible; if families would unite at least once a day in a brief, spirited hymn, as well as in other domestic devotions; if, instead of the choirs being burdened with *doing the singing*, they should simply be honored with *leading the singing*; and if the voices of *all* God's people should join heartily and understandingly, with grace not only in the notes but in the heart, the effect would surprise us all.[39]

Though no sales figures are extant, *Baptist Chorals* seems to have met with only limited success. The outbreak of war a year and a half later perhaps cut short the time required for a novel design to find acceptance.

## Hymnic Activity, 1859-1891

Though Manly did not serve as the principal editor of another collection until near the end of his life, he remained active as an author, composer, and consultant. At about the same time that *Baptist Chorals* was released, he moved to Greenville to become Professor of Biblical Introduction and Old Testament Interpretation at the newly-established seminary. As one of the institution's founders, he prepared two enduring writings: the "Abstract of Principles," the doctrinal statement governing each professor to the present day, and the seminary hymn, "Soldiers of Christ, in truth arrayed," which has been sung at every graduation. Stanzas one, four, five, and six of Manly's original appear in *The Baptist Hymnal,* 1991 (574).[40] The second and third, which have been omitted from 1871 forward, are:

> Forth to the realms of darkness go,
> Where, like a river's ceaseless flow,
> A tide of souls is drifting down,
> Blasted beneath th' Almighty's frown.

> No human skill nor power can stay
> That flood upon its gloomy way;
> But God's own love devised the plan
> To save the ruined creature, man.[41]

The text was unattributed in the first commencement program, but "By B. M., Jr." appears in his hand on a copy sent to his brother, Charles.[42] Though this hymn did not appear in a Southern Baptist hymnal until 1975, it was reprinted in other collections of 1891 and 1934.[43]

A text beginning, "Father, who in heaven hearest," appeared on the back of an undated pamphlet by John A. Broadus, "We Pray for You at Home."[44] Manly's letter of October 15, 1862, to his brother Charles, has the same text, headed "Prayer for the Loved Ones Far Away" and preceded by this note:

> I forget whether I ever sent you some lines I wrote to suit t[he] tune "Billow" in t[he] Chorals. At any rate, if I did, I'll send them again, as I h[ave] altd. t[he] 5th v[erse]. It began "On t[he] land or on t[he] ocean," as I had our privateers in mind then. But now, [illegible] are *nil* on t[he] ocean, so I h[ave] made a new verse instead, expr[essin]g a wish f[or] return again, too nat[ura]l to be omitted in such a course.[45]

During the hiatus of the seminary caused by the Civil War, Manly, as president of the Sunday School Board, oversaw the production and distribution of *The Little Sunday School Hymn Book*[46] and *The Confederate Sunday School Hymnal.*[47] There is no evidence that any of the contents of either is by Manly, though several items are unattributed.

There are many unpublished texts and tunes from all periods of Manly's life. Among the more interesting are several translations, one of which is dated October 27, 1864. "Maker of all, the glorious Lord" appears on a sheet with the original of Gregory, "Rex Christe, factor omnium," and the version from *The Sabbath Hymn Book*.[48] A similar, but undated, page has in parallel columns "Jesu, dulcis memoria," attributed to Bernard of Clairvaux; a German translation (marked by Manly as "Bibl. Sacra"); the English translation of Edward Caswall, as found in *The Sabbath Hymn Book*; and Manly's own translation, beginning "The memory of my absent Lord."[49] These items, though never published, are further evidence of his abilities and of his hymnological knowledge.

The next published hymnic item that can be clearly linked with Manly is an unnamed tune for a text that begins, "Only waiting till the shadows." This appeared in *Glad Tidings* (100-101),[50] a Sunday School song book edited by R. M. McIntosh, an associate of the Everett family who had contributed to *Baptist Chorals*. The tune is credited to "Rev. B. Manly Jr., D.D., of Greenville, S.C." and bears the footnote, "Composed expressly for this work."[51] This was reprinted in an altered form in *Kind Words* (31).

*Kind Words*[52] was a song book published in Memphis, in 1871 by the Sunday School Board. It borrowed the name of the historic periodical for children, which Manly had helped to found. This song book also includes four other tunes by him: HARK! THE HERALD ANGELS (29), which adds a refrain to Wesley's familiar text; JESUS, TENDER SAVIOUR (10); REALMS OF THE BLEST (21), revised from *Baptist Chorals*; and THE LAND WHERE JESUS DWELLS (15).[53]

In 1871, three new hymnals, *The Baptist Praise Book*,[54] *The Baptist Hymn Book*,[55] and *The Service of Song for Baptist Churches*,[56] competed to succeed *The Psalmist* and *The Baptist Psalmody* as the leading collection among Baptists.[57] Manly was directly involved in the first as a member of the editorial committee.[58] The book included only one of his texts, however: "God with us! oh, wondrous name!" (275), a revision of "God with us, O glorious name." He offered another of his texts, "Come, ye who feel your sins a load," to replace a hymn he found inadequate,[59] but this suggestion was not taken. *The Baptist Hymn Book* reprinted Manly's "Holy, holy, holy Lord" (133). He had no apparent connection to *The Service of Song*.

It was also in 1871 that Manly composed the tune ZINZENDORF as a setting for Frances Havergal's "I gave my life for thee."[60] In a letter of April 25, 1878, he responded to changes in the tune that had been suggested by William Howard Doane, the noted Baptist gospel song composer.[61] On the same date, Manly mentioned these changes to Crawford Toy of Southern Seminary, who had sought permission to reprint the hymn.[62] Toy's request was perhaps the genesis of the undated single-sheet printing found among the Manly papers at the South Carolina Baptist Historical Society.[63]

"Who is on the Lord's side," another text by Havergal, was also set by Manly, though the time of composition is uncertain. The printed version of the unnamed tune, published by the distinguished German firm of Breitkopf & Haertel, is undated.[64] A manuscript copy bears the date May 1881, but the date has been struck through.[65]

The next major hymnal to be published for Baptists—a book intended for South and North—was *The Baptist Hymnal* of 1883.[66] Manly served as a member of the consulting committee for this collection, though it included neither texts nor tunes by him. In an interesting, unaddressed document, he set forth his "Suggestions as to the New Hy. Book.," six pages of wisdom and practical advice.[67]

In 1884, Manly wrote what was to be his most widely published text—one that has never appeared in a Southern Baptist collection. "Work, for the day is coming" is clearly a parody of "Work, for the night is coming," by Annie Coghill. It was first written in an album for Mrs. L. H. Woodbury.[68] Manly included this text in a letter to his friend Doane,[69] who published it in *The Glad Refrain for the Sunday School* (6).[70] It appeared in 10 other hymnals and Sunday School song books.[71]

Manly's hymnological expertise was not limited to writing, composing, and editing. When Henry Burrage was researching his monumental *Baptist Hymn Writers and Their Hymns*,[72] he turned to Manly, along with John A. Broadus, for help in learning about Baptist hymnists in the South. Burrage reported to Broadus (who taught hymnology at Southern Seminary) that Manly had been most helpful.[73] When this significant volume was published, it included not only an article about Manly, but also a steel engraving of him.[74] This is remarkable, considering that only five Baptist hymnists were so honored, the others being John Fawcett, C. H. Spurgeon, S. F. Smith, and Emily Chubbuck Judson.

## Manly's Choice

Toward the end of his life, Manly turned again to the compilation of a collection. The product was *Manly's Choice*,[75] a small book containing 254 hymns. The words-only edition was published in 1891; the edition with tunes was published the following year, just after his death. His motivations for this undertaking were stated clearly in the preface:

> For some years it has been apparent that the rage for novelties in singing, especially in our Sunday-schools, has been driving out of use the old, precious, standard hymns.… .

We cannot afford to lose these old hymns. They are full of the Gospel; they breathe the deepest emotions of pious hearts in the noblest strains of poetry; they have been tested and approved by successive generations of those that loved the Lord; they are the surviving fittest ones from thousands of inferior productions; they are hallowed by abundant usefulness and tenderest memories.… .

• • •

…my attention has been directed specially to the subject of hymnology all my ministerial life. I think I know what our people need, and what they desire. To meet that need and that desire the present work is offered. It is cheap, and of convenient size for the pocket; it contains no trash, and no unreal sentiment or unsound doctrine: and while of course in so small a collection many good hymns and some general favorites must be omitted, not one is inserted which is not judged worthy of a special place among the *choice* hymns of the language.[76]

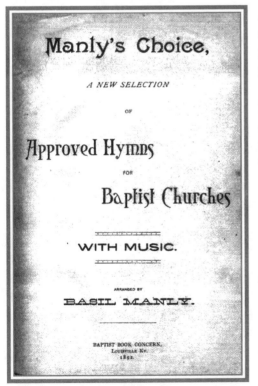

Title page from *Manly's Choice, A New Selection of Approved Hymns for Baptist Churches with Music* (Louisville, 1892).

Apparently Manly did not consider that any of his own texts met these criteria, for none is in *Manly's Choice.*

Manly can hardly be said to have opposed Sunday School songs—he wrote several and realized from his long devotion to Sunday School work that a simpler style related to the idiom of popular music had its role. Indeed, as he wrote to Doane, "I wish to restore [?] the old songs, not that I have any repugnance for the new ones, for some of them I admire greatly, and among these are a number of your compositions."[77] Yet as one who knew the breadth of the church's song, he did not want growing Christians to be deprived of the riches of classic hymnody.

In selecting music for the edition with tunes, Manly drew principally on traditional standard tunes.[78] He noted that he would have used some recent popular compositions, but that the expense required to cover copyright fees would have defeated his plan for an inexpensive book.[79] He also acknowledged one other source: "In a few cases, to meet an apparent necessity, the editor has inserted music of his own composition, for which he asks a lenient judgment."[80] *Manly's Choice* contains six of his own tunes: ZINZENDORF (22), from 1871; and GEORGETOWN (253), HARRIS (249), JOY (250), SUBMISSION (162), and WORK (144), all dated 1891. Two aspects of WORK are particularly interesting: it sets not his *contrafactum*, but Coghill's original; and the tune itself bears a striking resemblance to that of Lowell Mason, with virtually identical rhythm and similar harmony. In his review of the book, Broadus lamented the omission of Manly's text.[81]

In the preface to the text-only edition of *Manly's Choice*, Manly advised that he was planning a new large hymnal, to be called "Standard Hymns for Baptist Churches."[82] During the work on the tune edition, he may have realized that, because of his illness, such a goal would be unattainable, for it is not mentioned there. Rather, that preface ends with a statement of what he hoped this work would accomplish:

> Two great ends have been kept steadily in view. One is to promote universal congregational singing: "Let all the people praise God." The other is to do something towards the elevation and general culture of musical and poetic taste among the Baptist people whom I love, and to whom the best labors of my life have been given. May God bless this effort, and build up our churches in pure doctrine, and fervent piety, for Jesus' sake. Amen.[83]

## Conclusion

Manly's last words for publication may be read as a concise summary of his work as hymnist and hymnologist. His goal was the worship of God by *all* of the people in the churches. His chosen means were hymns that were sound theologically, devotionally, poetically, and musically. To that cause he devoted considerable time and energy, seeing this work as an important aspect of his vocation as pastor/teacher/equipper-of-the-saints.

Southern Baptists can take pride in the hymnic and hymnological contributions of Basil Manly, Jr. He edited the first collection of hymns published by the denomination and set a new standard for Baptist hymnbooks in America in the process. He compiled a tunebook in an innovative format to provide vehicles for effective singing. He applied himself to disciplined, critical study. He wrote texts and tunes in a variety of styles. One of his hymns, "Soldiers of Christ, in truth arrayed," endures.

Southern Baptists can also learn from Manly. He articulated and put into practice a philosophy of hymn use that balanced historic and contemporary styles of expression. He accepted variety without compromising quality. He selected hymns according to their appropriateness for the different functions of the church's ministry, considering in his selection not merely wants but needs.

Southern Baptists are fortunate in many ways to have had a leader with the wisdom, energy, and diverse interests of Basil Manly, Jr. What he accomplished as a pioneer in hymnody was and is significant.

[1]John A. Broadus, "[Funeral] Address of Dr. John A. Broadus," *The Seminary Magazine*, 5:314, March, 1892.

[2]Charles Manly, "Account of the Death of Basil Manly," unidentified newspaper (clipping in Manly papers, South Carolina Baptist Historical Society, Greenville, SC).

[3]The most thorough treatment of this subject is Joseph Powhatan Cox, "A Study of the Life and Work of Basil Manly, Jr." (Th.D. thesis, Southern Baptist Theological Seminary, 1954).

[4]See Hugh Wamble, "A Student Sees a Coming Split Among Baptists: Basil Manly, Jr., at Newton Seminary, 1844-45," *Baptist History and Heritage*, 5:123-130, July, 1970.

[5]The South Carolina Baptist Historical Society has more than 450 sermon manuscripts of Basil Manly, Sr.

[6]Letter, Basil Manly, Jr., to Charles Manly, October 8, 1869 (Manly papers, Southern Historical Association, University of North Carolina, Chapel Hill, NC).

[7]Letter, Basil Manly, Sr., to Basil Manly, Jr., November 22, 1844 (Manly papers, University of Alabama, Tuscaloosa, AL).

[8]Louise Manly, *The Manly Family: An Account of the Descendants of Captain Basil Manly of the Revolution and Related Families* (Greenville: [Keys Printing Co.], 1930), 198.

[9]Letter, Basil Manly, Sr., to Basil Manly, Jr., December 25, 1844 (Manly papers, UA).

[10]Letter, Basil Manly, Jr., to Basil Manly, Sr., May 9, 1845 (Manly papers, Southern Baptist Historical Library and Archives, Nashville, TN).

[11]Basil Manly and B. Manly, Jr., *The Baptist Psalmody: A Selection of Hymns for the Worship of God* (Charleston: Southern Baptist Publication Society, 1850). See David Louis Gregory, "Psalmody in the Mid-Nineteenth Century Southern Baptist Tradition" (M.C.M. thesis, Southern Baptist Theological Seminary, 1987).

[12]Baron Stow and S. F. Smith, *The Psalmist: A New Collection of Hymns for the Use of The Baptist Churches* (Boston: Gould, Kendall, and Lincoln, 1843).

[13]Jesse Mercer, *The Cluster of Spiritual Songs, Divine Hymns, and Sacred Poems,* 3d. ed. (Augusta: Hobby and Bunce, 1810). Earlier editions are not extant.

[14]William Dossey, *The Choice* (Philadelphia: Anderson and Mecham, 1820).

[15]B. Manly, B. Manly, Jr., "A New Hymn Book," *The Alabama Baptist,* October 31, 1849, 2.

[16]Letters, A. M. Poindexter to Basil Manly, Jr., December 17, 1849; Basil Manly, Jr., to A. M. Poindexter, January 21, 1850; M. T. Mendenhall to Basil Manly, Jr., February 20, 1850; M. T. Mendenhall to Basil Manly, Sr., March 23, 1850 (Manly papers, SCBHS).

[17]Letter, M. T. Mendenhall to Basil Manly, Jr., February 20, 1850 (Manly papers, SCBHS).

[18]Letter, A. M. Poindexter to Basil Manly, Jr., December 17, 1849 (Manly papers, SCBHS).

[19]Letter, Basil Manly, Jr., to A. M. Poindexter, January 21, 1850 (Manly papers, SCBHS).

[20]Letter, Basil Manly, Sr., to J. L. Reynolds, November 15, 1849, as quoted by Reynolds in the *Christian Index and South-Western Baptist,* May 6, 1869, 1.

[21]Letter, S. F. Smith to Basil Manly, Jr., May 29, 1850 (Manly papers, SCBHS).

[22]Letter, Gould, Kendall, and Smith to Basil Manly, Jr., January 9, 1850 (Manly papers, SCBHS).

[23]Basil Manly, Jr., "Fragments of Thoughts, No. 19" (Manly papers, SCBHS).

[24]Manly and Manly, *The Baptist Psalmody*, 297-98.

[25]Richard Fuller, E. M. Levy, S. D. Phelps, H. C. Fish, Thomas Armitage, E. T. Winkler, W. W. Everts, Geo. C. Lorimer, and Basil Manly, Jr., *The Baptist Praise Book: For Congregational Singing* (New York: A. S. Barnes & Company, 1871).

[26]*The Baptist Hymn Book: For Public Worship* (Philadelphia: The Bible and Publication Society, 1871).

[27]C. H. Spurgeon, *Our Own Hymn-Book* (London: Alabaster Press, 1866).

[28]Proceedings of the Southern Baptist Convention, 1851 (Richmond: H. K. Ellyson, 1851), 16.

[29]See Donald Clark Measels, "A Catalog of Source Readings in Southern Baptist Church Music: 1828-1890" (D.M.A. dissertation, Southern Baptist Theological Seminary, 1986).

[30]In 1847, an edition of *The Psalmist* was published with a *Supplement,* edited by Richard Fuller and J. B. Jeter, in an attempt to make the collection more appealing to Southern churches.

[31]Atlanta: Sheldon & Connor, 1870.

[32]Basil Manly, Jr., "Sketch of Rev. B. Manly, Jr., President of Georgetown College, Ky., for *Journal & Messenger,*" [ca. 1874] (Manly papers, Southern Baptist Theological Seminary, Louisville, KY).

[33]See "Andrew Broaddus and Hymnody," in Part II of this volume.

[34]John Courtney, *The Christian's Pocket Companion; Being a Collection of Hymns and Spiritual Songs for the Use of Christians, A Number Never Before Published* (Richmond: John Courtney, Jr., 1805).

[35]Letter, Basil Manly, Jr., to Basil, Sr., and Sarah Manly, April 10, 1857 (Manly papers, SBHLA).

[36]Letter, Basil Manly, Jr., to Basil Manly, Sr., January 4, 1859 (SCBHS).

[37]B. Manly, Jr., and A. Brooks Everett, *Baptist Chorals: A Tune and Hymn Book Designed to Promote General Congregational Singing; Containing One Hundred and Sixty-four Tunes, Adapted to about Four Hundred Choice Hymns* (Richmond: T. J. Starke and Company, 1859).

[38]Ibid., ii and iii.

[39]Ibid, iii.

[40]Wesley L. Forbis, editor, *The Baptist Hymnal* (Nashville: Convention Press, 1991).

[41]"Southern Baptist Theological Seminary. First Annual Commencement," May 28, 1860, 2.

[42]Ibid. This copy, on which is written a letter to Charles Manly, undated (Manly papers, UA).

[43]D. B. Towner, T. T. Eaton, and George H. Sommers, *Hymns Old and New, Revised* (Chicago: Fleming H. Revell, 1891), no. 16; John A. Lee, *Greatest and Lasting Hymns* (Glencoe, KY: John A. Lee, 1934), 446.

[44]John A. Broadus, "We Pray for You at Home" ([n.p.]:[n.p.],[n.d.]).

[45]Letter, Basil Manly, Jr., to Charles Manly, October 15, 1862 (Manly papers, UA).

[46]*The Little Sunday School Hymn Book* (Greenville: Sunday School Board, Southern Baptist Convention, 1863).

[47]C. J. Elford, *The Confederate Sunday School Hymnal* (Greenville: Sunday School Board, Southern Baptist Convention, 1863).

[48]Manuscript, signed "Translation of above by B. Manly, Jr.," October 27, 1864 (Manly papers, SCBHS).

[49]Manuscript, signed "Translation of above by B. M. Jr," undated. (Manly papers, SCBHS).

[50]R. M. McIntosh, *Glad Tidings: New Hymns and Tunes for Sunday-Schools* (Baltimore: T. Newton Kurtz, 1867).

[51]Ibid., 100.

[52]G. W. Linton and Howard M. Teasdale, *Kind Words* (Memphis: The Sunday School Board, Southern Baptist Convention, 1871).

[53]The text that this tune sets, beginning "We are going home," is unattributed in *Kind Words,* but there is an undated and unsigned manuscript in Manly's hand (Manly papers, SCBHS) of this text, with several different phrases, headed "The Land Where Jesus Dwells." This points toward Manly as author.

[54]See note 25.

[55]See note 26.

[56]S. L. Caldwell and A. J. Gordon, *The Service of Song for Baptist Churches* (Boston: Gould and Lincoln, 1871).

[57]See Measels, "A Catalog of Source Readings," for documents related to "The Hymnal War."

[58]Fuller, *et. al.*, *The Baptist Praise Book*, title page.

[59]Letter, Basil Manly, Jr., to Smith & McDougal, August 3, 1871 (Manly papers, SBTS).

[60]The dating is from the music edition of *Manly's Choice* (see note 75).

[61]Letter, Basil Manly, Jr., to William Howard Doane, April 25, 1878 (Manly papers, SBTS).

[62]Letter, Basil Manly, Jr., to Crawford H. Toy, April 25, 1878 (Manly papers, SBTS).

[63]E. [*sic*] R. Havergal and B. Manly, Jr., "I Gave My Life for Thee" ([n.p.]:[n.p.],[n.d.]) (Manly papers, SCBHS).

[64]F. R. Havergal and B. Manly, "Who is on the Lord's side" (Leipzig: Breitkopf & Haertel, [n.d.]).

[65]Manuscript, signed by Manly (Manly papers, SCBHS).

[66]W. Howard Doane, musical editor, and E. H. Johnson, associate editor, *The Baptist Hymnal, for Use in the Church and Home* (Philadelphia: American Baptist Publication Society, 1883).

[67]Basil Manly, Jr., "Suggestions as to the New Hy. Book" (Manly papers, SBTS).

[68]L. H. Woodbury, manuscript, states that it was written in an album for Mrs. Woodbury on January 20, 1884. An accompanying note is headed " 'Work for the day is coming'—how it was written" (Manly papers, SCBHS).

[69]Letter, Basil Manly, Jr., to William Howard Doane, April 5, 1884 (Manly papers, SBTS).

[70]Robert Lowry and W. Howard Doane, *The Glad Refrain for the Sunday School: A New Collection of Songs for Worship* (New York: Biglow and Main, 1886).

[71]The most recent publication was in *Hymns of Worship and Remembrance* (Fort Dodge, IA: Gospel Perpetuating Fund, 1950). Among the other books to include this text was *The Book of Common Praise, Being the Hymn Book of the Church of England in Canada* (Toronto: Henry Frowde [Oxford University Press], 1909), where the text is marked "anon."

[72]Henry S. Burrage, *Baptist Hymn Writers and Their Hymns* (Portland, ME: Brown Thurston & Company, 1888).

[73]Letter, Henry S. Burrage to John A. Broadus, October 25, 1886 (John A. Broadus papers, SBTS).

[74]Burrage, *Baptist Hymn Writers*, between 424 and 425.

[75]Basil Manly, Jr., *The Choice: A New Selection of Approved Hymns for Baptist Churches* (Louisville: Baptist Book Concern, 1891);...*With Music* (Louisville: Baptist Book Concern, 1892). Both were also issued later as *Manly's Choice*.

[76]Basil Manly, Jr., "Preface," *Manly's Choice* [text-only edition], 2-3.

[77]Letter, Basil Manly, Jr., to William Howard Doane, October 16, 1891 (Manly papers, SBTS).

[78]Basil Manly, Jr., "Preface," *Manly's Choice* [edition with music], iii.

[79]Ibid.

[80]Ibid.

[81]John A. Broadus, "President John A. Broadus on Dr. Manly's Last Work," *Religious Herald*, February 25, 1892, 1.

[82]Basil Manly, Jr., *Manly's Choice* [text-only edition], 3.

[83]Basil Manly, Jr., *Manly's Choice* [edition with music], iii. The change is contained in his letter to the engravers, Allison and Smith, of December 26, 1891 (Manly papers, SBTS).

# PART III:

# SINGING–SCHOOL TUNEBOOKS IN THE 19TH-CENTURY SOUTH

# Introduction
## Harry Eskew

THE AMERICAN SINGING SCHOOL, which originated in early 18th-century New England was an attempt to improve congregational psalm singing through teaching music reading. It emerged while Baptists and others were still engaged in lining-out—singing tunes passed along by word of mouth. In the 19th century, as singing schools increased in number and penetrated into the southern and midwestern regions of the country, they began to have a profound effect on the singing of Baptists.

In this century, especially in the period before the Civil War, hymnals were words-only collections. Hymn tunes were commonly published in wider than tall singing-school tunebooks. Southern tunebooks were published almost exclusively in shape notation, a system designed to simplify music reading which developed about 1800. The typical singing-school tunebook, compiled by an itinerant singing-school teacher, consisted of an introduction to the rudiments of music (perhaps 20 to 30 pages), followed by an anthology of up to several hundred psalm and hymn tunes, fuging tunes, and anthems. The singing school was the chief means of music education in the South, and singing-school tunebooks contained a sizable body of tunes for use in congregational singing.

Among the hymn tunes published in these southern tunebooks was a rich store of folk-hymn tunes, melodies reflecting the Anglo-American oral tradition. Recent American hymnals have included an increasing number of folk hymns and tunes from these early tunebooks, such as NEW BRITAIN ("Amazing grace! How sweet the sound"), WONDROUS LOVE, NETTLETON ("Come, thou fount of every blessing"), and RESTORATION ("Come, ye sinners, poor and needy"). Some of these folk hymns which developed in the camp-meeting revival tradition were simplified through repeated refrains, as in PROMISED LAND ("On Jordan's stormy banks"), with its familiar refrain, "I am bound for the promised land." Although most of the early tunebooks have not survived, several of them are still used in community singings, such as *The Sacred Harp* (1844), *Southern Harmony* (1835), and *Christian Harmony* (1867).

Baptists were active in compiling tunebooks during this period, and this section examines several of them: South Carolinian William Walker's *Southern Harmony* and *Christian Harmony*, Virginian Eli Ball's *The Manual of the Sacred Choir*, and Tennessean J. R. Graves' *The Little Seraph.* Two other significant Baptist-compiled tunebooks of this period are treated elsewhere. B. F. White and E. J. King's *The Sacred Harp*, the most popular tunebook yet in use, is described in books of Cobb and Jackson listed in the "Suggested Additional Readings in Baptist Hymnody" beginning on page 209 of this volume. Another Baptist tunebook of this era is John G. McCurry's *The Social Harp* (1855) treated in the facsimile reprint of this volume. The study of reprints or recent editions and participation in community singings using these tunebooks enable one to recognize more fully their impact upon Baptist congregational singing.

# PART III:
## SINGING–SCHOOL TUNEBOOKS IN THE 19TH-CENTURY SOUTH

# WILLIAM WALKER and His
# *Southern Harmony*
## Harry Eskew

Reprinted, with revisions, from *Baptist History and Heritage,* October 1986. Used by permission.

W HO WAS THE MOST FAMOUS Baptist musician in the pre-Civil War South? At that time Southern Baptists, who had become a separate denomination in 1845, had no denominational church music program, no graded-choir programs, and no full-time ministers of music, for these are 20th-century developments. The predominant type of church music for early Baptists of the largely rural South was congregational song, which flourished as the result of the separate efforts of preachers and musicians. Preachers compiled numerous hymn text collections, such as *Mercer's Cluster* (3rd ed., 1810), Dossey's *Choice* (1820), *Dover Selection* (1828), and *Baptist Harmony* (1834). The musicians, who were not organists or ministers of music but were singing-school teachers, compiled singing-school manuals which are now known as tunebooks, published in easy-to-read shape notation. Three well-known shape-note tunebooks compiled by Baptists before 1860 were: *Southern Harmony* (1835) by South Carolinian William Walker, *The Sacred Harp* (1844) by Georgians B. F. White and E. J. King, and *The Social Harp* (1855) by Georgian John G. McCurry.

Perhaps the most famous Southern Baptist musician during this era was William Walker of Spartanburg, South Carolina, known as "Singin' Billy" Walker. A letter from a singing-school teacher in French Camp, Mississippi, written in 1880, four years after Walker's death, gave the following remarkable tribute, the metaphors reflecting the predominance of agriculture in the South:

...Thousands and thousands have blessed the name of William Walker who has sent the *Southern Harmony* into almost every home in our Southern land, breaking up the fallow ground and creating at least, if nothing more, an incentive, a desire, a thirsting for sacred music in the masses such as the round note system never has nor never will accomplish... [1]

Lest this quote seem to be an isolated exaggeration of Walker's fame, note this similar tribute found in his obituary: "...The 'Southern Harmony' and his name, the distinguished name of the author, are as familiar as household duties, in the habitations of the South."[2]

Portrait of William Walker
1809–1875

Although William Walker's name may have been a household word in the South of his day, he is unknown to most of today's Southern Baptists and even to most Southern Baptist historians and musicians. Who was Walker and how did he become one of the South's best-known musicians?

### Biography

*Early Years.*—Walker was born in upper South Carolina on the Tyger River near Martin's Mills, about three miles from the village of Cross Keys, in Union County on May 6, 1809.[3] Walker's parents were Absalom and Susannah Jackson Walker, his mother being related to Thomas Jonathan "Stonewall" Jackson, the famous Confederate general. Among Walker's cousins were John B. O. Landrum, a pioneer historian of upper South Carolina, and Newton Pinckney Walker, the minister who founded South Carolina's Institution for the Deaf and Blind at Cedar Springs.

When William Walker was about 18 years of age, his family moved to Cedar Springs, a small community a few miles southeast of Spartanburg. There Walker received his only known formal education at the Word Academy, a school whose curriculum included not only English and mathematics but also Latin and Greek. Walker's musical experiences began at a very young age. By the time he was five his mother had taught him at least three hymns which reflected the Anglo-American folk style. He later published these hymns under the tune names SOLEMN THOUGHT ("Remember, sinful youth, you must die, you must die"), THAT GLORIOUS DAY ("That glorious day is drawing nigh"), and FRENCH BROAD ("High o'er the hills the mountains rise"). Walker probably received music training in singing schools, for by the age of 18 he had composed his first piece, SOLEMN CALL ("I sing a song which doth belong"), a folk-like fuging tune.

*Church Activities.*—Although the first Baptist church that Walker joined is not known, he did join the newly organized First Baptist Church of Spartanburg on October 2, 1839, when he was 30.[4] During his 36 years as a member of that church, Walker was a deacon, a frequent messenger to the association, and a leader of congregational singing. One of his sons, Miles T. Walker, was licensed as a minister by the church in 1865.

A. Merril Smoak, Jr., has described Walker's numerous activities in the Tyger River Baptist Association to which the Spartanburg church belonged.[5] Association minutes recorded Walker's activities in this association during 12 annual meetings between 1845 and 1869. These minutes identified him as "W. Walker, A.S.H.," the initials indicating his authorship of *Southern Harmony.* These initials also distinguished him from other William Walkers of his day. George Pullen Jackson reported that there were two other William Walkers at this time in the Spartanburg area.[6]

Walker's activities in the Tyger River Association included his service as a delegate from the Spartanburg First Baptist Church; he was also a messenger to other Baptist associations. His association appointed him as a delegate to the South Carolina Baptist Convention six times; once he was appointed to a Southern Baptist Convention meeting in Montgomery, Alabama, in 1855.[7] He served on several associational committees and at least once, in 1867, delivered an address to the association. The association recognized his competence as a church musician in 1855 by appointing him (along with three Baptist ministers) to a committee charged with reviewing a new hymnbook that had been published by the Southern Baptist Publication Society— Edwin T. Winkler's *Sacred Lute* (1855). The committee brought forth a resolution that the *Sacred Lute* be recommended to the churches of the association.

After Walker's death in 1875, the Tyger River Association disbanded so that several new associations could be formed. At the first annual meeting of the newly organized Spartanburg Association in 1876, the following memorial tribute was made to Walker:

> He occupied a large place in the affections of the Baptists, and indeed,
> of other denominations in the State and out of the State. His sweet
> songs have been resounded from the Hudson to the Gulf of Mexico,

and they will long continue to resound on earth and breathe the sentiments of Christian hearts, while he, Smith and Waters will doubtless be singing "a new song" in Heaven.[8]

*Family.*—In 1835 Walker married; he also published his first work. On January 20, now almost 26 years of age, he married Amy Shands Golightly (1811-1897) of Spartanburg. They had five sons and five daughters. Incidentally, Mrs. Walker's sister, Thurza Golightly, married B. F. White, the co-compiler of the most widely used shape-note tunebook still in use, *The Sacred Harp* (1844). In September 1835, Walker completed his first tunebook, *Southern Harmony.*[9]

*Tunebooks.*—In addition to *Southern Harmony,* Walker compiled three other shape-note collections. In 1846 his *Southern and Western Pocket Harmonist* was published by the Thomas Cowperthwait Company of Philadelphia. This smaller tunebook was intended to be a supplement to *Southern Harmony,* with more hymns suitable for revival use. Shortly after the Civil War (1867), Walker's other major tunebook, *Christian Harmony,* was published jointly by E. W. Miller and Walker in Philadelphia. *Christian Harmony* incorporated major changes from *Southern Harmony,* such as the switch from four to seven-shape notation and the selection of more pieces reflecting the influence of Lowell Mason and his colleagues of the Northeast. *Christian Harmony,* which was reprinted as recently as 1979, is still used in singings, especially in western North Carolina and Alabama.[10] Walker's last collection, published in 1873 by the J. B. Lippincott Company of Philadelphia, was a children's songbook, *Fruits and Flowers,* designed for use in both common schools and Sunday Schools. It included both secular and sacred songs.

*Later Years.*—Throughout most of his adult years, Walker was an active singing-school teacher. Although no specific records of his teaching are extant, his activities in this profession ranged widely. In 1866 he wrote, "...we have travelled thousands of miles in the Middle, Southern, and Western States, and taught a number of singing schools...."[11] From about the mid-1850s he also taught normal music schools designed to train singing-school teachers. His singing-school textbooks were his own tunebooks: *Southern Harmony* in the pre-Civil War years and *Christian Harmony* after the war.

Walker not only taught thousands to read music and sing, he also actively supported education in his community. In 1835 he was a trustee of the Spartanburg Male Academy and was one of a group who subscribed $1,300 to establish the Female Seminary in Spartanburg. In 1851 he took part in the cornerstone-laying ceremonies for Spartanburg's Wofford College. He also operated a bookstore and acquired a large personal library that included a number of rare volumes.

Walker was over 50 years of age by the time of the Civil War, so he did not fight in the war. In 1862, however, he was sent by Spartanburg's Soldiers' Aid and Relief Association to Richmond to nurse soldiers. While serving as a nurse, he became personally acquainted with General Stonewall Jackson. Among the soldiers Walker ministered to as a nurse was his own son, Absalom.

On September 24, 1875, Walker died at the age of 66. He was buried in Spartanburg's Magnolia Cemetery. His life is briefly summarized on his tombstone:

> In memory of William Walker, A.S.H. Died September 24, 1875 in the 67th year of his age. He was a devoted husband and kind father. A consistent Baptist 47 years. Taught music 45 years. The author of 4 books of sacred music. He rests from his labors. He died in the triumphs of faith. Sing praises unto the Lord.

### Southern Harmony

*General Description.—Southern Harmony,* William Walker's most important publication, was typical of the southern tunebooks of its time. It was a singing-school manual which contained an opening section of rudiments for teaching music reading. As described on the title page, this section provided "An Easy Introduction to the grounds of Music, the rudiments of Music, and

Title page from *Southern Harmony* (New Haven and Spartanburg, 1835).

THE

## SOUTHERN HARMONY, AND MUSICAL COMPANION:

CONTAINING A CHOICE COLLECTION OF

TUNES, HYMNS, PSALMS, ODES AND ANTHEMS:

SELECTED FROM THE MOST EMINENT AUTHORS IN THE UNITED STATES.

TOGETHER WITH NEARLY ONE HUNDRED NEW TUNES, WHICH HAVE NEVER BEFORE BEEN PUBLISHED; SUITED TO MOST

OF THE METRES CONTAINED IN

WATTS' HYMNS AND PSALMS, MERCER'S CLUSTER, DOSSEY'S CHOICE, DOVER SELECTION, METHODIST HYMN BOOK AND BAPTIST HARMONY;

AND WELL ADAPTED TO

CHRISTIAN CHURCHES OF EVERY DENOMINATION, SINGING SCHOOLS AND PRIVATE SOCIETIES.

ALSO, AN EASY

**Introduction to the grounds of Music, the rudiments of Music, and plain rules for beginners.**

BY WILLIAM WALKER.

Sing unto God, ye kingdoms of the earth; O sing praises unto the Lord.—DAVIS.
Speaking to yourselves in psalms and hymns, and spiritual songs, singing and making melody in your hearts to the Lord.—PAUL.

SPARTANSBURG, S. C.

Sold by the AUTHOR, at Spartanburg, S. C.; Rev. S. S. BURDETT, Pleasant Hill; MATTHEW LYON, Chester; ROBERTS and WADDELL, Union; WILLIAM RILEY, Charleston; J. R. and W. CUNNINGHAM, Columbia; and by MERCHANTS generally in the Southern States.

1835

plain rules for beginners." Music reading was simplified by the use of shape notes in the popular four-shape system standing for the old Elizabethan solmization (the use of syllables to denote the tones of a musical scale) with the syllables fa, sol, la, and mi.[12] *Southern Harmony* also contained an anthology of choral music for use in singing schools and churches, "a choice collection of tunes, hymns, odes, and anthems."

As was the case with other tunebooks of its day, *Southern Harmony* was multifunctional, as indicated on its title page: "Well adapted to Christian Churches of Every Denomination, Singing Schools, and Private Societies." Some indication of the diversity of functions intended for *Southern Harmony* appeared in the twofold division of its musical selections.

Part one, "Containing Most of the Plain and Easy Tunes Commonly Used in Time of Divine Worship," was the larger of the two. It contained basically the repertory of congregational hymns for church use, although these also certainly served the singing school. This first part included:

• Such older European tunes as OLD HUNDRED ("O come, loud anthems let us sing") and MEAR ("Will God forever cast us off?"), the New England composer Daniel Read's WINDHAM ("Broad is the road that leads to death"), Lowell Mason's MISSIONARY HYMN ("From Greenland's icy mountains"), and Thomas Hastings' ORTONVILLE ("Am I a soldier of the cross").

• American folk hymns, such as NEW BRITAIN (sometimes called AMAZING GRACE), KEDRON ("Thou man of grief, remember me"), HOLY MANNA

NEW BRITAIN ("Amazing Grace") from *Southern Harmony* (New Haven and Spartanburg, 1835).

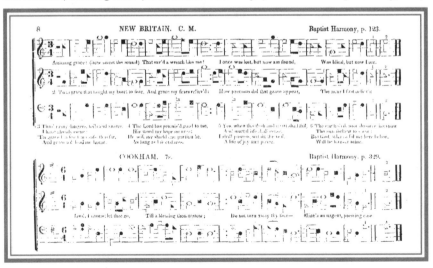

("Brethren, we have met to worship"), IDUMEA ("And am I born to die?"), and PISGAH ("Jesus, thou art the sinners friend").

• A few revival spirituals with choruses, such as THE PROMISED LAND ("On Jordan's stormy banks I stand"; refrain: "I am bound for the promised land"), WARRENTON ("Come, thou fount of every blessing"; refrain: "I am bound for the kingdom"), and Walker's tune HALLELUJAH ("And let this feeble body fail"; refrain: "And I'll sing hallelujah").

• Surprisingly, several fuging tunes requiring contrapuntal skills, such as LENOX ("Blow, ye the trumpet blow"), NINETY-FIFTH ("When I can read my title clear"), and EVENING SHADE ("The day is past and gone"), were included among "plain and easy tunes" for congregational use.

Part two, "Containing Some of the More Lengthy and Elegant Pieces, Commonly Used at Concerts, or Singing Societies," included all of the anthems in *Southern Harmony,* such as William Billings' EASTER ANTHEM ("The Lord is ris'n indeed!") and ROSE OF SHARON ("I am the Rose of Sharon") and Jacob French's HEAVENLY VISION ("I beheld, and lo a great multitude"). This latter part of the book also contained fuging tunes, some of which occupied more than one page. As in part one, there were revival spirituals, including Walker's THE GOOD OLD WAY ("Lift up your heads, Immanuel's friends"; refrain: "And I'll sing hallelujah") and his brother-in-law B. F. White's THE MORNING TRUMPET ("Oh when shall I see Jesus"; refrain: "Shout, O glory!") Although this second part contained more lengthy and challenging pieces, it also

THE PROMISED LAND ("On Jordan's stormy banks I stand") from *Southern Harmony* (New Haven and Spartanburg, 1835).

included simple hymn tunes, such as Lowell Mason's ROCKINGHAM ("Thy praise, O Lord, shall tune the lyre") and his arrangement of AZMON ("Plung'd in a gulf of dark despair").

In addition to these two main parts, the later editions of *Southern Harmony* usually added a variety of selections in an appendix, including pieces suitable for church, revival, or singing school.

*Editions.*—Although Walker published 3 prefaces to different editions of *Southern Harmony* dated 1835, 1847, and 1854, he actually published 5 distinctive editions in a total of at least 13 different printings. These 5 basic[13] editions were published as follows: [First] edition, 1835; [second] edition ("with an Appendix"), 1840; [third] edition ("with an Appendix"), 1847; [fourth] edition, ("New Edition, Thoroughly Revised and Greatly Enlarged"), 1854. From the initial edition of 1835 to the last one of 1854, Walker added 140 selections and deleted 20. *Southern Harmony* was first printed in New Haven, Connecticut, but all later printings through 1854 were made in Philadelphia. The 1854 edition was reprinted in 1939, 1966, and 1987.[14]

On the eve of the Civil War, Walker was making plans for a successor to his popular tunebook to be entitled *The New Southern Harmony*. In the Walker family papers is found a signed agreement between William Walker, A.S.H., and the J. B. Lippincott Company of Philadelphia to publish this new tunebook. The agreement was dated August 1, 1860. A few months later South Carolina became the first state to secede from the Union, so it is understandable that Walker's *The New Southern Harmony* was never published. Instead of this proposed tunebook, Walker turned shortly after the Civil War to one of his *Southern Harmony* publishers, E. W. Miller of Philadelphia, to publish his *Christian Harmony*. Although J. B. Lippincott did not publish *The New Southern Harmony,* this firm did publish Walker's last collection, *Fruits and Flowers* (copyright 1869, published 1873).

*Baptist Hymnals as Text Sources.*—*Southern Harmony* served as a musical companion to numerous words-only hymnals of its day. Walker credited these hymnals as sources for many of *Southern Harmony's* texts. His Baptist orientation in this respect was clear, for the three sources most often credited for texts in the 1854 edition of *Southern Harmony* were Baptist collections. Thirty-two hymns were credited to *Baptist Harmony,* a hymnbook by the South Carolina Baptist pastor Staunton S. Burdett that appeared in 1834, just a year before *Southern Harmony* was first published. The second of these three main text sources was *Dover Selection* (1828), compiled by the Virginia Baptist pastor Andrew Broaddus. The third main text source Walker used was *The Cluster,* the hymn collection of the Georgia Baptist pastor Jesse Mercer that had reached a third edition by 1810 and a fifth edition by 1835.[15]

*Folk Hymns.*—Although *Southern Harmony* included varied types of music ranging from psalm and hymn tunes to fuging tunes and anthems, the type that has aroused the greatest interest today is the folk hymn. Walker and other rural-oriented singing-school teacher-compilers drew from the rich store of Anglo-American folk songs that existed in oral tradition to provide melodies for many of the hymns. Sometimes the folk melody and hymn text were already associated with one another, and sometimes Walker and other compilers fitted secular folk melodies to hymns of Isaac Watts and other hymnists mainly from 18th-century England. Walker and others likely had so fully absorbed the Anglo-American folk song idiom that they themselves composed tunes in this style.

One of the most enduring of the early American folk hymns is WONDROUS LOVE, a tune first published in the 1840 [2nd] edition of *Southern Harmony.* Folk hymns such as WONDROUS LOVE have several distinctive musical traits:

1. The melody is often in one of the gapped scales, such as the pentatonic;

2. The melody is more frequently modal than in most types of hymn tunes;

3. The harmony is unorthodox, making common use of parallel fifths, octaves, and chords without thirds.

Another type of folk hymnody that grew out of the frontier camp-meeting

WONDROUS LOVE from *Southern Harmony* [2nd edition] (Philadelphia, 1840).

revivals of the early 1800s was what George Pullen Jackson called the "revival spiritual." Developed to meet the need for a simplified text for unlettered country folk, the revival spiritual often had a refrain or other repeated lines. One of the best-known revival spirituals, THE PROMISED LAND, first appeared in the initial edition of *Southern Harmony*. Some unknown American added the refrain, with its repetitions, to English Baptist minister Samuel Stennett's "On Jordan's stormy banks I stand":

> I am bound for the promised land,
> I'm bound for the promised land,
> O who will come and go with me?
> I am bound for the promised land.

It is noteworthy that THE PROMISED LAND was published in the pre-Civil War era in a minor mode. Only in the late 19th century was it changed to a major key to accommodate it to the newer gospel-hymn style in which it is widely known today.

*Continuing Influence.*—What impact have William Walker and his *Southern Harmony* had on recent Southern Baptist hymnals? A comparison of four major hymnals published by the Baptist Sunday School Board—*The Broadman Hymnal,* 1940; *Baptist Hymnal,* 1956; *Baptist Hymnal,* 1975; and *The Baptist Hymnal,* 1991—reveals that the first and second of these hymnals credit no hymns to William Walker or to his *Southern Harmony*. *The Baptist Hymnal,* 1991, credits *Southern Harmony* with three selections: RESIGNATION (No. 68, "My shepherd will supply my need"), RESTORATION (No. 323, "Come, ye sinners, poor and needy"), and WONDROUS LOVE (No. 143, "What wondrous love is this"). Two other selections in the 1991 hymnal may be properly credited to *Southern Harmony*. THE PROMISED LAND (No. 521, "On Jordan's stormy banks") first appeared in this 1835 tunebook. Although NEW BRITAIN had been published elsewhere to other texts, its first appearance in print to "Amazing grace! How sweet the sound" (No. 330, *TBH,* 1991) was in the first edition of Walker's *Southern Harmony*.[16] In terms of American folk hymnody in general, reflecting the influence of *Southern Harmony, The Sacred Harp,* and other early tunebooks, there was a marked increase in the *Baptist Hymnal,* 1975. *The Broadman Hymnal* has a dozen American folk hymns; the *Baptist Hymnal,* 1956, has only 10; *Baptist Hymnal,* 1975, has 24 different American folk hymns (not counting African-American spirituals). Three of these 24 tunes are used twice, giving a total of 27 folk hymns (text, tune, or both text and tune) in the *Baptist Hymnal,* 1975. Thus, much more of the Anglo-American folk hymnody of the repertory found in *Southern Harmony* and *The Sacred Harp* became available for congregational use among Southern Baptists through the 1975 *Baptist Hymnal.* The use of a larger number of these folk hymns and spirituals is a general trend in most major American hymnals published in recent years.

Like *The Sacred Harp, Southern Harmony* is still used in singings, but on a much smaller scale. In 1852, *Southern Harmony* was carried by settlers from the Carolinas to western Kentucky, and in 1884 a "Big Singing" was established in the town of Benton.[17] This *Southern Harmony* singing has been in existence for over one hundred years, meeting the fourth Sunday in May.

*Southern Harmony* marked its 150th anniversary in 1985. Baptists of the South can take justifiable pride in *Southern Harmony* and *The Sacred Harp.* Although no Southern Baptist hymnists have written hymns that have gained a place in most non-Baptist hymnals, the repertory of folk hymns compiled by William Walker, B. F. White, E. J. King, and John G. McCurry has gained a rightful place in the broad stream of present-day congregational song in America.

[1]J. A. Downing, French Camp, Mississippi, Letter to Editor, *Musical Million,* XI:135, September 1880.

[2]T. O. P. Vernon, "Late Prof. Walker of S. C.," *Musical Million,* VII:1ff, January 1876.

[3]Unless otherwise indicated, biographical data is based on Harry Eskew's "The Life and Work of William Walker" (M.S.M. thesis, New Orleans Baptist Theological Seminary, 1960), which refers to numerous primary and secondary sources.

[4]Mary Collins Green, *First Baptist Church, Spartanburg: A History, 1839-1982* (Spartanburg, SC: First Baptist Church, 1983), 213. This history, although valuable in many respects, erroneously credits Walker with the origination of shape notes.

[5]Alfred Merril Smoak, Jr., "William Walker's *Southern Harmony*" ( M.C.M. thesis, Southern Baptist Theological Seminary, 1975), 17-22.

[6]George Pullen Jackson, *White Spirituals in the Southern Uplands* (Chapel Hill: University of North Carolina Press, 1933; Reprint eds. Hatboro, PA: Folklore Associates, 1964; New York: Dover Publications, 1965), 55, 60.

[7]Walker likely did not attend this Southern Baptist Convention meeting, for the Convention minutes do not list him among the messengers from South Carolina.

[8]*Minutes*, Spartanburg Baptist Association, August 18-21, 1876, 11. Smith probably refers to Samuel Francis Smith (1808-1895), the Massachusetts Baptist minister who authored "My country, 'tis of thee" and compiled (with Baron Stow) *The Psalmist* (1843), the most widely used American Baptist hymnal of its time. Waters likely refers to Horace Waters (1812-1892), a New York piano merchant and publisher of popular Sunday School songbooks.

[9]A manuscript collection of pieces transcribed by Walker was made several years before his *Southern Harmony.* See Milburn Price, "Miss Elizabeth Adams' Music Book: A Manuscript Predecessor of William Walker's *Southern Harmony,* " *The Hymn,* 29:70-75, April 1978.

[10]For a study of *Christian Harmony* and its performance style in present-day singings, see Edith Bryson Card, "William Walker's Music Then and Now: A Study of Performance Style" (Ph.D. dissertation, Florida State University, 1975).

[11]William Walker, *Christian Harmony* (Philadelphia: E. W. Miller and William Walker, 1867), iii.

[12]See Harry Eskew, "Shape-Note Hymnody," *Encyclopedia of Southern Baptists,* 1982, IV, 2, 451.

[13]For a detailed description of these editions, see Harry Eskew, "William Walker's *Southern Harmony* (1835-1854): Its Basic Editions" beginning on page 129.

[14]The most recent reprint of the 1854 edition is available from The University Press of Kentucky, Lexington, KY 40506-1124.

[15]A recent detailed study is C. Ray Brewster, *The Cluster of Jesse Mercer* (Macon, GA: Renaissance Press, 1983).

[16]Two of the three tunes credited to *Southern Harmony* (1835) in *The Baptist Hymnal,* 1991, appeared in later editions. WONDROUS LOVE was first published in the 1840 [2nd] edition, and RESIGNATION was first published in the 1854 [5th] edition.

[17]For a detailed study of the famous singing, see Deborah Carlton Loftis, "Big Singing Day in Benton, Kentucky: A Study of the History, Ethnic Identity and Musical Style of Southern Harmony Singers." (Ph.D. dissertation, University of Kentucky, 1987).

# PART III:
## SINGING–SCHOOL TUNEBOOKS IN THE 19TH-CENTURY SOUTH

# WILLIAM WALKER'S
# *Southern Harmony:* Its Basic Editions
## Harry Eskew

Reprinted, with revisions, from *Latin American Music Review,* Fall/Winter 1986. Used by permission.

## Introduction

For over one hundred years in the county-seat town of Benton, Kentucky, groups of people have gathered annually to hold a "Big Singing." In 1983, when the 100th annual singing was held, I happened to be listening to National Public Radio and heard coverage of this historic event.

The shape-note tunebook used at Benton's singing is not from Kentucky, but originated in upper South Carolina, having been brought to western Kentucky by North Carolinian James R. Lemon in 1852. This tunebook is William Walker's *Southern Harmony,* first published in 1835. This western Kentucky singing is the only such institution in which this Carolina tunebook remains in regular use.

William Walker (1809-1875), probably the first to compile a shape-note tunebook in the Deep South, was born in Union County, South Carolina, on May 6, 1809. By age five his mother had taught him hymns reflecting the Anglo-American folk song tradition, which he later included in his tunebooks. Walker likely learned music through local singing schools, for at age 18 he composed his first original piece, SOLEMN CALL, a folklike fuging tune.[1] At age 20 Walker joined a Baptist church. He became convinced that his calling lay in the field of sacred music, as colorfully described by his biographer: "To perfect the vocal modes of praise became the leading ambition and cynosure of his long, laborious, and useful life. Determined, at once, he gathered and arranged into metre and melody a wonderful book, suitably adapted to the praise and glory of God."[2]

This "wonderful book" was *Southern Harmony*, the first and most popular of Walker's four collections.[3] Although no exact circulation figures are available, it seems likely that *Southern Harmony* was the South's most popular tunebook during the pre-Civil War period. In the preface to *Christian Harmony,* Walker expressed thanks "for the very hearty and unparalleled patronage given to the various editions of the *Southern Harmony*, there having been sold (as we understand from one of the publishers) about six hundred thousand copies."[4]

How many editions did the reportedly six hundred thousand copies of *Southern Harmony* encompass? The last known edition lists three prefaces:

> Preface to Former Edition...September 1835
> Preface to New Edition...January 1847
> Preface to Revised Edition...July 1854

In his pioneering *White Spirituals in the Southern Uplands,* published in 1933, George Pullen Jackson describes four editions of *Southern Harmony*, but his description is incomplete and confusing.[5] Richard J. Stanislaw's *A Checklist of Four-Shape Shape-Note Tunebooks,* published in 1978, lists nine dated issues of *Southern Harmony*. However, even Stanislaw's extensive list is incomplete and does not clearly distinguish between editions and reprints. In spite of the widespread attention given to *Southern Harmony*, there has remained uncertainty and confusion in regard to its editions.

The purpose of this chapter is to describe basic editions of *Southern Harmony* and their significance in the shape-note tradition. The term "basic editions" is used to indicate the first edition and later issues with significant changes in terms of number of pages added and pieces of music added or deleted. A minor change will be regarded as a variant issue of the same edition. I have assigned the numberings of the basic editions.

### [First] Edition, 1835

Although *Southern Harmony* was first published in 1835, Walker composed his first original tune in 1827[6] and produced a manuscript collection dated 1832 and 1833 whose pieces are largely found in *Southern Harmony*.[7] Walker, who lived in Spartanburg, South Carolina, during his adult years, had to have *Southern Harmony* printed where music fonts were available for the widely used four-shape notation of Little and Smith. Why he went as far as New Haven, Connecticut, to have *Southern Harmony* printed is a puzzle, for shape-note tunebooks had been printed in locations such as Harrisonburg, Virginia, Baltimore, Maryland, and at Harrisburg and Philadelphia, Pennsylvania. It is also strange that no other shape-note tunebooks appear to have been printed in New Haven. After this initial edition, Walker yielded to geographical convenience and had all later editions printed in Philadelphia.

The 1835 edition, printed by Nathan Whiting, contains 32 pages of introductory material followed by general and metrical indexes; these pages are indicated in Roman numerals. The rest of this initial edition consists of 216 pages of music, concluding with "Farewell Anthem."

In 1838 Walker issued a "Stereotype Edition, Corrected and Improved," a variant issue of the first edition. Produced at Philadelphia (as were all known issues after 1835), this variant's copyright page indicates that it was printed by T. K. and P. G. Collins and stereotyped by L. Johnson. Walker himself is listed as the sole publisher on the title page. Other than corrections, only three minor changes distinguish this variant's contents: (1) its indexes are transferred from the close of the introductory material (xxxi and xxxii) to added pages 217 and 218; (2) in place of the indexes at the close of the introductory material are the two-page "Introductory Remarks, from the Columbian Harmony" (xxx and xxxi); (3) the tune WARRENTON is added on page 94. Because of the transfer of the two pages of indexes to the end of this variant, it has a total of 218 numbered pages after the introductory materials.

## [Second] Edition, 1840

The first significant revisions in *Southern Harmony* occurred in its 1840 edition, published (as indicated on its title page) jointly by Walker and "E. King, Esq., Flat Rock, N.C." A check of courthouse records and local histories for Henderson County (where Flat Rock is located) has not turned up the identity of E. King. Like the 1838 issue, this edition was printed by T. K. and P. G. Collins and stereotyped by L. Johnson. As in all later editions, the theoretical introduction remained unchanged in content and length. This edition is enlarged by an appendix of 16 pages, which contains 13 additional pieces. The appendix includes such well-known folk hymns as WONDROUS LOVE (attributed to Christopher, 220) and THE SAINTS BOUND FOR HEAVEN (attributed to J. King and W. Walker, 226).[8] Significantly, this is the earliest known printing of WONDROUS LOVE. In *Christian Harmony* (359) Walker described WONDROUS LOVE as "a very popular old Southern tune" and indicated it was "arranged by James Christopher, of Spartanburg, South Carolina." Christopher has not been further identified. Since B. F. White accused Walker, his brother-in-law, of not crediting him as a coauthor of *Southern Harmony*,[9] it is no surprise that Walker's name is omitted as a composer of THE SAINTS BOUND FOR HEAVEN in the first edition (1844) of White and E. J. King's *The Sacred Harp* (224). The identity of J. King is unknown. J. King is apparently not E. J. King, for Walker clearly identified E. J. King elsewhere.[10] In 1843, 1844, and 1845, the second basic edition of *Southern Harmony* was reprinted.[11] All second edition copies examined have the following indication on the final page (metrical index, p. 232): "Whole number of pages 264."

## [Third] Edition, 1847

The next revision of *Southern Harmony* was the first 1847 edition, published jointly by Thomas, Cowperthwait and Company, and by Walker. This first of two 1847 editions carried the same edition designation as that of 1840: "Stereotype Edition, Corrected and Improved. With an Appendix." The Library of Congress has a copyright deposit copy of this edition with what appears to be Walker's signature and dated April 22, 1847. This edition also contains an inserted errata sheet listing corrections for time signatures in 26 of the pieces added. It has 272 pages, an increase of 40 pages, and 51 additional pieces of music.

These 51 added tunes, three times the number added to the 1840 edition, constitute a variety of traditions. Older tunes of European origin include Arne's ARLINGTON ("And must I be to judgement brought"), Hatton's DUKE STREET (" 'Tis by the faith of joys to come"), and the psalm tune AYLESBURY ("And am I born to die"). Early New England tunes include Swan's CHINA ("Why do we mourn departing friends?"), Holden's CORONATION ("All hail the power of Jesus' name"), and Ingalls' fuging tune NORTHFIELD ("How long, dear Jesus, Oh! how long"). Tunes in the Mason-Hastings idiom include Webb's COME, YE DISCONSOLATE, Hastings's ROCK OF AGES, and Mason's arrangement from a Gregorian chant entitled RIPLEY ("Jesus, I my cross have taken"). Pieces in the rural folk hymn style include Lewis' DUNLAP'S CREEK ("My God, my portion, and my love"), David Walker's HEBREW CHILDREN ("Where are the Hebrew children?"), and Chapin's ROCKBRIDGE ("Life is the time to serve the Lord"). Pieces bearing William Walker's name added to this edition include PARDONING LOVE ("In evil long I took delight") and FRENCH BROAD ("High o'er the hills the mountains rise"). This last tune has a text that Walker wrote while traveling on the French Broad River in North Carolina and Tennessee in 1831.[12]

Ten of the 51 pieces added in this 1847 edition appeared in the first edition of *The Sacred Harp* (1844). A comparison of the voice parts and stanzas of these eight pieces reveals none of them to be close enough to have been clearly taken from *The Sacred Harp*. Twelve of the 51 new pieces had also been previously published by Walker in his second tunebook, *Southern and Western Pocket Harmonist* (1846), which he intended as a supplement to *Southern Harmony* that was suitable for revival use.

## [Fourth] Edition, 1847

Not content with one revision of *Southern Harmony* issued in 1847, Walker brought out a "New Edition, Improved, and Enlarged," published in Philadelphia by E. W. Miller, Ranstead Place. The following booksellers listed after publisher E. W. Miller on the title page give some idea of the geographical distribution of *Southern Harmony* by this time: "And for sale by Thomas, Cowperthwait & Co., Lippincott, Grambo & Co., Troutman & Hayes.—New York: A. S. Barnes & Co., Pratt, Woodford & Co., R. B. Collins, Geo. F. Cooledge & Bro.—Charleston, S.C.: A. Carter, McCarter & Allen: and booksellers generally throughout the United States. Spartanburg S.C.: William Walker, author and proprietor."

Both 1847 editions have the same number of pages, but they are numbered differently. The Thomas, Cowperthwait edition is numbered xxxii plus 272, a total of 304 pages. The Miller edition follows the same numbering through page 216, which bears the note, "Whole number of pages including Gamut, 248." From this point the Miller edition follows the new pagination, beginning with page 249 and continuing through page 304.

Although both 1847 editions have 304 pages, the Miller edition has 15 additional pieces. Space for these 15 pieces was gained by printing two tunes on a page (the stanza being placed between staves to provide additional space), whereas only one had been placed earlier. Three of these 15 pieces—Mason's MISSIONARY HYMN ("From Greenland's icy mountains," with a treble by James Langston), the anonymous folk hymn SWEET AFFLICTION ("In the floods of tribulation"), and Walker's THE GOOD OLD WAY ("Lift up your heads, Immanuel's friends")—appear in identical form in *The Sacred Harp,* an indication that Walker may have taken them from this tunebook. In *The Sacred Harp,* however, THE GOOD OLD WAY appears as an anonymous tune.

In 1850 and 1851, additional issues of *Southern Harmony* appeared. Both issues were published jointly by Thomas, Cowperthwait and Company, and Walker. They bear the title page designation of the 1847 E. W. Miller edition: "New Edition, Improved and Enlarged." A comparison of the indexes of the 1850 and 1851 issues with the 1847 fourth edition published by E. W. Miller shows them to be identical.

## [Fifth] Edition, 1854

The last known edition of *Southern Harmony*, designated "New Edition, Thoroughly Revised and Greatly Improved," was published in 1854 in Philadelphia by E. W. Miller (later Miller & Burlock). The title page lists more northern than southern firms from which *Southern Harmony* could be purchased: "And for sale by H. Cowperthwait & Company, J. B. Lippincott & Company, Hayes & Zell. Philadelphia—New York: A. S. Barnes & Company, R. B. Collins, Mason & Brothers—Charleston, S.C.: McCarter & Company, A. Carter: and booksellers generally throughout the United States. Spartanburg, South Carolina: William Walker, author and proprietor."

The 1854 edition has xxxii and 344 pages, an additional 32 pages of music. Unlike the second through fourth editions, in which changes consisted only of additional pieces of music, this edition also involved the deletion of music, as stated by Walker in his preface (p.ii):

> Since the *Southern Harmony* was first published, many of the tunes having gone out of use, the *author* determined to revise the work, and leave out those pieces, and supply their places with *good new tunes,* which have been selected for their intrinsic worth, and great popularity, and highly devotional character. He has also enlarged the work with thirty-two pages of excellent music, many of the tunes being suitable for revival occasions.

Twenty pieces that Walker judged to have gone out of use were deleted from the 1854 edition. Eighteen of these had appeared in *Southern Harmony,* beginning with its first edition of 1835.

Two pieces, PACOLET ("Shall men pretend to pleasure") and HEAVENLY TREASURE ("Friendship to every willing mind"), had been in *Southern Harmony* since the second edition of 1840. Only two of these 20 deleted pieces, SOLITUDE IN THE GROVE ("O, were I like a feather'd dove") and NEW LEBANON ("Great God, the Heav'n's well order'd frame"), appeared in earlier (1844 and 1850) editions of *The Sacred Harp*.[13] The deleted pieces are predominantly New England pre-Lowell Mason tunes and rural folk hymns, being about equally divided between these categories.

Seventy-three pieces were added to the 1854 edition, almost twice the number added to any single earlier edition. Sixteen of these had appeared in *The Sacred Harp*. Seven of the 16 are identical in all voice parts; nine have different voice parts. Five of the seven identical pieces are by two persons closely associated with *The Sacred Harp:* CROSS OF CHRIST (WSH, 35; WKH, 123), HAPPY LAND (89; 354), and MERCY'S FREE (304; 337) by Leonard P. Breedlove, and BOUND FOR CANAAN (193; 82) and WEEPING SAVIOUR (7; 33) by co-compiler E. J. King.[14]

Slightly over half of the 73 selections added to the 1854 edition of *Southern Harmony* are in the style of the folk hymn, such as J. T. White's ALL IS WELL ("What's this that steals, that steals upon my frame?"), RESIGNATION ("My Shepherd will supply my need"), SAMANTHRA ("His voice as the sound of a dulcimer sweet"), and S. Hill's YOUNG CONVERT ("When converts first begin to sing"). The only other types of music represented significantly are the hymns (approximately 20 percent) in the style of Lowell Mason and Thomas Hastings, such as Mason's HARWELL ("Hark! ten thousand harps and voices"), Webb's BENEVENUTO ("While with ceaseless course, the sun"), and Hastings' ORTONVILLE ("Am I a soldier of the cross").

Eight of the 73 added pieces bear Walker's name. Two of these are joint attributions: BOWER OF PRAYER ("To leave my dear friends and with neighbors to part") by Richerson and Walker, and THE SAILOR'S HOME ("When for eternal worlds we steer") by William M. Caudill and Walker.[15] Choruses typical of the revival spiritual are found in THE SAILOR'S HOME (chorus: "The soul, for you then claps her wings") and in three of the other Walker tunes, CHRISTIAN PROSPECT ("We have our trials here below"; chorus: "O glory, hallelujah"), COME AND TASTE WITH ME ("Come and taste, along with me"; chorus: "'Tis religion we believe"), and IN THAT MORNING ("Jesus, my all, to heav'n is gone"; chorus: "In that morning, in that morning"). Thirty-nine pieces in the 1854 edition are attributed to Walker, many of which are in the style of Anglo-American folk hymnody.[16]

### Summary

The basic editions of *Southern Harmony* are summarized in table 1. Five basic editions were published in at least 12 issues by 1854.[17] These editions show Walker to be less bound by tradition than his brother-in-law, B. F. White. In White and King's *The Sacred Harp,* each edition merely added texts and tunes; at no point were pieces deleted, as was the case with Walker's 1854 edition, from which he took out 20 pieces. Furthermore, White and King held to earlier four-shape notation, whereas Walker became convinced that the seven-shape system was preferable. Instead of publishing *Southern Harmony* in seven-shape notation, Walker published a seven-shape tunebook, *Christian Harmony* (1867) after the Civil War.[18] Whereas *Southern Harmony*

## TABLE I. SOUTHERN HARMONY EDITIONS

| BASIC EDITION | YEAR | LATER ISSUES | PUBLISHER AND PLACE | PRINTER/TYPOGRAPHER AND PUBLISHER | PAGES | PIECES ADDED OR DELETED | LIBRARY LOCATIONS |
|---|---|---|---|---|---|---|---|
| [1st] | 1835* | | Walker, Spartanburg, SC | Nathan Whiting, New Haven, CT | xxxii, 216 | | Eskew, SCSp |
| | | 1838 "Stereotype edition Corrected and Improved" | Same | Printed by T.K. & P.G. Collins; stereotyped | xxxii, 218 | +1 | MWA |
| [2d] "With an Appendix" | 1840* | | Walker, Spartanburg, SC, & E. King, Flat Rock, NC | As in 1838 | xxxii, 232 | +13 in "Appendix" | Shull |
| | | 1843 | Walker, Spartanburg,SC, & Thomas, Cowperthwait & Co., Philadelphia, PA | As in 1838 | Same | Same | LNB, NcD |
| | | 1844* | As in 1843 | King & Baird,Printers, Philadelphia, PA | Same | Same | Shull, KyBB (inc.) |
| | | 1845 | As in 1843 | Not indicated | Same | Same | KyLos |
| | | Undated* | As in 1840 | As in 1838 | Same | Same | CLU |
| | | Undated | As in 1843 | As in 1838 | Same | Same | Eskew (inc.) SCSp |
| [3d] "With an Appendix" | 1847* | | As in 1843 | | xxxii, 272 [=304] | +51 | DLC, CLU (inc.), TXFS, KyBB |
| [4th] "New Ed. Improved & Enlarged" | 1847* | | E. W. Miller, Philadelphia, PA | | xxxii, 216 [xxxii + 216 = 248] | +15 | DLC, NNUT |
| | | 1850 | As in 1843 | Not indicated | Same | Same | CNY, Shull |
| | | 1851 | As in 1843 | Not indicated | Same | Same | ICN |
| [5th] "New Ed. Thoroughly Rev. and Greatly Improved" | 1854* | | As in 4th ed, 1847, Miller & Burlock | Miller & Burlock | Same xxxii, 216,248-336 | +73 -20 | CLU, ICN Eskew, NcD, TXFS |

*Personally examined.

### LIBRARY ABBREVIATIONS FOR TABLE 1

CLU: University of California at Los Angeles
CNY: Yale University Music Library, New Haven, CT
DLC: Library of Congress
Eskew: Personal Library of Harry Eskew, New Orleans, LA
ICN: Newberry Library, Chicago
KyBB: Berea College, Berea, KY

KyLos: The Southern Baptist Theological Seminary Library, Louisville, KY
LNB: New Orleans Baptist Theological Seminary, Martin Music Library
MWA: American Antiquarian Society Library, Worcester, MA
NcD: Duke University Library, Durham, NC

NNUT: Union Theological Seminary Library, New York
SCSp: Public Library, Spartanburg, SC
Shull: Personal Library of Carl Shull, Elizabethtown, PA (on loan to Eastern Mennonite College Library, Harrisonburg, VA)
TXFS: Southwestern Baptist Theological Seminary Library, Fort Worth, TX

was a formidable competitor to *The Sacred Harp* in its early history, Walker's espousal of the seven-shape system and its more modern idiom inevitably meant that efforts previously devoted to *Southern Harmony* were given to *Christian Harmony.* It therefore is no surprise that after 1854 *Southern Harmony* was no longer issued during Walker's lifetime.

Nevertheless, *Southern Harmony* appeared in five basic editions in 19 years, whereas *The Sacred Harp* took 25 years to appear in four editions. Although we have no exact circulation figures for these tunebooks, it seems reasonable, on the basis of their respective number of editions in this period, to surmise that *Southern Harmony* was the most popular tunebook of the Deep South before the Civil War and that only in the decade following the war was it overtaken by *The Sacred Harp.*

[1]Harry Eskew, "William Walker, 1809-1875: Popular Southern Hymnist," *The Hymn* 15, no. 1 (January 1964): 5.

[2]T. O .P. Vernon, "Late Prof. Wm. Walker, of S.C.," *Musical Million* 7 (January 1878).

[3]Walker's other three collections are *Southern and Western Pocket Harmonist* (Philadelphia: Cowperthwait & Co., 1846), *Christian Harmony* (Philadelphia: E. W. Miller and William Walker, 1867), *Fruits and Flowers* (Philadelphia: Lippincott & Co., 1873).

[4]Walker, *Christian Harmony,* iii.

[5]Jackson's undated edition of xxxii and 232 pages is the second basic edition. The 1854 edition, which he lists as containing xxxii and 236 pages, actually has xxxii and 336 pages.

[6]This was a fuging tune, SOLEMN CALL ("I sing a song which doth belong"), dated by Walker in *Christian Harmony,* no. 155.

[7]See Milburn Price, "Miss Elizabeth Adams' Music Book: A Manuscript Predecessor of William Walker's *Southern Harmony,*" *The Hymn* 28, no. 2 (April 1978): 70-75.

[8]These two folk hymns appeared four years later in the initial edition of B. F. White and E. J. King's *The Sacred Harp* (Philadelphia: S. C. Collins, 1844) on pages 159 and 224, respectively, with identical voice parts and stanzas of text but *without* composer attributions. Eight of the 13 pieces in Walker's appendix appeared in the first edition of *The Sacred Harp* with identical voice parts and stanzas, five of which appear on pages 157, 158, 159, 161, and 162, a strong indication of their having been borrowed from this appendix.

[9]See Jackson, *White Spirituals in the Southern Uplands* (Chapel Hill: University of North Carolina Press, 1933; Reprint eds. Hatboro, PA: Folklore Associates, 1964. New York: Dover Publications, 1965), 83-84.

[10]In *Christian Harmony,* a note with the tune FULFILLMENT [*sic*] says, "This beautiful old tune was set to music by E. J. King, junior author of the 'Sacred Harp,' who died in a few weeks after its publication, in 1844, much lamented by his Christian brethren and musical friends" (330).

[11]The 1843 issue bears this date on its inside title page and 1844 on its cover. The 1844 issue bears on its copyright page the name of a different printer: "King and Baird, printers, No. 9, George Street, Philadelphia." The 1845 issue bears no printer's name.

[12]Walker, *Southern Harmony* (Philadelphia: Thomas, Cowperthwait & C., Spartanburg, S.C.: William Walker, 1847), no. 233.

[13]B. F. White and E. J. King, *The Sacred Harp* (1859; reprint, Nashville: Broadman Press, 1968), 138 and 202.

[14]Breedlove was one of the eight members of the committee that produced the 1850 revised edition of *The Sacred Harp,* listed on page 263 of the Broadman reprint of the 1859 edition.

[15]BOWER OF PRAYER appears in a different version in *The Sacred Harp* (100), attributed to E. J. King.

[16]In five of these Walker is listed as co-composer. In addition, he is listed as composer of the treble part in two pieces and of all harmony parts in one piece.

[17]The 1854 edition has been reprinted three times in this century: in 1939 by Hastings House,

New York; in 1966 by Pro Musicamericana of Los Angeles; and in 1987 by the University Press of Kentucky.

[18]On the eve of the beginning of the Civil War, Walker was making plans for a successor to his popular tunebook to be entitled *The New Southern Harmony*. In the Walker family papers is a signed agreement between William Walker, A.S.H., and the J. B. Lippincott Company of Philadelphia to publish this new tunebook. The agreement is dated August 1, 1860. A few months later, South Carolina became the first state to secede from the Union, so it is understandable that Walker's *The New Southern Harmony* was never published.

# PART III:
## SINGING–SCHOOL TUNEBOOKS IN THE 19TH-CENTURY SOUTH

# ELI BALL, of Virginia
## Paul A. Richardson

Reprinted, with revisions, from *The Virginia Baptist Register,* 1986. Used by permission.

"ELI BALL, OF VIRGINIA"—It was in this manner that this venerable minister, though a native of Vermont, identified himself on the title page of his magnum opus, *The Manual of the Sacred Choir.*[1] This chapter will examine the man, his contributions to Baptist life, especially in his adopted commonwealth, and the hymnbook that forms his most enduring monument.

### The Man and His Work

Eli Ball was born on November 2, 1786, in Marlborough, Vermont.[2] He was reared in a Christian home, but was not converted until age 19. For two years thereafter he struggled with a sense of call to ministry. He preached his first sermon in December 1807, in Boston, and was licensed seven months later. His previous education having prepared him but little, he immediately began to study for the ministry. His instructors were Daniel Stanford, a teacher of classics in Boston, and Caleb Blood, pastor of that city's Third Baptist Church, who instructed him in theology. During this time of training, Ball served a church in Malden, near Boston. This pastorate and his studies were both brief, however; by December 1809 he had moved to Harwich. The next few years saw him in pastorates in Wilmington, Massachusetts; Lansingburg, New York; and Middletown, Connecticut. He was ordained while in Wilmington.

Ball came to Virginia in June 1823 and was present at the first meeting of the General Association. Jeremiah Bell Jeter, a young man at that time, recalled later that this newcomer was well received by such leaders as Semple, Rice, and Baptist.[3] In July, only a few weeks after his arrival, he was called as pastor of the Baptist church in Lynchburg. His standing and that of his church may be gauged by their selection as hosts of the 1824 annual meeting of the General Association.[4]

Because the Lynchburg church did not adequately support him, Ball was obliged to conduct a school for girls during this period. His advertisement read:

> FEMALE EDUCATION: Mr. Ball will open a school in this place on the first Monday in September, for the reception of young ladies exclusively. As he intends that every pupil shall be under his own immediate instruction, no more will be received than can well be attended to. Terms: for reading, writing, and arithmetic, $12.00 a session; for Arithmetic, English, Grammar, and Geography, with the use of Globes, $15.00; for Rhetoric, History, Astronomy, Moral Philosophy, etc., etc., $18.00; for any or all of the above branches, with the rudiments of French and Latin languages, $20.00.[5]

The offering of such a curriculum by one instructor whose own education was modest is, to say the least, remarkable!

In July 1825, Ball left Lynchburg[6] to accept the call of the Deep Run church in the Dover Association. He remained at Deep Run for 10 years, serving concurrently for various periods at smaller churches and providing pastoral leadership for several of the congregations split by the Reform movement. When Richard Claybrook resigned as pastor at Bruington, Ball was called as his successor and served through 1839. He left Bruington to become General Agent for the General Association.[7] From this point he did not hold a continuing position with a congregation, though he preached frequently and served two prominent churches as *ad interim* minister. He was at Hampton for nearly a year during the absence of J. R. Scott and supplied the pulpit at First Baptist, Richmond, for three months in 1844 while Jeter was away.[8] Ball was a member of First, Richmond, from 1844 until his death.[9]

Ball's parish work was nearly always augmented by other forms of service. He was instrumental in the formation and governance of many of the important cooperative ventures of this period. He was also active as a fund-raising agent for many of these organizations. As an editor, a publisher, and a bookseller, he was an advocate of many significant causes.

Ball played a variety of roles in the field of publication. Most significant of these was as editor of *Religious Herald* from 1831 until 1833. He came to this position at a particularly difficult time, when the Campbell controversy was raging. It had been suggested that his predecessor, Henry Keeling, left under pressure for providing too much access to Campbell and his supporters.[10] Published statements by Keeling, Ball, and William Sands, the paper's owner, certainly allow room for this interpretation, but cited another reason for the change. The stated reason was the desire by Sands that the editor share in the financial obligations of the publication, a responsibility that Ball was willing to accept when Keeling would not.[11] Ball made his editorial position clear at the onset:

> Believing as he most conscientiously and firmly does, that the important doctrines believed and professed by the great body of the denomination to which he belongs, are clearly taught in the Bible, and are essential to true religion, he will feel it his duty at all times, to inculcate them and when assailed, to defend them.[12]

Underscoring his support of cooperative ministries, he pledged that "The Herald will continue to be, as it always has been, the firm advocate of all the great enterprises of Christian benevolence."[13] His primary objective in this role would be "to promote experimental and practical piety."[14]

Not all who had dealings with the *Herald* during this time were pleased with his stewardship. In 1832, John Hersey published a 36-page pamphlet charging that Ball had misrepresented him and "mutilated" his correspondence.[15] Ball acknowledged his critics, but did not give in to them. In his final column as editor, he wrote, "I have always supposed that truth never had but one side."[16]

Ball left the editorship in May 1833 to accept a teaching position at the Virginia Baptist Seminary. Actually, as he noted in announcing his departure, Sands had been directing publication during the previous year while Ball conducted an agency for the Bible Society.[17]

During the late 1840s, Ball was for a time associate editor and partial proprietor, along with Keeling, of another periodical, *The Baptist Preacher.* This subsequent venture would indicate that no hard feelings resulted from their roles with *Religious Herald.* Indeed, Keeling's memorial tribute to Ball in the latter publication is both affirming and affectionate, referring to him as "An intimate acquaintance for thirty years" and "an eminent servant of God."[18]

Prior to his work with *Religious Herald,* Ball had been co-editor with Abner Clopton of *Wisdom's Voice to the Rising Generation,*[19] a volume of essays, sermons, and other materials on temperance.

For several years after leaving the pastorate, Ball participated in the operation of a bookshop. Notices and advertisements in *Religious Herald* show his participation, successively, in Perkins, Harvey, & Ball; Ball & Perkins; Eli Ball (apparently alone for a few months); and Ball, Harrold, & Co. According to the notice in the August 5, 1847, issue, the dissolution of the last-named partnership was occasioned "by the withdrawal of Eli Ball for the purpose of devoting all of his time to the ministry."[20] This parting also seems to have been on good terms, for the successor firm, Harrold & Murray, was the publisher, two years later, of his tunebook.

Another area in which Ball figured prominently was higher education. In 1828 he served as agent in South Carolina and Georgia for Columbian College, raising funds to enable its reopening.[21] At the chartering of Richmond College, in 1840, he was listed as one of its first trustees.[22] During the intervening years he was often cited in the minutes of the Virginia Baptist Education Society.[23]

When the Education Society was formed at Second Baptist Church of Richmond in 1830, Ball was elected Second Vice President and was appointed to the Board of Managers.[24] In subsequent years he served on committees for examining prospective students, establishing a manual labor system, designing the curriculum, choosing a permanent site, raising funds, preparing regulations, purchasing books, and hiring instructors.[25] In 1831, before a school was formally established, he took students into his home for instruction, following the pattern of Edward Baptist.[26]

At the organization of the Virginia Baptist Seminary in 1833, Ball was hired as Assistant Teacher to Robert Ryland. In this role, it was his duty "to conduct the Biblical studies of the Beneficiaries and to assist in the direction of the other studies as far as may be necessary."[27] He did not continue long in this position, though. In an address delivered in 1891, Ryland recalled that

> [Ball's] ideas of education inclined him to take "short cuts" for advancing the young men, and this, together with a thirst for more evangelical labors, caused him, after one year, to resign his office.[28]

His enthusiasm for the endeavor does not seem to have been diminished, however, for he was quickly appointed agent for the seminary, though this service also lasted only a few months. Alley proposes that he left this position in deference to his health.[29]

Ball was active in the affairs of the Dover Association, perhaps the leading such body in the United States at that time. He frequently accepted committee assignments, twice prepared the corresponding letter to other associations, and authored the group's circular letter in 1836.[30] His topic was "Sunday Schools," another area in which he had proven to be a progressive leader. In reporting Ball's death for the association's obituary committee, James B. Taylor averred that "Brother Ball was among the oldest and most esteemed of the Virginia Baptist ministry."[31]

Ball's involvement in Baptist life went beyond his state. He was one of those representing Virginia in Augusta, Georgia, in 1845, at the formation of the Southern Baptist Convention. At that meeting he was chosen to be Vice President for Virginia of the Foreign Mission Board.[32] In the next year, when the Convention held its first triennial meeting in Richmond, Ball was continued on the Board of Managers of the Foreign Mission Board and was also appointed to the Committee on Colportage of the Home Mission Board.[33]

During the last several years of his life, Ball's energies were largely directed toward missions. From 1849 until his death, he served as agent for the Foreign Mission Board in Georgia.[34] When the board could find no one else to inspect the mission in Liberia, Ball, aged 65, volunteered.[35] He departed from Savannah in January 1852, and spent six months in Africa, preaching as well as carrying out his duties as the board's representative.[36] Upon his return, his account of the work was a boon to the mission effort.[37] He was preparing for a second African journey when stricken by his final illness.[38]

Ball worked beyond the bounds of his own denomination. He was one of the founders of the Virginia Society for the Promotion of Temperance. He preached at the organizational meeting at Ash Camp in 1826,[39] and later served as the group's president.[40] Deep Run, which already boasted its own temperance society, was the site of the state body's first annual meeting in 1827.[41]

Eli Ball died on July 21, 1853, after a brief illness. He was quite active until shortly before his death, taking time from his preparations for a return trip to Liberia to serve on the presbytery and to preach the ordination sermon for a young man in Petersburg on June 14.[42] His grave is in the cemetery on Richmond's Shockoe Hill, not far from where he had operated his bookstore for many years.

Ball was married twice, but did not father any children.[43] He was survived by his second wife, the former Martha Bowles, whom he had wed in Hanover County on November 23, 1829.[44]

Ball was an exceedingly industrious man. His many avocations did not, however, detract from his efforts to proclaim the gospel. Keeling wrote that[45]

> Not only in Lynchburg and Hampton, but at Rehoboth, Bruington, Deep Run, and every church in Virginia—on the seaboard—in the valley—beyond the mountains—in every vale and on every hill top—has been heard the voice of brother Ball, encouraging believers in Christ, and exhorting sinners to repentance.

His tireless work is reflected in his meticulous recordkeeping. An 1851 entry in his diary records: "In prosecuting the duties of my agency, during this year, I have traveled 10,487 miles, and preached 141 sermons."[46] He proceeded to summarize his life's work to that point:

> During my whole ministry, I have preached 5,891 sermons. Since 1831 I have travelled while prosecuting my public labors as a minister, 84,873 miles—a distance, I may add, more than three times the circumference of the globe.[47]

It seems that Ball was willing, even eager, to serve in any way that he could. Taylor recounted the great demand for his services and also Ball's response: "With quenchless ardor he readily embraced all such opportunities of preaching the Word."[48] A correspondent of the *Herald,* one J. F. K., wrote of Ball's service above and beyond the call when asked to fill in at a baptism for an indisposed pastor.

> Our last baptismal service was quite novel and interesting, for although the day was cold and windy, we had to break the ice (nearly two inches thick) on the side of the Creek, yet Bro. Ball went down into the water singing, and there stood and prayed before the candidates descended into the liquid grave.[49]

Ball was one of the most outspoken opponents of Alexander Campbell and the Reform movement. As noted above, his coming to the editorship of the *Religious Herald* was, to some degree, occasioned by the controversy. While serving in that position he issued a stinging rebuke of Campbellism in a *Herald* column headed "The Crisis."[50] He was one of the consultants to the Dover Association committee that, in 1832, produced a strong condemnation of the movement.[51] As a pastor he was often called upon to guide the remnants of churches divided by the Campbell forces. It was in these circumstances that he served Bethlehem (formed out of Chickahominy) and Rehoboth (later Sharon, formed out of Upper College.)[52]

In Jeter's view, Ball's greatest success was as an agent soliciting financial support for various religious efforts.[53] Already mentioned have been Columbian College, the Virginia Baptist Seminary, the Bible Society of Virginia, the Baptist General Association of Virginia, and the Foreign Mission Board. He also served the Baptist Mission Society in this capacity.[54]

The sole physical description of Ball is from Taylor:

> In stature small, his whole form, rather inclined to corpulency, was compact and well proportioned, indicating vigor and the power of endurance. His face round, his features regular, he impressed the beholder with the idea of one genial and happy.[55]

This outward appearance of happiness was sometimes deceiving, according to Jeter, who had access to his private papers.[56] He apparently suffered from bouts of depression, but hid these to avoid diminishing his ministry.[57]

Despite his accomplishments as a writer and editor and his devotion to the cause of education, the evidence concerning his intellectual gifts is mixed. In his *Recollections*, Jeter mentions Ball in his role as seminary teacher as "a brother whose scholarship was various rather than profound, but whose attainments were, doubtless, equal to the demands of the pupils."[58] Robert Ryland's assessment, quoted above, is similarly tepid in tone. But Taylor at least offers testimony to his industry in this area:

> Every leisure moment, when not engaged in the active duties of the ministry, was spent in study and preparation. By his own endeavors he had made himself somewhat acquainted with the learned languages, and had taken some discursive flights over the fields of literature. To theological studies he had given more attention, and in these he may be said to have been proficient.[59]

In one of the few personal letters that are extant, Ball makes his point by arguing from the Greek New Testament.[60]

Ball's eulogizers unanimously cite his gentleness and goodness. Keeling, a man with whom he had worked for many years, described him as "a diligent student, an agreeable companion, a confiding and trustworthy friend, a courteous gentleman, and a devout Christian."[61]

### The Manual of the Sacred Choir

On December 28, 1848, a letter from Eli Ball appeared in *Religious Herald* announcing that a new "compilation of sacred music for public worship, for social meetings and for revival seasons"[62] was at the printer and would be available for sale in a short time. He gave his reasons for producing a new hymnal.

> I have endervored [*sic*] to furnish what I have for many years seen was needed, a book of tunes as well as of hymns to be carried to meeting. Many of our best singers in country congregations cannot always recollect the tunes which they have learned, and having no note book before them, sacred music rather grates than delights the ear.[63]

THE

## MANUAL OF THE SACRED CHOIR:

A SELECTION OF

### TUNES AND HYMNS,

FROM THE MOST APPROVED AUTHORS,

ADAPTED TO PUBLIC WORSHIP, TO REVIVALS, TO PRAYER
MEETINGS, AND TO FAMILY WORSHIP.

BY

ELI BALL, OF VIRGINIA.

RICHMOND, VA.:
PUBLISHED BY HARROLD & MURRAY, 177 BROAD STREET
PHILADELPHIA:
THOMAS, COWPERTHWAIT & CO., 253 MARKET STREET.
1849.

Title page from Eli Ball's *The Manual of the Sacred Choir* (Richmond and Philadelphia, 1849).

He went on to describe the book's contents:

> *The Manual of the Sacred Choir* contains more than 80 [sic] tunes, in patent notes; and will be portable so as to be conveniently carried to places of worship; of such notes that nearly every hymn in the Virginia Selection, Psalmist, with the Supplement, Dover Selection, Baptist Hymn Book, &c., &c., may be sung.[64]

All of these books were text-only volumes, typical of the time. There were some tunebooks available, but, as Ball wrote in his preface, he found none suited to the country congregations of the South and West.

> The note books that are in use in our singing schools, are too large and inconvenient in form to be carried and used by singers in public worship.[65]
>
> • • •
>
> Some laudable attempts have been made to supply the various defects in our note books, but these efforts have almost wholly failed to meet our wants. The Christian Lyre, Spiritual Songs for Social Worship, Hymns for Family Worship, Jocelyn's Zion's Harp, Revival Melodies, &c., &c., have successively appeared, but they have never found their way into our public assemblies on Lord's days, and few of them have been known in our social or revival meetings.
>
> All, except the last named compilation, are too large and expensive; the tunes are not generally known, nor are they favourites among us, and all of them are printed with round notes, which are not as extensively known as the patent notes. *We are still without the book we need.* [Italics original.]

The tunebooks that Ball mentions were all prepared in the North and did not, by and large, contain the tunes that would have been known and appreciated in rural Southern churches. The "patent notes" to which he refers are those of the system using four shapes (triangular, round, square, and diamond-shaped) to show the degrees of the scale.

It is interesting that Ball does not name among the "note books" either *The Southern Harmony*[66] or *The Sacred Harp,*[67] shape-note books used widely in singing schools in the South. That he would not have known these collections, both compiled by Baptists, seems highly unlikely. Indeed,

William Walker, compiler of *The Southern Harmony,* is cited as the source of the treble part of THE TRUMPET,[68] one of only two such citations in Ball's book. Ball's remarks, quoted on page 147, indicate that he found all singing-school books inappropriate for his purposes. This may have been because they seldom included complete texts, as did *The Manual.*

What expertise did Ball bring to the compilation of a hymn- and tune-book? That he could have had much training in music seems doubtful, given the limits of his formal education. Hymn singing does appear to have been an area of long-standing interest. Taylor records that:

> ...his fine taste and talent for vocal music rendered him popular as a leader in social meetings, and welcome as a guest in the homes of his friends. He took a lively interest in the improvement of the young in this department of worship. Being well acquainted with the science of music, and possessing a fine, flexible voice, he never failed to render agreeable those religious meetings in which he took a prominent part.[69]

It is likely that his experience gave him practical knowledge that enhanced his innate talent. Evidently his opinions on hymnody were respected. He served as chair of the committee appointed in 1835 by the Dover Association to review a new hymnal by Andrew Broaddus.[70] A note appended to its report advised that "Several members of the Committee had previously examined this Compilation."[71] It seems probable that Ball was among these.

The listing of text-only books given in the *Herald* letter is amplified in *The Manual's* preface. Also mentioned there are Mercer's *Cluster,* Dossey's *Choice,* and *Village Hymns.*[72] These lists show that Ball was quite familiar with hymnals in use among Baptists at that time.

*The Virginia Selection*[73] was compiled in 1836 by Ball's neighbor, Broaddus. *The Psalmist*[74] was a Boston publication of 1843, edited by Massachusetts Baptist pastors Baron Stow and S. F. Smith (author of "My country, 'tis of thee"). *The Supplement* cited in its title was the work of Jeremiah Jeter and Richard Fuller, a Baltimore pastor, and was added in 1847 to make the book more attractive to churches in the South. Broaddus was also the compiler of *The Dover Selection,*[75] an anthology prepared in 1828 for the churches of that association. *The Baptist Hymn Book*[76] was edited by Louisville pastor William C. Buck in 1842. *The Cluster,*[77] by 1835 in its fifth edition, was the work of Georgia pastor Jesse B. Mercer. William Dossey, pastor at Society Hill, South Carolina, produced his *The Choice*[78] in 1820. *Village Hymns for Social Wor-*

*ship*[79] was a Northern book of wide circulation edited in 1824 by Asahel Nettleton. Ball would have encountered all of these as a bookseller and may have used many of them in the congregations which he visited.

The availability of *The Manual* for sale was announced May 24, 1849, in an advertisement by Harrold & Murray. They advised that "Conductors of singing in country churches will be well to provide themselves with this book."[80]

*The Manual of the Sacred Choir* is a small book, measuring 4¾ inches wide by 5¾ inches tall, which might conveniently be carried to worship or to social gatherings. It contains 62 tunes rather than the 80 promised in Ball's letter to the paper. Each tune is supplied with a multistanza text. The inclusion of full texts enabled it to serve alone if none of the large text-only books (most of which contained hundreds of hymns) were available.

No authors or composers are named, though two harmonizers are identified.[81] The single index lists tunes in alphabetical order. This index also indicates poetic meter so that a tune can be matched quickly to a text from another source. True to his purpose, Ball includes a wide variety of meters—31 in all—with a still wider variety of patterns involving repeats, refrains, and other devices.

Forty-five of the tunes are scored in three parts, with the tune in the middle voice (called the tenor), a descant above (called the treble), and a bass line beneath. The other 17 tunes have but two parts, the tune above and the bass below.

Though aimed at Southern rural congregations, the book is remarkably eclectic in its selection of tunes. It contains not only tunes that have been identified as belonging to the core repertory of the Southern oral tradition, such as PARTING HAND and SUPPLICATION, but tunes found in both oral and written traditions, such as GREEN FIELDS and BALERMA.[82] It also contains tunes from the Northern "scientific" music of Lowell Mason and Thomas Hastings, such as HAIL TO THE BRIGHTNESS and SAFELY THROUGH ANOTHER WEEK. Almost half of the tunes (29 of 62) can be found in one or both of the Southern shape-note books mentioned earlier. Sixteen are in both, while 11 are only in *The Southern Harmony* and two are only in *The Sacred Harp*.

Three texts and two tunes from *The Manual* are found in *The Baptist Hymnal*, 1991.[83] The enduring texts are Charles Wesley's "Jesus, lover of my soul," Thomas Ken's "Glory to Thee, my God, this night" (with the first line "All praise to You, my God, this night"), and Philip Doddridge's "O happy day that fixed my choice." The surviving tunes are THE MORNING LIGHT IS BREAKING (now called WEBB) and HARWELL. Another tune in Ball's collection, GOOD SHEPHERD, bears a

GOOD SHEPHERD ("Let thy kingdom, blessed Saviour") from Eli Ball's *The Manual of the Sacred Choir* (Richmond and Philadelphia, 1849).

strong resemblance to the familiar melody, NETTLETON. Much greater is the relationship with the *Baptist Hymnal,* 1956,[84] which includes no fewer than 10 of the same tunes and 14 of the same texts. Among these are "Awake, my soul in joyful lays," by British Baptist Samuel Medley, set to LOVING KINDNESS; "How tedious and tasteless the hours," by John Newton, set to GREEN FIELDS (called CONTRAST in the 1956 hymnal); "The morning light is breaking," by Samuel Smith; and "When I can read my title clear," by Isaac Watts, set to PISGAH.

In all, six Baptist authors can be identified: John Blain ("My Christian friends, in bonds of love"), John Fawcett ("Lord, dismiss us with thy blessing"), Enoch Freeman ("Rouse ye at the Saviour's call"), John Leland ("O when shall I see Jesus"), Samuel Medley ("Awake, my soul in joyful lays" and "Hark, how the gospel trumpet sounds"), and Samuel Smith ("The morning light is breaking"). Besides Medley, the authors appearing more than once are John Newton (6), Charles Wesley (5), Isaac Watts (4), Thomas Hastings (3), Philip Doddridge (2), and Reginald Heber (2). There are 24 identifiable hymnists with a single text each. Among the more prominent of these are William Cowper, Thomas Kelly, Thomas Ken, and Henry Milman. Fourteen texts are by unknown authors.

The texts included address a variety of topics. These may indicate the needs which Ball perceived and, to some extent, the practices of churches that would use such a book. The two largest groups are those celebrating salvation ("Hail, sov'reign love that first began") and the fellowship of Christians ("My Christian friends, in bonds of love"). Others speak of God's providence ("Through ev'ry age, eternal God"), the joy of the Christian life ("O how happy are they"), or of the life to come ("There is a land of pleasure"). Some 8 to 10 are addressed specifically to those outside the church ("Stop, poor sinner, stop and think"), and there are a few "modern" missions hymns ("From Greenland's icy mountains") that reflect Ball's strong interest in that work. It is notable that there are no hymns related either to baptism or to the Lord's Supper, those occasions at which hymn singing has been introduced among Baptists.

*The Manual of the Sacred Choir* was reviewed briefly by *Religious Herald* in its May 24, 1849, issue:

> This little volume was gotten up to supply a desideratum long felt in our churches, and contains many familiar tunes, adapted to public and social worship. The author designs, if he should meet with sufficient encouragement, to publish an enlarged and revised edition. There are several errors in the typography, which mar the harmony of some of the sweetest tunes.[85]

Apparently, "sufficient encouragement" was not forthcoming, for there was no subsequent edition. The unnamed reviewer is accurate in his observation of typesetting problems; there are many.

The same issue of the *Herald* also reviewed *The Baptist Harp,*[86] just released by the American Baptist Publication Society, a book also directed toward "the closet, the family, social worship, and revivals," according to its title page. Though it is a much larger collection, containing 583 hymns, and a text-only book, it is interesting to note that it includes 30, or almost half, of Ball's text choices. There is a similar commonality of material (26 of the same texts) with *The Baptist Psalmody,*[87] a book for worship use designed by Basil Manly, Sr., and Basil Manly, Jr., and published by the Southern Baptist Publication Society in the following year.

The absence of later editions of *The Manual* indicates that the book was not a financial success. Perhaps its aims or its markets were too limited. It is unfortunate that its influence was thereby limited as well. Ball accomplished what he set out to do: he provided a small, inexpensive book balancing tunes from a variety of traditions with those that were well known, including complete versions of texts, so that the book might serve alone, should the larger text anthologies not be available. Situated between the popular singing-school tunebooks of the oral/rural tradition and the more learned text collections of the written/urban stream, *The Manual* provides a unique perspective on the corpus of hymnody that may actually have been in use in churches such as those found in the country sections of the Dover Association.

## Conclusions

Eli Ball was a man of many abilities, great energy, and generous service. He came to Virginia as a mature minister and moved in a circle of ministers who were giants in the life of Baptists in the South. His skills were employed in the organization and promotion of the many cooperative ventures that Virginia Baptists began in the second quarter of the 19th century. His hymn and tunebook, though not a commercial success, was a significant attempt to meet a need in the worship and devotional life of churches in the rural South. That he is not as well known today as many of his contemporaries lacks a clear reason.

His place may best be estimated by quoting the views of his peers. At Ball's death, Sands, as editor of *Religious Herald,* asserted that "Few men have rendered more essential service to the Baptist church in the South."[88] Taylor wrote in summation: "Doubtless Eli Ball will long be remembered by Virginia Baptists as one of their soundest, best, more useful proclaimers of the glorious gospel."[89] These are significant evaluations from respected and proven judges. But, given the way in which Ball identified himself in *The Manual,* he might be most pleased with Keeling's assessment that, "Elder Ball, although a native of New England, was by adoption, a thorough Virginian."[90]

---

[1]Eli Ball, *The Manual of the Sacred Choir: A Selection of Tunes and Hymns, From the Most Approved Authors, Adapted to Public Worship, To Revivals, To Prayer Meetings, and to Family Worship* (Richmond, 1849).

[2]J. B. Jeter, "Sketch of the Life and Labors of Rev. Eli Ball," *Religious Herald,* August 4, 1853. This is excerpted from Jeter's address at Ball's funeral. It is the principal source for biographical information (though some of this is erroneous and must be corrected from other sources) and is quoted extensively in Taylor (see note 21). All biographical data not otherwise documented is from this source.

[3]Ibid.

[4]Blanche Sydnor White, compiler, *First Baptist Church, Lynchburg, 1815-1965,* ([n.p.], [n.d.]), 24.

[5]Ibid.

[6]Ibid.

[7]*Minutes of the Dover Association,* 1825-1840, *passim.*

[8]*Religious Herald,* April 18, 1844.

[9]Blanche Sydnor White, *First Baptist Church, Richmond: 1780-1955* (Richmond, 1955), 90.

[10]Reuben Edward Alley, *A History of Baptists in Virginia* (Richmond, [1973]), 208.

[11]*Religious Herald,* February 11 and April 29, 1831.

[12]*Religious Herald,* April 29, 1831.

[13]Ibid.

[14]Ibid.

[15]John Hersey, *A Connected View of a Correspondence between Eli Ball, Editor of the Richmond Religious Herald, and John Hersey on the Subject of Baptism* (Baltimore, 1832).

[16]*Religious Herald,* May 31, 1833.

[17]Ibid.

[18]Henry Keeling, "Rev. Eli Ball, Brief Biographical Sketch, by the Editor," *The Baptist Preacher,* June, July, and August, 1853, 134.

[19]Abner W. Clopton and Eli Ball, *Wisdom's Voice to the Rising Generation: Being a Selection of the Best Addresses and Sermons on Intemperance, from Dwight, Rush, Kittredge, Porter, Beecher, Sprague, and Others* (Philadelphia, [n.d.]).

[20]*Religious Herald,* August 5, 1847.

[21]James B. Taylor, *Virginia Baptist Ministers,* Series II, 1859, 339. Frequent letters from Ball in *Religious Herald* advise of his experiences in this endeavor.

[22]Minutes of the Virginia Baptist Education Society, 240.

[23]Ibid., *passim.*

[24]Ibid., 8.

[25]Ibid., *passim.*

[26]Ibid., 24.

[27]Ibid., 82-83.

[28]Robert Ryland, *The Virginia Baptist Education Society* (Richmond, 1891), 12.

[29]Reuben E. Alley, *History of the University of Richmond, 1830-1971* (Charlottesville, 1977), 24.

[30]*Minutes of the Dover Association,* 1825-1839, *passim.*

[31]*Minutes of the Dover Association,* 1853, 10.

[32]*Proceedings of the Southern Baptist Convention* (Richmond, 1845), 6-7.

[33]*Proceedings of the First Triennial Meeting of the Southern Baptist Convention* (Richmond,1846), 2, 7.

[34]*Religious Herald,* July 28, 1853.

[35]Taylor, *Virginia Baptist,* 340.

[36]Ibid.

[37]Jeter, "Sketch of the Life."

[38]Taylor, *Virginia Baptist,* 341.

[39]Garnett Ryland, *The Baptists of Virginia, 1699-1926* (Richmond, 1955), 217.

[40]*Religious Herald,* December 19, 1828.

[41]Ryland, *The Baptists,* 218.

[42]*Religious Herald,* June 23, 1853.

[43]Keeling, "Rev. Eli Ball,"134.

[44]*Religious Herald,* December 11, 1829.

[45]Keeling, "Rev. Eli Ball," 135.

[46]Quoted in Jeter, "Sketch of the Life." Unfortunately, this diary is no longer extant.

[47]Ibid.

[48]Taylor, *Virginia Baptist,* 337.

[49]*Religious Herald,* December 22, 1842.

[50]*Religious Herald,* April 13, 1832.

[51]*Minutes of the Dover Association,*1832, 6.

[52]*Minutes of the Dover Association,*1833, 10, and 1834, 13.

[53]Jeter, "Sketch of the Life."

[54]Alley, *A History of Baptists,* 18.

[55]Taylor, *Virginia Baptist,* 347.

[56]Jeter, "Sketch of the Life."

[57]Ibid.

[58]Jeremiah Bell Jeter, *The Recollections of a Long Life* (Richmond, 1891), 220.

[59]Taylor, *Virginia Baptist,* 345.

[60]Letter from Eli Ball to James D. McGill, February 28, 1835, now in the files of the Virginia Baptist Historical Society.

[61]Keeling, "Rev. Eli Ball," 135.

[62]*Religious Herald,* December 28, 1848.

[63]Ibid.

[64]Ibid.

[65]Ball, *The Manual,* 3-4.

[66]William Walker, *The Southern Harmony and Musical Companion: Containing a Choice Collection of Tunes, Hymns, Psalms, Odes and Anthems: Selected from the Most Eminent Authors in the United States* (Spartanburg, 1835).

[67]B. F. White and E. J. King, *The Sacred Harp, A Collection of Psalm and Hymn Tunes, Odes, and Anthems, Selected from the Most Eminent Authors: Together with Nearly One Hundred Pieces Never Before Published; Suited to Most Metres, and Well Adapted to Churches of Every Denomination, Singing Schools, and Private Societies, with Plain Rules for Learners* (Philadelphia, 1844).

[68]Ball, *The Manual,* 30.

[69]Taylor, *Virginia Baptist,* 337.

[70]*Minutes of the Dover Association,* 1835, 5.

[71]Ibid., 6.

[72]Ball, *The Manual,* 4.

[73]Andrew Broaddus, *The Virginia Selection of Psalms, Hymns, and Spiritual Songs. From the Most Approved Authors. Adapted to the Various Occasions of Public Worship and Social Meetings* (Richmond, 1836).

[74]Baron Stow and S. F. Smith, *The Psalmist: A New Collection of Hymns for the Use of the Baptist Churches* (Boston, 1843).

[75]Andrew Broaddus, *The Dover Selection of Spiritual Songs; With an Appendix of Choice Hymns, on Various Occasions: Compiled by the Recommendation of the Dover Association,* Richmond, 1828.

[76]W. C. Buck, *The Baptist Hymn Book; Original and Selected* (Louisville, 1842).

[77]Jesse Mercer, *The Cluster of Spiritual Songs, Divine Hymns, and Sacred Poems; Being Chiefly a Collection* [3rd edition], August, 1810. This is the earliest edition extant. The date of the first edition is not known.

[78]William Dossey, *The Choice; In Two Parts* (Philadelphia, 1820).

[79]Asahel Nettleton, *Village Hymns for Social Worship. Selected and Original. Designed as a Supplement to the Psalms and Hymns of Dr. Watts* (Hartford, 1824).

[80]*Religious Herald,* May 24, 1849.

[81]Ball, *The Manual.* William Walker is cited as composer of the treble to THE TRUMPET, 30-31. James Langston is credited with the treble of MISSIONARY HYMN, 38-39.

[82]Irvin Henry Murrell, Jr., "An Examination of Southern Ante-Bellum Baptist Hymnals and Tunebooks as Indicators of the Congregational Hymn and Tune Repertories of the Period with an Analysis of Representative Tunes." (D.M.A. dissertation, New Orleans Baptist Theological Seminary, 1984), 53-55.

[83]Wesley L. Forbis, editor, *The Baptist Hymnal* (Nashville, 1991).

[84]W. Hines Sims, editor, *Baptist Hymnal* (Nashville, 1956).

[85]*Religious Herald,* May 24, 1849.

[86]*The Baptist Harp: A New Collection of Hymns for the Closet, the Family, Social Worship, and Revivals* (Philadelphia, 1849).

[87]Basil Manly and Basil Manly, Jr., *The Baptist Psalmody: A Selection of Hymns for the Worship of God* (Charleston, 1850).

[88]*Religious Herald,* July 28, 1853.

[89]Taylor, *Virginia Baptist,* 348.

[90]Keeling, "Rev. Eli Ball," 134.

# J. R. GRAVES' *The Little Seraph* (1874): A Memphis Tunebook

## David W. Music

Reprinted, with revisions, from *The West Tennessee Historical Society Papers,* October 1981.
Used by permission.

T HE FIRST MUSIC BOOK to be compiled in the state of Tennessee— Alexander Johnson's *Tennessee Harmony* (Cincinnati: Morgan, Lodge & Co., 1818)—was published two years before the founding of Memphis. This book, drawing from the shape-note tradition which originated at the end of the 18th century, became quite popular in Middle and West Tennessee and went through at least three editions. Johnson's tunebook was soon followed by those of other Tennesseans, and by 1860 at least 13 tunebooks had been issued bearing a Tennessee imprint or the name of a Volunteer State compiler. Some of these books went through several editions and most used some sort of shape-note notation.[1]

Portrait of J. R. Graves
1820–1893

Memphians appear to have played little part in the compiling and publishing of tunebooks during the first three quarters of the 19th century. The relatively late settling of the town, its frontier nature, and the lack of local religious publishing enterprises probably contributed to the seeming lack of interest in compiling tunebooks exhibited by early Memphians. Nevertheless, by the early 1870s the stage was set for the publication of a book of religious music compiled by a resident of Memphis and published in the Bluff City. This tunebook was James Robinson Graves' *The Little Seraph.*

J. R. Graves was born in Chester, Vermont, on April 10, 1820. His father died when he was only two weeks old, and his mother was defrauded of her share of the estate by the machinations of her husband's former business partner. Graves was unable to acquire a good formal education, a deficiency which he made up in part by diligent self-study.

Graves' parents were Congregationalists, but James joined the Baptist church at the age of 15. In 1839 he moved with his mother and sister to Ohio, where he became principal of a school. Two years later he moved again, taking charge of a school near Nicholasville, Kentucky. While in Kentucky he joined the Mount Freedom Baptist Church, which licensed and ordained him to preach.

Graves moved to Nashville in 1845 to continue his teaching. Soon after his arrival he was called to the pastorate of the Second Baptist Church of that city, a position he filled for about a year. In 1846 he became assistant editor, copublisher, and a depository agent for a monthly newspaper called *The Baptist.* In 1848, R. B. C. Howell, the founder and editor of the paper, resigned, and Graves was chosen to succeed him, thus beginning a long and distinguished career as a journalist, author, and editor.

Graves changed the name of the newspaper to the *Tennessee Baptist,* and due to indifference on the part of the board of directors, eventually became the owner of the paper. In 1855 he organized the publishing firm of Graves, Marks & Co., which adopted the trade name of South-Western Publishing House, and continued to publish the *Tennessee Baptist.* This publication quickly became one of the most widely read Southern Baptist newspapers.

In addition to his publishing activity, Graves was one of the leaders in the formation of the Southern Baptist Sunday School Union, which was founded in 1858 and located in Nashville. The occupation of Nashville by Federal troops during the Civil War brought an end to this organization and forced Graves, Marks & Co. to move to Memphis. The *Tennessee Baptist* had been discontinued in 1862, but was revived in Memphis in 1867, and the name of the firm was changed to Graves, Jones and Co. The next year a stock company called the Southwestern Publishing Company was formed to publish the newspaper and other materials. However, several financial reverses brought about the dissolution of this company in 1871.

In his attempt to become the primary publisher and agent of Sunday School materials for Southern Baptists, Graves persuaded the Big Hatchie Baptist Association to form the Southern Baptist Publication Society, which was established at Memphis and began printing in the fall of 1873. In 1877 this venture also collapsed, but Graves continued to publish the *Tennessee Baptist* until 1889. He died in Memphis in 1893.[2]

Graves was one of the founders of the so-called "Landmark" movement among Southern Baptists. According to Landmark doctrine, the only "true" churches were Baptist churches; consequently, all other denominations were not churches, but "societies." The Landmarkers were strongly opposed to open communion, the trading of pulpits with non-Baptist ministers, and the organization of mission boards, which they saw as usurpers of local church prerogatives.

In addition to his other activities, Graves maintained an interest in the church's hymnody, particularly as it related to Southern Baptists. His first hymnal, *The Southern Psalmist,* was published in Nashville in 1858 with the collaboration of another Landmarker, J. M. Pendleton. This collection contained words only. In 1873 the Memphis-based Southern Baptist Publication Society issued Graves' second hymnal, *The New Baptist Psalmist.* Like *The Southern Psalmist,* this was a words-only collection.

Graves seems to have been content mainly to anthologize the hymns of others. One hymn, "Jesus only—dark the cloud," which appeared anonymously in *The Southern Psalmist,* was attributed to Graves in *The New Baptist Psalmist.* This seems to have been Graves' only serious effort at hymn writing.

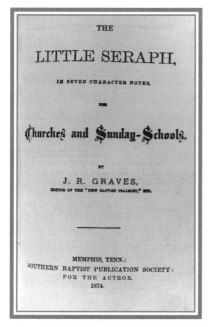

Title page from J. R. Graves'
*The Little Seraph* (Memphis, 1874).

Graves' interest in the hymnody of the church was not restricted to the words of the hymns, but also included the tunes to which they were sung. This concern prompted him to compile and publish *The Little Seraph,* a tunebook "in seven character notes, for Churches and Sunday-Schools."[3] The date of *The Little Seraph* is usually given as 1873. Indeed, the copyright notice reveals that the book was "Entered, according to Act of Congress, in the year 1873, by Mrs. J. R. Graves." However, the book was evidently not actually published until 1874, for that is the date which appears on the title page of every copy known to the present writer. The work was published in Memphis by the Southern Baptist Publication Society. *The Little Seraph* opens with some "Explanatory Remarks" concerning its use of the "doremi" system of musical notation. According to the editor,

> The system of Seven Characters to represent the Seven Degrees of
> the Natural Scale, now so deservedly popular, has been adopted in this
> work. Nothing is more easily demonstrable than the superiority of this,
> for vocal music, to the ordinary notation.

This "deservedly popular" system was, however, under copyright; thus, a note on the *verso* of the title page informed the public that "The Seven Character notes [were] secured for this Work by special contract with the proprietor."

The fact that *The Little Seraph* was copyrighted in the same year as Graves' *The New Baptist Psalmist* suggests that the former might have been intended as a musical companion to the words-only hymnal. Indeed, an advertisement on the back cover of *The Little Seraph* lists an edition of the "New Baptist Psalmist, with Music," which means that the two books were bound together into one volume, though each preserved a separate identity.

Nevertheless, a study of the contents of the two books reveals that *The Little Seraph* is not simply a musical version of *The New Baptist Psalmist*. Of the 194 tunes printed in *The Little Seraph*, 103 are set to texts which are not found in *The New Baptist Psalmist*. A large number of texts from the words-only hymnal are not supplied with tunes in *The Little Seraph*. Thus, Graves does not seem to have intended *The Little Seraph* to be simply a musical companion to *The New Baptist Psalmist*, though its use in that role cannot be ruled out.

One interesting feature of *The Little Seraph* is Graves' occasional use of the same tune in two different parts of the book, with the tune bearing a different name at each appearance. Thus, George F. Root's BECAUSE HE LOVED ME SO (165) is the same as his ZELLA (129). Likewise, the tunes MEMPHIS (35) and MELODY (19) are identical, as are I DO BELIEVE (26) and THE GOLDEN RULE (118). One tune, NO SORROW THERE by E. W. Dunbar, was printed twice (39, 134) but received the same name both times.

The music of *The Little Seraph* was drawn mainly from four traditions of church song: (1) English and American psalm and hymn tunes of the 17th and 18th centuries, (2) the Mason-Hastings-Bradbury school of American composers, (3) the gospel song, and (4) the American folk-hymn tune. Conspicuously absent are familiar hymns from the German tradition, such as "Ein feste Burg" ("A mighty fortress") and "Nun danket alle Gott" ("Now thank we all our God"); many other hymns that are well-known to modern church congregations are likewise omitted. It should be remembered that Graves' tunebook was designed not only for the church service, but also for the Sunday School, and its contents suggest that the editor considered the latter function the most important.

The major hymnic tradition which provided the smallest number of tunes to *The Little Seraph* was that of English and American music of the 17th and 18th centuries. Among the English tunes included in the book are the anonymous AMERICA (originally "God save the king"), T. A. Arne's ARLINGTON, John Randall's CAMBRIDGE, Simon Browne's MEAR, Ralph Harrison's PETERBORO', EVENING HYMN by Thomas Tallis, and ST. THOMAS by Aaron Williams. Four of these tunes—AMERICA, ARLINGTON, EVENING HYMN, and ST. THOMAS—can still be found in most American hymnals. A few other tunes in the book were of English origin, but became hymn tunes only when they were arranged by an American tunebook compiler from some larger work. An example is the tune ANTIOCH, which is familiar as the setting for Isaac Watts' hymn "Joy to the world! The Lord is come." The tune was arranged by the American Lowell Mason from several passages found in George Frederick Handel's famous oratorio *Messiah*.[4]

Slightly fewer in number than the tunes from English sources are those derived from 18th-century American psalmody. However, some of these tunes—Timothy Swan's CHINA, Oliver Holden's CORONATION, Lewis Edson's LENOX, and Daniel Read's WINDHAM—were easily the most popular ones from that period of American history. The only one which regularly continues to appear in American hymnals is CORONATION.

To these more-or-less "classic" English and American tunes may be added several other standard melodies from different, though related, traditions. These include Hugh Wilson's AVON, F. H. Barthélemon's BALERMA, GREENVILLE by Jean Jacques Rousseau, Louis Bourgeois' OLD HUNDRED, and Ignaz Pleyel's PLEYEL'S HYMN. Many of these tunes have retained their popularity to the present day.

Lowell Mason, Thomas Hastings, and William B. Bradbury were three American music teachers and composers who exerted a strong influence on the course of American music during the 19th century. Mason and Hastings were particularly interested in raising the level of music understanding and performance in the church. Their approach was to arrange hymn tunes from the secular works of the great European composers, thus making the music of Handel, Beethoven, and others available to the average congregation. They also sought to compose original tunes in the style of their arrangements.

William B. Bradbury was connected with the work of Mason and Hastings, but he excelled primarily in writing simple songs for the use of Sunday Schools. Indeed, he is often given credit for having invented the Sunday School song. His music is generally more elevated in character than that written for the Sunday School in later years; thus, he is grouped with Mason and Hastings rather than the gospel song composers.

The influence of Mason, Hastings, and Bradbury on *The Little Seraph* was quite strong. At least 51 of the 194 tunes in the book are known to have been composed or arranged by one of these men. Add to this figure some seven or eight tunes by other composers which were first printed in a book compiled by one of the three and the extent of their influence becomes apparent. Mason, with 28 tunes and arrangements in *The Little Seraph,* is the most conspicuous of the trio, followed by Bradbury and his 19 tunes. Hastings' four contributions should not be disdained because of their small number, for they include the ever-popular tunes ORTONVILLE, RETREAT, ROCK OF AGES, and ZION.

In marked contrast to the sturdy psalm and hymn tunes from early England and America and the suave grace of the Mason-Hastings-Bradbury compositions are the lively, enthusiastic melodies of the gospel song composers. The gospel song was an answer to the musical needs of two different religious gatherings: the Sunday School and the revival meeting. The Sunday School, geared as it was toward the religious education of children, demanded a type of song that was both simple and memorable. The revival meeting was aimed at the person-in-the-street; therefore, its music also had to be simple and direct. In order to meet these needs, certain composers began writing catchy, repetitious songs that were frequently based on the dance-hall music style of the day. These songs enjoyed tremendous commercial and popular success and eventually found their way into the church sanctuary, though their presence was not always welcomed.

Some of the most popular composers of gospel songs were represented in *The Little Seraph*, including Robert Lowry (eight tunes), W. H. Doane (eight tunes), T. E. Perkins (six tunes), George F. Root (five tunes), S. J. Vail (two tunes), J. R. Murray (two tunes), and Hubert P. Main and P. P. Bliss with one tune each. It is interesting to note the large number of tunes by Lowry and Doane since these composers, like J. R. Graves, were Baptists. No tunes by

Ira D. Sankey, the musical half of the famous Moody-Sankey revival team, were printed in the book (Sankey's first collection being published as recently as 1873, and by an English publisher at that).[5] However, Graves' knowledge of the newer gospel songs is evident from his inclusion of J. E. Gould's SAVIOUR PILOT ME (also known as PILOT) and William G. Fischer's TRUSTING, both of which were first printed in the 1871 *Baptist Praise Book* (New York: Barnes and Co.).[6]

Most of the gospel songs in *The Little Seraph* were of a general nature and were suitable for both the revival meeting and the Sunday School, but some were designed especially for the latter function. These include WE HAVE COME REJOICING, WHAT MAKES US HAPPY, WALK IN THE LIGHT, THE GOLDEN RULE, SWEET REST IN HEAVEN, LEARNING OF JESUS, and ONE MORE HYMN. The refrain of THE GOLDEN RULE can serve as an example of the type of text encountered in a Sunday School song:

> The Sunday-School, the Sunday-School,
>> It is the place I love;
> For there I'll learn the golden rule,
>> Which leads to joys above.[7]

Some of the gospel songs found in *The Little Seraph* are still employed in modern hymnals: SAVIOUR PILOT ME, THE OLD, OLD STORY, PASS ME NOT, BEAUTIFUL RIVER, NEAR THE CROSS, and SWEET BY AND BY.

Perhaps the most interesting feature of *The Little Seraph* is the presence of a large number of American folk-hymn tunes. The earliest known American publication of folk-hymn tunes occurred in Amos Pilsbury's *United States' Sacred Harmony* (Boston: Thomas and Andrews, 1799). This collection used the round-note notation that is most common today, but the folk hymn quickly became identified with shape-note notation. A large number of shape-note books containing folk hymns appeared in the South, culminating in the "classic" collections by William Walker (*Southern Harmony,* 1835) and B. F. White and E. J. King (*Sacred Harp,* 1844).

The inclusion of a number of folk hymns in *The Little Seraph* is of interest primarily because the book also relied heavily upon the gospel song. The folk hymn had its origin in the isolated rural areas of the nation, while the gospel song was born in the crowded urban centers. As America tended to become more and more industrialized, the gospel song gradually began to replace the folk hymn as the accepted musical utterance of the country people. The two styles were not mutually exclusive, for the gospel song took on some of the characteristics of the earlier folk hymn. Nevertheless, the folk hymn and the gospel song were directed toward different audiences and fulfilled different functions. For this reason, few books were published during the 19th century that included both a large number of folk hymns and a large number of gospel songs. *The Little Seraph,* however, was one of those that contained a fair representation of both.

As might be expected, Graves' choice of folk hymns represents a sort of "cream-of-the-crop" selection. The continuing popularity of some of these melodies can be seen in the following table, which lists folk-hymn tunes from *The Little Seraph* that appear in two recent Baptist books: *Baptist Hymnal* (Nashville: Convention Press, 1975) and *The Baptist Hymnal* (Nashville: Convention Press, 1991).

| *The Little Seraph* | *Baptist Hymnal,* 1975 | *The Baptist Hymnal,* 1991 |
|---|---|---|
| WE'LL WAIT | ———————— | O LAND OF REST |
| SAY BROTHERS | BATTLE HYMN (ref.) | BATTLE HYMN (ref.) |
| HOW I LOVE JESUS | OH, HOW I LOVE JESUS | OH, HOW I LOVE JESUS |
| SWEET LAND OF REST NO. 1 | LAND OF REST | LAND OF REST |
| MELODY (MEMPHIS) | TWENTY-FOURTH | ———————— |
| ALL IS WELL | ALL IS WELL | ———————— |

It is somewhat startling to note that two of the most popular American folk hymns, AMAZING GRACE and WONDROUS LOVE, are missing from *The Little Seraph.* However, William J. Reynolds has pointed out that AMAZING GRACE, though printed in several southern fasola tunebooks, did not become generally popular until the first two decades of the 20th century.[8] Similarly, WONDROUS LOVE does not seem to have been as popular in the 19th century as it is in the 20th.[9]

One of the folk-hymn tunes printed by Graves has sometimes been attributed to an early Tennessee composer named William Caldwell. This tune, LOVING-KINDNESS, was claimed by Caldwell in his four-shape tunebook *Union Harmony* (Maryville: F. A. Parham, 1837).[10] However, the tune had appeared in at least two previous publications, Joshua Leavitt's *The Christian Lyre* (New York: Jonathan Leavitt, 1831)[11] and J. H. Hickok's *The Sacred Harp* (Lewistown, PA: Shugert and Cummings, 1832). The attribution to Caldwell in his *Union Harmony* probably means that he simply set it in harmony, or perhaps indicates that he transcribed it from oral tradition and was unaware of its earlier printings in the North.

Another name in *The Little Seraph* which is of interest is the title of the tune MEMPHIS, obviously named for the Bluff City. However, as has been noted above, this tune also appears in *The Little Seraph* under one of its more common names, MELODY. Since the tune was first printed in John Wyeth's *Repository of Sacred Music, Part Second* (Harrisburg, PA: John Wyeth, 1813),[12] there is little reason to connect its origin to the Volunteer State.

There are no records to tell us how widely Graves' little tunebook was used. Though no denominational restriction is evident in the title or contents of the book, its usage was in all likelihood limited primarily to Southern Baptist churches. Graves was a prominent figure in Baptist life during the late 19th century, and it is probable that his reputation secured a wide circulation for his tunebook among the Baptists, particularly in areas where his Landmark doctrine held sway. Indeed, the Arkansas Baptist Convention, over which Graves had considerable influence, received a recommendation from its "Committee on Publications" at the 1874 meeting that the Baptist Sunday Schools of the state adopt *The New Baptist Psalmist* and *The Little Seraph*. Undoubtedly, many Arkansas churches followed the recommendation of this committee.

The collapse of the Southern Baptist Publication Society three years after *The Little Seraph* was issued undoubtedly affected the distribution of the book. However, there was evidently a continuing demand for the work, since it was reprinted in 1890 by J. R. Graves & Son (Memphis).

Another factor which suggests a wide distribution for *The Little Seraph* is that, except for the rural fasola books of men like Walker and White and King, Graves' was one of the first tunebooks compiled and published by a Southern Baptist. The first Southern Baptist tunebooks of a general character seem to have been Eli Ball's *Manual of the Sacred Choir* (Richmond, 1849) and Basil Manly, Jr., and A. B. Everett's *Baptist Chorals* (Richmond: T. J. Starke, 1859). It is evident that there was need of an "official" Southern Baptist tunebook and Graves may have sought to fill that need, though how well he succeeded in this is open to question. Nevertheless, *The Little Seraph* marks an important step in the transference of the folk hymn from the fasola collections to those of a more general appeal and provides an interesting juxtaposition of the gospel song, folk hymn, and other styles of church song.

---

[1]In addition to Johnson's book, Tennessee-compiled collections included A. D. Carden's *Western Harmony* (Nashville, 1824) and *United States Harmony* (Nashville, 1829), William Moore's *Columbian Harmony* (Cincinnati, 1825), William Caldwell's *Union Harmony*

(Maryville, 1837), John B. Jackson's *Knoxville Harmony* (Maryville, 1838), John M'Collum and J. P. Campbell's *Cumberland Harmony* (Nashville, 1834), Andrew W. Johnson's *American Harmony* (Nashville, 1839) and *Western Psalmodist* (Nashville, 1853), John B. Seat's *St. Louis Harmony* (Cincinnati, 1831), William B. Gillham's *Aeolian Lyrist* (Cincinnati, 1854), M. L. and W. H. Swan's *Harp of Columbia* (Philadelphia, 1848), and L. C. Everett's *Wesleyan Hymn and Tune Book* (Nashville, 1859).

[2]For further biographical data on Graves, see Homer L. Grice's valuable article, "Graves, James Robinson," in *Encyclopedia of Southern Baptists* (Nashville: Broadman Press, 1958), Vol. 1, and the works cited in the bibliography of Grice's article.

[3]J. R. Graves, *The Little Seraph* (Memphis: Southern Baptist Publication Society for the Author, 1874), title page.

[4]William Jensen Reynolds, *Hymns of Our Faith: A Handbook for the Baptist Hymnal* (Nashville: Broadman Press, 1964), 107-108.

[5]Ibid., 398.

[6]Ibid., 105, 73. Louis F. Benson gives the date of the *Baptist Praise Book* as 1872. Cf. *The English Hymn* (Richmond: John Knox Press, 1962; reprint of 1915 edition), 559.

[7]The tune to which this is set is not a gospel-song melody, but one from the American folk tradition.

[8]Reynolds, *Hymns,* xxix, 16.

[9]Cf. Ellen Jane Porter, *Two Early American Tunes: Fraternal Twins?*, No. 30 of The Papers of the Hymn Society of America (New York: The Hymn Society of America, 1975), 1-2, and Ellen Jane Porter and John F. Garst, "More Tunes in The Captain Kidd Meter," *The Hymn*, 30 (October, 1979), 253.

[10]Reynolds, *Hymns,* 20.

[11]George Eliga Webb, Jr., "William Caldwell's *Union Harmony* (1837)," (M.C.M. thesis, Southern Baptist Theological Seminary, 1975), 76. Webb gives the date of *The Christian Lyre* as 1830, as does Theron Brown and Hezekiah Butterworth's *The Story of the Hymns and Tunes* (Grosse Pointe, MI: Scholarly Press, 1968; reprint of 1906 edition), 277, but most other authorities place it in the year 1831. Cf. Benson, *The English Hymn,* 377.

[12]William J. Reynolds, *Companion to Baptist Hymnal* (Nashville: Broadman Press, 1976), 220.

[13]J. S. Rogers, *History of Arkansas Baptists* (Little Rock: The Executive Board of Arkansas Baptist State Convention, 1948), 537.

# PART III:
## SINGING–SCHOOL TUNEBOOKS IN THE 19TH-CENTURY SOUTH

# *Christian Harmony* Singing in Alabama: Its Adaptation and Survival
## Harry Eskew

Reprinted, with revisions, from *Inter-American Music Review,* Spring-Summer 1989. Used by permission.

THE SOUTH CAROLINA SINGING-school teacher and tunesmith William Walker (1809-1875) compiled four collections in shape notation, the better known of which are *Southern Harmony* (1835) and *Christian Harmony* (1867). Both of these tunebooks remain in use. *Southern Harmony* survives in the annual "Big Singing" at Benton, Kentucky, held each fourth Sunday in May. The year 1983 marked the centenary of this famous singing. *Christian Harmony* survives in sections of North Carolina, Georgia, Mississippi, and Alabama. The state with the largest number of singings and the only one with a state Christian Harmony singing convention is Alabama.

This chapter focuses on the historical development of Christian Harmony singing in Alabama, and on the adaptation of Christian Harmony singing to changing conditions in the last quarter of the 20th century.

### Basic Description

In contrast to *Southern Harmony* and B. F. White and E. J. King's *The Sacred Harp* (1844), Walker's *Christian Harmony* was published in seven-shape notation. Because the seven shapes of Jesse B. Aikin were protected by a patent, Walker published *Christian Harmony* with three additional shapes of his own devising. Along with this necessary change came his inclusion of a greater number of tunes of the Lowell Mason school and tunes from Europe. However, numerous early American folk hymns and fuging tunes were retained in *Christian Harmony*. The first edition, published for

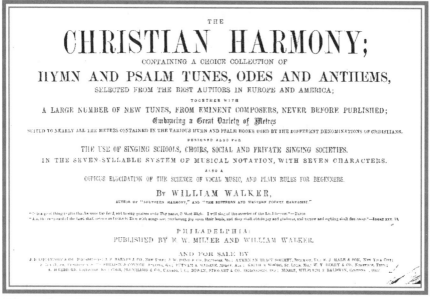

Title page from William Walker's *The Christian Harmony* (Philadelphia, 1867).

Walker at Philadelphia by E. W. Miller in 1867, contained 16 pages of musical rudiments and 473 pieces of music. In 1873 a revised second edition, the last publication edited by Walker, was issued by Miller's Bible and Publishing House of Philadelphia. Walker added the following sentence to the preface of this second edition: "We have added the most beautiful and desirable of modern tunes, thus bringing this work up to the present and latest date, July 1, 1873."

A comparison of these editions shows that all 473 pieces of the first edition were retained and 59 pieces were added, making a total of 532 pieces of music. The 59 pieces added to the revised edition include several gospel-type northern Sunday School songs, such as Lowell Mason's "Work for the night is coming," William G. Fisher's "I love to tell the story," and William Howard Doane's setting of Fanny Crosby's "Pass me not, O gentle Savior." This revised edition was reprinted by the Edward W. Miller Company of Philadelphia in 1901. In 1933 this firm was still selling *Christian Harmony* for $1.50 to people in and around Walker's hometown of Spartanburg.[1]

### Geographical Range

The use of *Christian Harmony* spread to much of the rural South in the late 19th century. In 1875 W. E. White, writing in *Musical Million,* reported that

Here in the mountain region of North Carolina with the exception of the primary school books… the sales of *Christian Harmony* are more than quadruple that of any other book of the kind. Indeed, the demand for the book is so great that merchants, who do not deal in books, keep it in stock to supply the demand. Music teachers have difficulty in many of the mountain counties in getting singing schools to use any other book.[2]

*Christian Harmony* also spread to the midwestern sections of the South. Both *Southern* and *Christian Harmony* were popular around Kentucktown (or Kentucky Town), Texas, shortly after the Civil War. *Christian Harmony* was one of the favorite books of the Central Arkansas Vocal Musical Convention at Toledo, Cleven County, Arkansas, in August of 1886.[3] In 1892 the "State Convention" of Louisiana, meeting in Ruston, used *Christian Harmony*.[4] In 1930 J. H. Hall reported that Christian Harmony singings had met annually in southern Missouri for 41 years.[5] In 1967 Jean Geil described some of the last of these Christian Harmony singings in the Ozarks.[6] A few Christian Harmony singings have survived to the present day in northern Georgia and in Newton County, Mississippi. Two Georgia singings and two Mississippi singings were announced for 1987.[7] In Mississippi, Christian Harmony singing has continued so tenaciously that *Christian Harmony*, along with *The Sacred Harp*, "have been designated as the official books of the Mississippi Sacred Harp Singing Convention."[8]

In Alabama, the Warrior River Vocal Singing Convention used *Christian Harmony* as early as 1891. This organization held its 17th annual session on August 9, 10, and 11 of 1901 (which would place its first convention in the year 1885). The present-day Warrior River Christian Harmony Convention began in 1891. A typescript copy of its minutes for July 31 and August 1 and 2 of 1891 has the title "Proceedings of the First Convention of the Second District of the Warrior River Vocal Singing Convention Held with Oak Grove Singing Society." During this 1891 convention, *Christian Harmony* was adopted as its official textbook.

The earliest extant minutes of the Alabama State Christian Harmony Musical Association (now called a Singing Convention) are dated August 15, 16, and 17, 1930.[9] The state convention, which met at the courthouse in Tuscaloosa, was the 11th such annual gathering, making 1920 its first year. Also included with the printed state convention minutes of 1930 are those of eight Alabama area conventions held in that year (Four Mile Creek, Tallapoosa, Bibb County, Hale County, Tuscaloosa County, Jefferson County, Mount Olive, and County Line). The minutes for Bibb County list John Deason among the Executive Committee members. He was a 25-year-old singer who was to play a significant role in the Christian Harmony singing movement.

## The 1958 Revision

As early as 1930, Alabama Christian Harmony singers mooted a revision of their tunebook. The minutes of the 1930 Alabama State Christian Harmony Musical Association list a seven-person "Board of Directors of Birmingham Christian Harmony Publishing Company" and a nine-person "Committee to Select Music for the Christian Harmony Song Book." These committees are again listed in the extant minutes for both 1934 and 1935. The 1936 minutes are missing, and the 1937 minutes no longer list the board of directors or the music selection committee. In all probability, the Great Depression of the 1930s kept this revision project from coming to fruition. The revision of *Christian Harmony* awaited the warmer economic climate of the 1950s. The 1958 edition bears the names of two men as the revisers: John Deason and O. A. Parris.

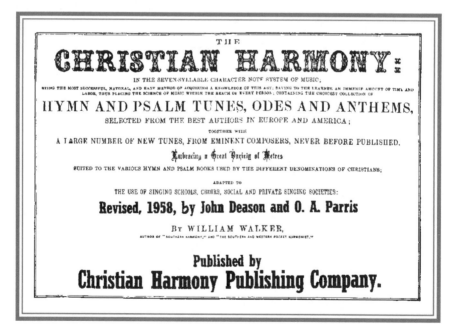

Title page from the Deason-Parris revision of William Walker's *The Christian Harmony* (Birmingham, 1958).

## O. A. Parris

Oren Adolphes Parris, born December 26, 1898, near Warrior in Jefferson County, Alabama,[10] was one of five children of Oscar Hayden and Ada Ovelia Morris Parris. He was reared a Missionary Baptist (his home congregation being the Liberty Baptist Church of Helicon). In the same community and same school was brought up another famous Alabama shape-note composer, Otis L. McCoy (*b* 1897), who in 1987 at the age of 90 lived in Addison, Alabama.[11] Parris attended the Vaughan School of Music, Lawrenceburg, Tennessee. His teachers included James D. Vaughan, S. M. Denson, C. A. Brock, J. D. Wall, V. O. Stamps, W. W. Combs, W. B. Walbert, and Adger M. Pace. In 1919 Parris married Mae Lewis; they had two sons and two daughters.[12]

Like many other shape-note musicians, Parris grew up singing the older Sacred Harp and Christian Harmony music along with the newer southern shape-note gospel music, commonly referred to as "new book" repertory (publishers released new paperback songbooks for singing conventions once or twice a year). In 1932 Parris established the Parris Music Company at Arley, Alabama, which he operated until 1945. By 1937 he had composed more than 300 gospel songs. In the 1930s, Parris also helped prepare the Denson revision of *The Sacred Harp*, serving on the music committee for *The*

THE HEAVENLY THRONG from the Deason-Parris revision of William Walker's *The Christian Harmony* (Birmingham, 1958).

*Original Sacred Harp* of 1936. Although Parris seems to have favored fuging tunes (three of his own fuging tunes were published in the 1936 edition and two more were added in the 1969 edition), he also composed songs in both the Sacred Harp tradition and in the new book style. Hugh McGraw recalls O. A. Parris stating that although he loved Sacred Harp music, he made his living from new book songs. Three of Parris's convention songbooks date from the 1930s: *Music Waves* and *Golden Cross,* both published in 1937, and *Saints Delight,* published in 1939.[13] (The title *Saints Delight* is also the name of a familiar revival spiritual found in *The Sacred Harp*.)

A representative tune composed by O. A. Parris is "The Heavenly Throng" (CH-43), which was recorded in 1974 by a group of singers directed by John Deason in *Christian Harmony Album No. 1.* The tenor melody is hexatonic and all voice parts exhibit a typical melodic vitality.

From 1947 to 1962, Parris managed the southeastern office of the Stamps Quartet Music Company. In 1963 he organized the Convention Music Company and was president until his death, April 13, 1966.

### John Deason

John Henry Deason—seven years younger than O. A. Parris—was born December 30, 1905, at Brent, Bibb County, Alabama. The eldest of nine children, he was the son of Wiley Ezra Deason and Mary Souvella Elam Deason, who were Primitive Baptists. Wiley Deason lined out the hymns for their congregation from Benjamin Lloyd's *Primitive Hymns* (1841).[14] At an early age John began singing and directing songs. He attended singing schools taught by Elder J. D. McElroy (a Primitive Baptist minister) and by Barney Thompson. These schools were held at Little Hope Primitive Baptist Church and at Pleasant Hill Cumberland Presbyterian Church, both in Bibb County. While still in his teens, John began teaching singing schools. According to his sister, Clara Deason Smith, John at age 15 would gather several friends at home to sing and learn singing.[15]

It was at a singing school at Pleasant Hill Church taught by Elder McElroy that John Deason met his bride-to-be, Ressie Kornegay (married December 23, 1922). Although Deason was brought up in a Primitive Baptist Church, he joined his wife's church, being baptized at Old Pleasant Hill Cumberland Presbyterian Church near Centreville, Alabama, in 1925. In 1927 he was elected an elder of this Presbyterian congregation. The Deasons had one child, Henry Martin Deason (1925-1971).

John Deason taught his first Christian Harmony singing school (at Elam

School near Brent, Alabama) in 1923. He continued to teach singing schools each summer at churches and schools in his area. One of the largest singing schools taught by him was at the Tuscaloosa County courthouse in 1924. A few years later, after deciding to learn more about song writing, he attended the Vaughan School of Music in Lawrenceburg, Tennessee.

Upon moving to Birmingham in 1934, Deason met people who used the paperback songbooks of Showalter, Vaughan, and Stamps-Baxter. He thereupon formed his own quartet, which traveled throughout Alabama, singing at church services and all-day singings, and giving concerts at schools and churches on Friday and Saturday evenings. This quartet used primarily the "new book" collections published by the Vaughan Music Company of Lawrenceburg and the Stamps-Baxter Music Company of Dallas, Texas.

From 1936 through 1939, Deason lived in Centreville, Alabama. During these years his quartet of singers from Bibb County began a regular Sunday morning program on radio station WJRD in Tuscaloosa. This quartet also sang for Missionary Baptist minister J. T. Swan's program on station WACT in Tuscaloosa. After Deason moved in 1941 to Flomaton in south Alabama, Swan used recordings of Christian Harmony singing directed by John Deason on his program.[16]

While singing was John Deason's first love, his lifetime vocation was life insurance. From 1937 until his retirement in 1971, Deason worked for Liberty National Insurance Company. Over the years his insurance business took him to such Alabama cities as Flomaton, Fort Payne, Leeds, Calera, Jackson, Mobile, and Albertville. Deason served as agent-manager in most of these cities and received awards from Liberty National for his outstanding work as a salesperson and agent-manager for the company (including election to their Torch Club). When Deason was asked to give a devotional talk for the Torch Club, he began by asking the group to sing "Amazing grace." The tradition of singing "Amazing grace" at Torch Club meetings of Liberty National has continued to the present as one way of paying tribute to John Deason.

After decades of having been active in Christian Harmony singings, John Deason, in the 1950s, became increasingly sought for leadership posts (he was elected president of the state convention in 1954 and 1955). A blue paperback volume in a taller-than-wide format entitled *Christian Harmony Book One* appeared in 1954. Its subtitle reads "A partial revision of the original Christian Harmony published by William Walker nearly 100 years ago, together with a number of new songs in the old-style harmony." This revision lacks a musical rudiments section, but contains 138 pieces of music, all in Aikin's seven-shape notation as adopted by O. A. Parris, whose name alone appears as compiler. Many 20th-century shape-note composers are represented. The name of O. A. Parris appears with 21 pieces; the name of William Walker appears with a mere 13 selections. Reportedly, *Christian Harmony Book One* enjoyed little popularity, mainly because it did not have the accustomed appearance of a tunebook.

Four years later, in 1958, the full revision of *Christian Harmony* was published in traditional, wider-than-tall tunebook format, with both Parris and Deason listed as revisers. The actual editing was done by Parris; Deason underwrote the publication costs.

### Basic Changes

The 1958 full revision of *Christian Harmony* represents a marked departure from Walker's compilation. Changes in the Deason and Parris edition include the following:

1. There are no musical rudiments. Several Christian Harmony singers maintain that the rudiments section should have been included, if only to continue the time-honored pedagogic function of shape-note tunebooks.

2. The revisers shifted to the widely accepted seven-shape notation of Jesse B. Aikin, thus bringing *Christian Harmony* into conformity with more recent singing convention songbooks. Significantly, Walker himself—according to William Hauser—had at first sought to use Aikin's shapes for *Christian Harmony*. However, he was denied permission to do so.[17] The 1958 revision thus belatedly fulfills Walker's wishes, so far as Aikin's system of seven-shape notation is concerned.

3. The 1958 revision is a somewhat smaller book, containing only 458 selections of music as opposed to the 532 of Walker's 1873 edition. The revisers removed 179 songs which they found to be seldom if ever used. Of the 458 selections in the new book, 348 (76%) were carried over from the 1873 edition.

4. There were 109 pieces (24%) added in the 1958 edition. Among them were four songs from the 1854 edition of *Southern Harmony* that Walker did not carry over into his *Christian Harmony*.[18] The leading contributor of the new songs was Parris, with 28 selections bearing his name. Of these 28, he wrote words and music to 10, music alone to 12, words alone to 4, and the added

alto part to 2. In comparison with Parris, the contributions of other 20th-century composers were proportionally small: seven songs each bear the names of J. D. Wall and John Deason; four, John T. Hocutt; and three each that of G. S. Doss, John Dunagan, J. Elmer Kitchens, and W. Bennie Rigdon.

In addition to the contributions of composers living at the time that *Christian Harmony* was revised, the new edition drew upon both shape-note tunebooks and paperback convention songbooks. The publication supplying the largest number of pieces added to *Christian Harmony* was the "Supplement" to the 1911 fourth edition of J. L. White's *Sacred Harp,* an edition that had been used for several decades in northern Alabama and northern Mississippi.[19] Seven songs from the 1911 "Supplement" were added to the *Christian Harmony* in 1958.[20] Three songs added in 1958 had been previously published in Anthony J. Showalter's *Class, Choir and Congregation* (1888), a songbook that had been used monthly for singings at the Tuscaloosa (Alabama) County courthouse from the mid-1930s to at least 1940.[21] Two pieces in the 1958 revision were taken from Aldine S. Kieffer's *The Temple Star* (1878).[22]

An example of one of the more popular added songs (in what George Pullen Jackson called the "gospel-hymn tinged" style[23]) is the anonymous

NOT MADE WITH HANDS from the Deason-Parris revision of William Walker's *The Christian Harmony* (Birmingham, 1958).

song "Not Made with Hands." Although the tenor melody is hexatonic (omitting the leading tone), the harmony and echo voices are clearly in the style of gospel hymnody.

## Impact of the 1958 Revision

The 1958 revision reflected the song choices of Alabama shape-note singers, and as a result its acceptance has largely been limited to central and north central Alabama, along with Newton County, Mississippi, and northern Georgia. Most Christian Harmony singers in North Carolina still use earlier editions (a reprint of the 1873 edition) rather than the 1958 revision. (I still recall the words of the late Earle W. Justice of Rutherfordton, North Carolina, a grandson of William Walker. I visited him in 1959 just after the new revision had come out. He would have nothing to do with the revision, calling it "a travesty on *Christian Harmony*.")

Although comprehensive statistics are not available, it appears that since the introduction of the 1958 revision the number of Christian Harmony singings in Alabama has remained about constant. However, Alabama Christian Harmony singing suffered a heavy blow when John Deason died in 1975. Since his death, no one of comparable leadership ability has arisen. Although younger singers are being drawn to Sacred Harp singing, relatively few children and youth appear to be involved in Christian Harmony singing. Grants from the National Endowment for the Humanities enabled Christian Harmony singing schools to be held in Alabama in 1980, 1981, and 1982. Several of them were taught by Arthur L. Deason of Centreville, a cousin of John Deason. But the singing schools do not seem to have sparked noticeably increased attendance at Christian Harmony singings.

*Christian Harmony* is now published (1987) by W. Bennie Rigdon, 543 West Lake Drive, Bessemer, AL 35020. He reports three reprints of the 1958 revision:

> 1973-1029 copies
> 1977-1000 copies
> 1981-1100 copies.[24]

He adds that some 100 copies a year are being sold. Unless a new leader of John Deason's stature arises, the prospects for further growth of Christian Harmony singing seem dim.

Just as Walker's *Southern Harmony* survives in Benton's Big Singing in western Kentucky because of family support, so also *Christian Harmony* and *The Sacred Harp* have been published in new 20th-century editions through the efforts of families. The Denson family's efforts were crucial to the 1936 Denson revision called *The Original Sacred Harp.* So also the Deason family's support, especially that of John Deason, was a key factor in the publication of the 1958 revision of *Christian Harmony.* It should also be noted that in those areas where Sacred Harp singers attend Christian Harmony singings (and vice versa), the crossovers seemingly experience little difficulty in switching from one shape notation system to another. (Perhaps the threat of urbanization has served to unite those shape-note singers.)

Walker's tastes in song obviously evolved through the various editions of *Southern Harmony* and *Christian Harmony.* So also evolving tastes of Alabama Christian Harmony singers have now resulted in their embracing late 19th- and 20th-century shape-note gospel song. Indeed, there is more of the gospel song idiom in the 1958 revision of *Christian Harmony* than in any other shape-note tunebook in current use. *Christian Harmony* has thus been adapted to the changed musical environment of mid-20th century Alabama shape-note singers—an adaptation that may possibly enable this singing tradition to survive through the remainder of the 20th century.[25]

[1]George Pullen Jackson, *White Spirituals in the Southern Uplands,* reprint of original 1933 edition (Hatboro, PA: Folklore Associates, 1964), 336.
[2]*Musical Million,* VI (1875), 71. Quoted in Jackson, 334.
[3]*Musical Million,* XVII (1886), 42, 158 (Jackson, 335).
[4]*Musical Million,* XXII (1892), 12 (Jackson, 335).
[5]*Daily News Record,* Harrisonburg, VA, May 10, 1930. (Jackson, 335)
[6]Wilma Jean Geil, "Christian Harmony Singing of the Ozarks" (M.M. thesis, University of Illinois, 1967).
[7]*1986 Minutes of the Alabama State Christian Harmony Singing Convention* (ed. Cecile D. Cox, 504 37th St., Tuscaloosa, AL 35405), 12-13.
[8]*Minutes of the Thirty-Eighth Annual Session of the Mississippi Sacred Harp Singing Convention* (August 27 and 28, 1966), 12.
[9]Copies of extant minutes of Alabama Christian Harmony singing conventions are in the Martin Music Library of the New Orleans Baptist Theological Seminary.
[10]"O. A. Parris" in *Gospel Song Writers Biography,* compiled by Mrs. J. R. (Ma) Baxter and Violet Polk (Dallas, TX: Stamps-Baxter Music & Printing Co., 1971), 17-18; Otis J. Knippers, *Who's Who among Southern Singers and Composers* (Lawrenceburg, TN: James D. Vaughan Music Publisher, 1937), 108. I am also indebted to Ronald B. Parris of Maryville, Tennessee, a grandson of O. A. Parris, for additional biographical details.
[11]Telephone conversation with Otis L. McCoy, Addison, AL, March 30, 1987.
[12]They are Elvin B. Parris (d. 1990) Chickasaw, AL; Heflin Parris, Winona, TX; Edith Parris Ivey, Jasper, AL; and Aurelio Parris Larsen, Lillian, AL.
[13]O. A. Parris, *Music Waves* (Arley, AL: Parris Music Co., 1937); *Golden Cross* (Joseph, AL: Parris Music Co., 1937); and *Saints Delight* (Jasper, AL: Parris Music Co., 1937). These songbooks, which once belonged to Ruth Denson Edwards, are in the Sacred Harp Museum, Carrollton, GA.
[14]See R. Paul Drummond, *A Portion for the Singers: A History of Music among Primitive Baptists since 1800* (Atwood, TN: The Christian Baptist Library & Publishing Co., 1989), 73-79.
[15]Manuscript of Clara Deason Smith and Ruth Wyers given to Harry Eskew at Tuscaloosa, AL,

February, 1987. The Deason children (listed in order of birth) are Clara Deason Smith, J. C. Deason (d. 1992), Elvin Deason Morris, Bryan Deason (died 1971), Cecile Deason Cox, Ola Deason Meadows, Mary Deason Thompson, and Carl Elam Deason.

[16]Much of this biographical information is from "John Deason" (unpublished typescript), compiled from family records by Cecile Deason Cox, Tuscaloosa, AL, 1987. Mrs. Cox, a sister of John Deason, is current secretary-treasurer of the Alabama State Christian Harmony Singing Convention.

[17]William Hauser, *Musical Million,* VII (1876), 55. (Quoted in Jackson, *White Spirituals,* 332).

[18]James Scholten, "William Walker's *Christian Harmony* in Alabama: A Study of the Tunebook and its Traditions" (typescript paper presented to the Music History Special Interest Group Session of the Society for Research in Music Education, National Convention, Music Educators National Conference, Miami Beach, FL, April 11, 1980).

[19]Buell E. Cobb, Jr., *The Sacred Harp: A Tradition and Its Music* (Athens: The University of Georgia Press, 1978; reprint with new preface, 1988) 108-10.

[20]These seven pieces and their page numbers in *Christian Harmony* are: ALONE (261), BABYLON IS FALLEN (165), DON'T GRIEVE YOUR MOTHER (284), GOSPEL WAVES (82), LADY, TOUCH THY HARP AGAIN (82), MOTHER TELL ME OF THE ANGELS (274), and NOT MADE WITH HANDS (109).

[21]Published by the A. J. Showalter Co., Dalton, GA, and the Showalter-Patton Co., Dallas, TX. Joel F. Reed, "Anthony J. Showalter (1858-1924): Southern Educator, Publisher, Composer" (Ed. D. dissertation, New Orleans Baptist Theological Seminary, 1975), 132. The three songs added from this songbook are ONE BY ONE (189), THAT BEAUTIFUL LAND (178), and THE SINLESS SUMMERLAND (180). (I am indebted to Mr. Rupert Yarbrough of Tuscaloosa, AL, for assistance in identifying this source.)

[22]Published by Ruebush, Kieffer & Co, Singers Glen, VA. These two selections are TWILIGHT IS FALLING (248) and WATCHMAN (255). For a detailed study of this firm, see Charles Edwin Morrison, "Aldine S. Kieffer and Ephraim Ruebush: Ideals Reflected in Post-Civil War Ruebush-Kieffer Company Music Publications" (Ed. D. dissertation, Arizona State University, 1992).

[23]Jackson, *White Spirituals,* 345.

[24]W. Bennie Rigdon, Letter to Harry Eskew, February 18, 1987.

[25]As of the fall of 1994, there are new reasons for encouragement in the Christian Harmony singing movement. A new, slightly revised edition of the 1958 revision of *Christian Harmony* is scheduled to be published by the Christian Harmony Singers, Centerville, Alabama, in the fall of 1994. Information on this edition can be obtained from Arthur Deason, P. O. Box 535, Centerville, AL 35042. Another reprint of the 1873 edition of *Christian Harmony* is also scheduled to be released in the fall of 1994 by the Folk Heritage of North Carolina, Inc., Asheville. Information on this edition can be obtained from Ms. Willie Israel, 124 Brucemont Circle, Asheville, NC 28806.

# PART IV:

# SOUTHERN BAPTIST HYMNODY

# PART IV:
## SOUTHERN BAPTIST HYMNODY

# Introduction
## Harry Eskew

B Y THE TIME THE SOUTHERN BAPTIST Convention was organized in 1845, congregational singing had become an important part of Baptist life and worship. It is from this point that the particular history of singing among Southern Baptists can be charted. Part IV explores two facets of Southern Baptist hymnody: its use of hymnals and its writing of hymns.

The history of the development and use of hymnals for Southern Baptist churches remains somewhat sketchy. However, the extant collections of congregational song reveal the variety of contexts for which they were written, including revivals, Sunday Schools, and worship services. The compilers of these collections were mostly pastors. The early collections contained only the hymn texts. The music was provided by the tunebooks compiled by singing-school teachers for use in their singing schools. After the Civil War, Sunday School and revival songbooks and church hymnals commonly included words and music to hymns as they do today.

In addition to their activity in compiling hymnals and tunebooks, Southern Baptists have also been active in the creation of hymn texts and tunes. The second chapter focuses on the hymns of this tradition which remain in use and describes how gospel hymnody came to dominate congregational singing through much of its history, especially in the early 20th century under the leadership of Robert H. Coleman and B. B. McKinney, and culminating in McKinney's *Broadman Hymnal* of 1940. The emergence of a large number of Southern Baptists whose hymns appeared in recent editions of *(The) Baptist Hymnal* completes this story. A list of Southern Baptists and their hymns found in the 1956, 1975, and 1991 editions of *(The) Baptist Hymnal* can be found beginning on page 205.

PART IV:
SOUTHERN BAPTIST HYMNODY

# Use and Influence of Hymnals in Southern Baptist Churches Up to 1915

## Harry Eskew

Reprinted, with revisions, from *Baptist History and Heritage,* July 1986. Used by permission.

THE TWO MOST IMPORTANT BOOKS found in Southern Baptist churches are undoubtedly the Bible and the hymnal. These books are used regularly by thousands of Southern Baptist congregations in worship. Hymnals have become so commonplace that it seems surprising to learn that they have not always been in the hands of worshiping congregations. It may also come as a surprise to many that the now familiar large hymnal with both texts and tunes was not used by Baptist congregations in early America.

Although much is still to be learned concerning the evolution of hymnals among Southern Baptists, current knowledge constitutes a fascinating variety of different forms of hymn collections created in response to the needs of different generations. In this chapter, a hymnal will be regarded as any collection that contains primarily hymns, regardless of its shape, size, or type of cover, and whether or not it contains music. For convenience, this account of Baptist hymnals will be divided into two periods: the earlier period through the Civil War and the later period from 1865 up to 1915.

### Through the Civil War

*Contexts and Shapes*—Baptist hymnals were used in at least three different settings in the early 19th-century South: worship services, revivals, and singing schools. Different types of hymn collections emerged for use in these settings.

In worship services and in revival meetings, the pocket-sized, words-only hymnal was found. Hymnals designed for revival use included hymns which were categorized as spiritual songs, a type often made more accessible to unlettered frontier folk by adding refrains, such as:

Turn to the Lord and seek salvation,
  Sound the praise of his dear name.
Glory, honor, adoration!
  Christ, the Lord, to save us came.[1]

In the singing school, the chief means of music education in the pre-Civil War rural South, another shape of hymnal was used—a much larger and wider-than-tall collection known as a tunebook. Although tunebooks were published in shape notation and designed to teach music, in this early period they contained almost exclusively settings of sacred texts. A very important function of tunebooks was to provide tunes for the hymns found in the numerous words-only hymnals of this period. Although tunebooks were probably little used in congregational singing, many of their tunes became a part of the repertory of congregations through singing schools. Conversely, tunes which first existed orally (including those that emerged in frontier revivals) were written down by singing-school teachers and published in their tunebooks.

*Performance: Unaccompanied Lining-Out*—The earlier period might well be characterized as the oral period of congregational singing—a time when hymns in most Baptist churches were given out orally to congregations by a leader line by line. Brought over from Britain to the colonies, this method was known as lining-out.[2] Many Baptists were unable to read,[3] so lining-out was a necessity. During the period prior to 1865, musical instruments were not generally accepted in Southern Baptist worship services.

*Representative Hymnals*—Since Isaac Watts' hymns were those widely sung among Baptists in America prior to 1865, it is no surprise that his hymnals were in common use. Published in 1818 and reprinted as late as 1858 was *An Arrangement of the Psalms, Hymns and Spiritual Songs of Dr. Watts,* edited by James Winchell, pastor of First Baptist Church of Boston, popularly known as "Winchell's Watts." Another widely influential edition of Watts was that of the English Baptist pastor, John Rippon, which was published in 1787 with Rippon's *Selection of Hymns from the Best Authors, Intended to Be an Appendix to Dr. Watts' Psalms and Hymns;* it was reprinted in America in 1792 and through the early decades of the 19th century. These editions of Watts and Rippon were the prime sources of hymns in most Baptist hymnals prior to 1865.

By the time of the formation of the Southern Baptist Convention in 1845, many hymnals had been compiled by Baptist pastors and were generally in use in limited geographical areas. Some Baptists were probably still using

Jesse Mercer's *The Cluster of Spiritual Songs, Divine Hymns, and Sacred Poems*,[4] published in Augusta, Georgia, as early as 1810 and republished in 1823 and 1835. Another Baptist hymnal which was probably still being used in the 1840s was *The Dover Selection*, compiled by Andrew Broaddus at the request of Virginia's Dover Association (the largest Baptist association of its time) and published in 1828, 1829, and 1831. A third representative Baptist hymnal likely being used in 1845 was *Baptist Harmony*, compiled by the then South Carolina pastor Staunton S. Burdett, and published in 1834, 1836, and 1842. In 1835 Baptist layman William Walker, a fellow South Carolinian, used *Baptist Harmony* as the primary source for hymn texts for his *Southern Harmony*,[5] probably the South's most popular tunebook before the Civil War. The closest rival to *Southern Harmony's* popularity in this era was *The Sacred Harp*,[6] published in 1844 by the Georgia Baptists B. F. White and E. J. King. *The Sacred Harp* eclipsed the *Southern Harmony* after the Civil War and remains the most widely used tunebook even to the present time.[7] Although used in singings rather than in church services, *The Sacred Harp* and *Southern Harmony* have served as source collections for most major American hymnals of recent decades, especially providing folk hymn tunes such as BEACH SPRING and WONDROUS LOVE.

Although Baptists before 1865 were much more regional than now and used many different hymnals, attempts were made to provide a hymnal which would win general acceptance and bring about more unity among Baptists through singing from a common hymnal. Two such attempts occurred just prior to the establishment of the Southern Baptist Convention, one in Kentucky and one in Massachusetts.

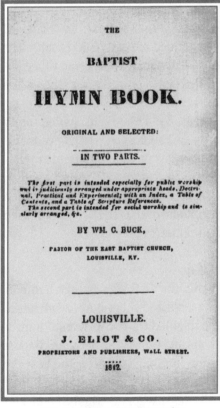

Title page from William C. Buck's
*Baptist Hymn Book* (Louisville, 1842).

In 1842 William C. Buck, editor of the Kentucky state Baptist paper, published his *Baptist Hymn Book* in Louisville. He hoped this hymnal would be adopted by the denomination at large.[8] Only a year after Buck's hymnal, a Baptist hymnal with similar aims was published in Boston under the auspices of the American Baptist Publication Society. Entitled *The Psalmist,* this collection of almost 1,200 hymns was compiled by Baron Stow and Samuel F. Smith as a replacement for "Winchell's Watts." While it met with ready acceptance in the North, several editors of state Baptist papers in the South, including William C. Buck, raised objections to *The Psalmist.*[9] Even though *The Psalmist* was republished in 1847 with a supplement of hymns popular in the South—selected by the southern pastors Richard Fuller and J. B. Jeter—it failed to gain widespread acceptance among Southern Baptists.

While *The Psalmist* became the Baptist hymnal most widely used in the North in the mid-19th century, Buck's *The Baptist Hymn Book* did not achieve that distinction in the South. In 1847 the Southern Baptist Publication Society was established at Charleston, South Carolina, and three years later published its first hymnal. Entitled *The Baptist Psalmody* and compiled by Basil Manly and Basil Manly, Jr., it contained almost 1,300 hymns. The Southern Baptist Convention meeting in Nashville in 1850 voted to recommend *The Baptist Psalmody* to its churches, and it gained acceptance in the South comparable to *The Psalmist* in the North.

Just before the outbreak of the Civil War, Basil Manly, Jr., joined forces with the well-known Virginia musician, A. Brooks Everett, to produce a "tune and hymn book" entitled *Baptist Chorals*[10] with hymn number references to both *The Baptist Psalmody* and *The Psalmist.* In the same year, 1860, *The Psalmist with Music,* "collated by B. F. Edmunds,"[11] appeared in Boston. These two collections were forerunners of the Baptist hymnals with music that were to become common in the latter 19th century.

### The Half Century Following the Civil War

*Contexts and Shapes*—In the period after the Civil War, Baptist hymnals were used in an expanding number of contexts and shapes. Although small, words-only hymnals continued to be published for use in worship, most hymnals of this period contained both texts and tunes. The Southern Baptist Publication Society had ceased operation in 1863, and after the War the American Baptist Publication Society of Philadelphia supplied Sunday School materials and hymnals through Sunday School missionaries in the South and West and through branch offices in Atlanta, Dallas, and St. Louis. The slower pace of the development of Sunday School work and publications such as hymnals in the South was due to a combination of factors, including the vast distances between population centers, poor transportation, resulting isolation of churches, small church memberships, inadequate church buildings, stratification of society, widespread illiteracy, delayed establishment of public schools, uneducated ministers, scarcity of teachers, abruptly shifting political conditions, difficult financial conditions, and paper shortages.[12] Considering these obstacles, it is no surprise that the primary thrust of new hymnals came from the North. Among the northern composers and compilers assuming leadership in the publication of Sunday School music were Baptists William B. Bradbury, Robert Lowry, and W. Howard Doane.[13]

A second movement which originated in the North during the 1870s and gained increasing momentum was urban revivalism, associated with the remarkable mass meetings in Great Britain and America of Dwight L. Moody and Ira D. Sankey. Urban revivalism produced the gospel hymns and gospel songbooks which were to have far-reaching influence on the singing of Southern Baptists.

The shape-note tunebook continued to have a place in the southern rural or small town singing school, as well as in the singing conventions established to foster shape-note singing. The older conventions sang the older repertory from *The Sacred Harp.* William Walker published a somewhat more modern tunebook, *The Christian Harmony* (1867), in seven-shape notation,[14] but still retained a significant body of folk hymnody.

Gradually the lighter style of hymnody from the Sunday School and urban revivals superseded or modified the older folk hymns. The folk-tune setting of "On Jordan's stormy banks I stand," for example, first appeared in print in 1835 in Walker's *Southern Harmony* in a minor key. In the later 19th century, this tune of frontier revivalism was changed to major to accommodate it to the style of the newer hymnody of the Sunday School and urban revivalism.[15] The shape-note tunebook gradually gave way in the later 19th century to the newer gospel songbooks which were often published in seven-shape notation for southern use.

The later 19th-century types of hymnals with words and music were distinctive in shape. The Sunday School songbooks were wider than tall, but much smaller than the tunebooks. The gospel songbooks were taller than wide, thinner, and generally of slightly smaller dimensions than the full-sized hymnals, which were of similar size and shape to the 20th-century hymnals.

*Performance: Toward Use of Hymnals by the Congregation as a Whole—* During the middle decades of the 19th century, a change began to take place which has had a tremendous impact on the worship practices of Southern Baptists. The practice of lining-out hymns, involving an organic exchange between leader and congregation, gradually but surely conceded to the current practice of singing directly from the written word, a passive stimulus requiring literacy and dictating more unanimity in hymn singing among Baptists, but simultaneously eroding the individualism which characterized the older singing practices. The lining-out of any one hymn varied sometimes significantly, depending on the leader and his musical expertise and background.

This change among Southern Baptists from lining-out hymns to singing directly from hymnals is documented in the records of the prestigious First Baptist Church of Richmond, Virginia. Pastor John Courtney, himself a compiler of two hymnals, objected to the congregational use of hymn books, preferring to line-out the hymns to his congregation. Nevertheless, by 1822 the members had overcome Courtney's objection to the congregational use of hymnals.[16] Their ambivalence toward the change is illustrated by their records, which indicate that in 1880 they were without hymnals again and were using "hymn slips" containing words of the hymns for the Sunday morning and evening services.[17]

In some churches the number of hymnals made available seems to have been relatively small. In the Jones Creek Baptist Church of Long County, Georgia, for example, a dozen hymnals were donated in 1854, whereas for comparison this same church authorized two years later the construction of two dozen spit boxes![18]

The political division between the North and the South did not go unreflected in the singing practices of the southern churches. Although Montgomery, Alabama's, First Baptist Church may have been using the northern published *The Psalmist* as early as 1844, pastor Basil Manly, Sr., persuaded the congregation to switch to his *The Baptist Psalmody* in 1861 because, among other reasons, *The Psalmist* was "owned and published in a foreign country."[19]

Although congregation-wide use of hymnals was gaining impetus, as evidenced, for example, by the decision in 1857 of the First Baptist Church of Nashville, Tennessee, to purchase hymnals "to be placed in the pews throughout the church,"[20] there was still no consensus of opinion regarding the value of these hymnals containing the music to accompany the words. From this same church came the following argument against securing a hymnal with music for use in evening worship and prayer meetings:

It is very questionable whether it would be good policy to introduce among us any collection of hymns accompanied with written music. To a very large majority of those who make up our evening congregations, music notes are of no more use than is a Latin Bible to a Roman Catholic. Those who can read music are very few in number, and, under the circumstances, it seems scarcely worthwhile to adopt a tune book, with its inevitable disadvantages of a restricted choice of tunes for hymns of regular metres, and increased bulk cost.[21]

Many Southern Baptist churches during the later 19th century opted for a compromise—they purchased words-only hymnals for the congregation and hymnals with music for the musicians. In 1887, for example, the First Baptist Church of Livingston, Alabama, purchased 36 copies of *The Baptist Hymn Book* (1871) and only 6 copies of *The Baptist Hymn and Tune Book* (1871).[22] And in 1889, the Hephzibah Baptist Church in Georgia purchased eight hymnals without music and one with music.[23]

The records of the Hephzibah Baptist Church also reflect another, possibly parallel, shift in church music practices. Their records indicate that in 1889 the church was in the process of selling their old organ and purchasing a new one. The combined existence of the multiple hymnals and the organ suggests a shift from unaccompanied singing to singing with instrumental accompaniment, frequently with the pump organ. Both the shift from lining-out to singing from the hymnal and the shift from unaccompanied singing to accompanied singing probably occurred simultaneously, for it becomes clear from the preceding documentation that most church members were a long way from musical literacy. The aural stimulus of lining-out was replaced by another aural stimulus, and very often the replacement in these late 19th-century Baptist churches was the harmonium, also called the pump-style reed organ,[24] some of which were still being used in rural churches in the mid-20th century. It is for other historians to ferret out the instrumental choices available to Baptists of this period and ascertain why the pump organ gained ascendancy.

*Representative Hymnals*—Among the types of hymnals published in the decade after the Civil War, probably none exceeded the popularity of the songbooks published for the growing Sunday School movement. Typical of these numerous songbooks was *Pure Gold for the Sunday School. A New Collection of Songs, Prepared and Adapted for Sunday School Exercises.* Published in New York in 1871, 1877, and 1899, *Pure Gold* was compiled by Bap-

Title page from Robert Lowry and William H. Doane's *Pure Gold* (New York and Chicago, 1871).

tists Robert Lowry and W. Howard Doane; it contained over 170 songs and hymns, including the first publication of "Take the name of Jesus with you" and "To the work! To the work! We are servants of God." These songbooks thus not only served the Sunday School but also introduced hymns that were taken up in revivalism and have remained in Baptist hymnals of later times.

From the mid-1870s the "Gospel Hymns Series,"[25] compiled by Philip P. Bliss, Ira D. Sankey, and others associated with the revivals of Dwight L. Moody, made a major impact upon the congregational song of Baptists and other Evangelicals. Representative of Baptist publications that included many of the new hymns for Sunday School and revival use, Lowry and Doane's *Gospel Hymn and Tune Book* was published in 1879 in Philadelphia by the American Baptist Publication Society.

Quite isolated from the stream of gospel hymnody associated with the Moody-Sankey revivals was that introduced by Baptist evangelist W. E. Penn in Texas, and the Southwest through his gospel songbook series *Harvest Bells,* first published in 1881.[26] This revival collection's numerous gospel hymns included many of southern authorship, such as those of Penn himself, whose "The Sheltering Rock" ("There is a rock in a weary land") is in the *Baptist Hymnal,* 1975. *Harvest Bells* begins with several pages of musical rudiments, a feature unusual for a gospel songbook and usually reserved for singing-school tunebooks.

The first major Baptist hymnal to reflect the impact of both the Sunday

School hymnody in the decade after the War and the gospel hymnody from the mid-1870s was *The Baptist Hymnal for Use in the Church and Home,* published in Philadelphia by the American Baptist Publication Society in 1883. In place of the 1,200 or 1,300 hymns of earlier words-only hymnals, there were only 704 in *The Baptist Hymnal,* providing space for a great variety of hymn tunes as described in its preface:

> All sources have been laid under contribution for the music. The animated Sacred Songs of Lowry, Bliss, and others; Psalm-tunes hallowed by use for more than a generation; the familiar Church Psalmody of Mason, Bradbury, Kingsley, and Woodbury; the stately Ancient Chorals of Europe, and the free melodies and rich harmonies from the school of church music represented in England by Dykes and Barnby; on the Continent by Gounod and Hiller, and in America by Cutler and Cornell; all will be found here represented (iii).

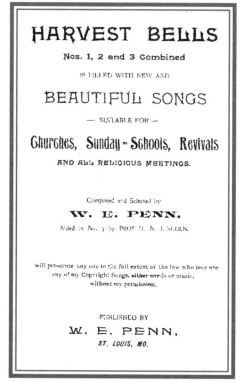

Title page from W. E. Penn's *Harvest Bells Nos. 1, 2, and 3, Combined* (Cincinnati, 1892).

The Baptist Hymnal represented an effort to provide a hymnal acceptable to Baptists of both the North and South. Of the 14 members of this hymnal's consulting committee, five were from the South: H. H. Tucker of Atlanta, Georgia; T. T. Eaton of Petersburg, Virginia; Basil Manly, Jr., of Louisville, Kentucky; E. T. Winkler of Marion, Alabama; and T. S. Pritchard of Wake Forest, North Carolina. While *The Baptist Hymnal* was widely used in the North, it found less acceptance in the South as had been the case with *The Psalmist* 40 years earlier. Among the reasons which could be cited for the limited acceptance of *The Baptist Hymnal* in the South were sectional pride and differences in worship practices and musical tastes. The familiar southern tunes to well-known hymns were missing, such as those to "Amazing grace," "How firm a foundation," and "On Jordan's stormy banks." Furthermore, the closing section of 60 Anglican-style chants was undoubtedly too foreign to the musical orientation and worship practices of Southern Baptists. Many had come to prefer the lighter style of hymnody exemplified in the non-denominational songbooks. In 1891, Basil Manly, Jr., expressed the age-old conflict between the old and the new, identifying its realization in the contents of recently published hymn collections: "For some years it has been apparent that the rage for novelties in singing, especially in our Sunday schools, has been driving out of use the old precious, standard hymns. They are not even contained in the undenominational songbooks which in many churches have usurped the place of our old hymn books."[27]

Manly wrote these words in the preface of *Manly's Choice,* the words-only hymnal in which he attempted to turn his fellow Baptists back to the old standard hymnody. As announced in his preface, he planned to follow *The Choice* with a music edition and then a larger hymnal to be entitled "Standard Hymns for Baptist Churches," but his death in 1892 precluded the realization of these dreams.

The seeds planted by Manly in his 1891 hymnal were to bear fruit in the first hymnal of the Southern Baptist Sunday School Board, which had been established in that same year. Rather than publishing a Sunday School songbook with emphasis on "novelties in singing," the Board chose to publish a full-sized classified hymnal with words and music. Although the newer hymns of the Sunday School and urban revivalism were included, the editor of this book, *The Baptist Hymn and Praise Book* of 1904, left no doubt in his preface as to its orientation: "The basal idea in this

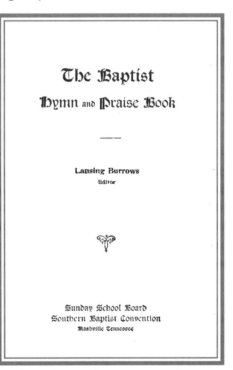

The Baptist

Hymn and Praise Book

Lansing Burrows
Editor

Sunday School Board
Southern Baptist Convention
Nashville Tennessee

Title page from Lansing Burrows' *Baptist Hymn and Praise Book* (Nashville, 1904).

*For Nancy,*
*and for Christopher, Sarah, Thomas, and Heather*

# Contents

Preface   ix

Introduction   xiii

## PART 1
## History: Using DNA to Understand the Past

  1. Abraham Lincoln: Did He Have Marfan Syndrome?   3

  2. Kings and Queens: Genetic Diseases in Royal Families   15

  3. Toulouse-Lautrec: An Artist despite His Genes   27

  4. Old Bones: DNA and Skeletons   39

## PART 2
## Justice: The DNA Revolution in the Courts

  5. DNA Detectives: The New DNA Evidence   53

  6. Cold Hits: The Rise of DNA Felon Databanks   65

  7. Genes and Violence: Do Mutations Cause Crime?   79

  8. Wrongful Birth: What Should the Doctor Know?   93

## PART 3
## Behavior: Do Genes Make Us the Way We Are?

  9. Mental Illness: How Much Is Genetic?   105

  10. Personality: Were We Born This Way?   117

  11. Talent: Nature or Nurture?   131

  12. Gay Genes: What's the Evidence?   145

## PART 4
## Plants and Animals: Genetic Engineering and Nature

  13. Genetically Modified Organisms: The Next Green Revolution?   157

  14. Transgenic Animals: New Foods and New Factories   173

  15. Endangered Species: New Genes Beat Extinction   187

  16. Xenotransplantation: Animal Organs to Save Humans   199

PART 5
## Diseases: The Genetic Revolution in Medicine

17. Cystic Fibrosis: Should Everyone Be Tested?     213
18. Breast Cancer: The Burden of Knowing     223
19. Alzheimer Disease: Are You at High Risk?     235
20. Gene Therapy: The Dream and the Reality     247

PART 6
## Dilemmas: Genetic Technologies and Individual Choice

21. Genetic Testing and Privacy: Who Should Be Able to
    Know Your Genes?     263
22. Frozen Embryos: People or Property?     277
23. Cloning: Why Is Everyone Opposed?     289
24. Eugenics: Can We Improve the Gene Pool?     303

Bibliography     317
Index     331